Personal Best

Student's Book

B1
Pre-intermediate

Series Editor
Jim Scrivener

Authors
Bess Bradfield with
Graham Fruen

Richmond

CONTENTS

		LANGUAGE			SKILLS	
		GRAMMAR	PRONUNCIATION	VOCABULARY		
1 **All about me**		▪ simple present and adverbs and expressions of frequency ▪ present continuous and simple present	▪ final -s/-es sound ▪ -ng sound	▪ personality adjectives ▪ hobbies and socializing ▪ useful verbs	**LISTENING** ▪ a video about our hobbies and how we socialize ▪ listening for the main idea ▪ contractions	**WRITING** ▪ making notes ▪ expressing reasons and results (so, because, that's why) **PERSONAL BEST** ▪ a blog post about personal objects
1A	The only friends you need p4					
1B	21st century hobbies p6					
1C	Famous families p8					
1D	Me in three objects p10					
2 **Stories and pictures**		▪ simple past and time expressions ▪ question forms	▪ -ed endings ▪ question intonation	▪ -ed/-ing adjectives ▪ life stages	**READING** ▪ a text about Andrew Jackson's parties at the White House ▪ approaching a text ▪ sequencers (after, later, then)	**SPEAKING** ▪ showing interest ▪ telling a personal story **PERSONAL BEST** ▪ talking about a personal story
2A	That's me in the photo! p12					
2B	Party like it's 1829 p14					
2C	Behind the camera p16					
2D	That reminds me of … p18					
1 and 2 REVIEW and PRACTICE p20						
3 **Keep on traveling**		▪ comparatives, superlatives, (not) as … as ▪ past continuous and simple past	▪ sentence stress ▪ was/were	▪ useful adjectives ▪ vacation activities	**LISTENING** ▪ a video about the popularity of staycations ▪ identifying key points ▪ sentence stress	**WRITING** ▪ writing a narrative ▪ adverbs of manner **PERSONAL BEST** ▪ a story about a travel problem
3A	Tourist or traveler? p22					
3B	Staycation or vacation? p24					
3C	A traveler's tale p26					
3D	Travel problems p28					
4 **The working world**		▪ will, may and might for predictions ▪ be going to and present continuous for plans and arrangements	▪ want/won't ▪ going to and want to	▪ jobs ▪ phrases about work	**READING** ▪ a text about how boredom can improve creativity ▪ skimming a text ▪ pronoun referencing	**SPEAKING** ▪ dealing with difficulties ▪ telephone language **PERSONAL BEST** ▪ making arrangements by phone
4A	The future of work p30					
4B	I'm so bored! p32					
4C	The secret boss p34					
4D	Can I leave a message? p36					
3 and 4 REVIEW and PRACTICE p38						
5 **Mind and body**		▪ should/shouldn't (for advice and suggestions) ▪ first conditional	▪ should/shouldn't ▪ 'll contraction	▪ health and medicine ▪ verb collocations (do, make, have and take) ▪ emotions and feelings	**LISTENING** ▪ a video about how we react to stress ▪ listening in detail ▪ linking consonants and vowels	**WRITING** ▪ writing an informal e-mail ▪ modifiers **PERSONAL BEST** ▪ an informal e-mail to a friend asking for advice
5A	Should I see a doctor? p40					
5B	Modern life is stressful p42					
5C	How to be happy p44					
5D	I need your advice p46					
6 **Risks and experiences**		▪ present perfect with ever and never ▪ second conditional	▪ irregular past participles ▪ sentence stress	▪ phrasal verbs ▪ the natural world	**READING** ▪ an article about Aron Ralston's survival story ▪ guessing the meaning of words from context ▪ linkers to add extra information (and, also, as well, and too)	**SPEAKING** ▪ taking turns ▪ agreeing and disagreeing **PERSONAL BEST** ▪ having a group discussion
6A	Try something new! p48					
6B	An amazing story p50					
6C	Into the wild p52					
6D	Would you take the risk? p54					
5 and 6 REVIEW and PRACTICE p56						

Language App, unit-by-unit grammar and vocabulary games

		LANGUAGE			**SKILLS**	
		GRAMMAR	PRONUNCIATION	VOCABULARY		
7	City living	• present perfect with *yet* and *already* • present perfect with *for* and *since*	• *just* and *yet* • *for* and *since*	• city features • transportation	**LISTENING** • a video about commuting around the world • listening for facts and figures • final /t/ sound	**WRITING** • writing an essay • giving opinions **PERSONAL BEST** • an opinion essay about a problem
7A	Life in the city p58					
7B	The daily commute p60					
7C	A life in three cities p62					
7D	I think it's a great idea! p64					
8	Food for thought	• *too, too many, too much,* and *(not) enough* • *have to, not have to,* and *can't*	• *too much sugar* • sentence stress	• food and drink • adjectives to describe food	**READING** • an article about a course offered by a Gelateria in Bologna • scanning for specific information • linkers to contrast information (*although, but, however*)	**SPEAKING** • sounding polite • making and responding to invitations **PERSONAL BEST** • making plans to go out with a friend
8A	Sweet, but dangerous p66					
8B	Ice cream university p68					
8C	You have to eat your vegetables! p70					
8D	First dates p72					
7 and 8	REVIEW and PRACTICE p74					
9	Money and shopping	• *used to* • the passive: simple present and past	• *used to/use to* • sentence stress	• money verbs • shopping	**LISTENING** • a video about the importance of shopping centers • identifying attitude and opinion • filler expressions	**WRITING** • writing a formal e-mail • noun forms of verbs **PERSONAL BEST** • an e-mail complaining about a purchase
9A	He used to be poor p76					
9B	What a bargain! p78					
9C	Going, going, gone! p80					
9D	I'd like a refund! p82					
10	Sports and fitness	• past perfect • reported speech	• *'d* and *hadn't* • weak form of *that*	• sports and competitions • parts of the body	**READING** • an article about wheelchair rugby • finding information in a text • giving examples	**SPEAKING** • being helpful • making inquiries **PERSONAL BEST** • asking for information about a service or product
10A	Winning is everything! p84					
10B	Rock 'n' roll on wheels p86					
10C	He said it had changed his life p88					
10D	Could you tell me …? p90					
9 and 10	REVIEW and PRACTICE p92					
11	At home	• *-ing*/infinitive verb patterns • articles (*a/an, the,* no article)	• sentence stress • *the*	• household items • housework • words to describe materials and clothes	**LISTENING** • A video about what we really think of housework • understanding and interpreting information • omission of words	**WRITING** • making writing interesting • adjective order **PERSONAL BEST** • writing an interesting description of a house
11A	Dream home p94					
11B	The truth about housework p96					
11C	Technology you can wear p98					
11D	House exchange p100					
12	People and relationships	• defining relative clauses • uses of the *-ing* form and the infinitive	• sentence stress • word stress	• relationships • relationship verbs	**READING** • an infographic showing how much time we spend on different activities • interpreting data • expressing approximate quantities	**SPEAKING** • responding modestly • saying thanks **PERSONAL BEST** • thanking someone for a favor
12A	Bring your parents to work p102					
12B	In our lifetime p104					
12C	Long-distance love p106					
12D	Thanks a million! p108					
11 and 12	REVIEW and PRACTICE p110					

Grammar practice p112   Vocabulary practice p136   Communication practice p158   Irregular verbs p175

All about me

LANGUAGE | simple present and adverbs and expressions of frequency ■ personality adjectives

1A The only friends you need

1 Here are some words to describe a good friend. Order the words from 1 (very important) to 6 (less important).

> honest   funny   patient   nice   polite   generous

Go to Vocabulary practice: personality adjectives, page 136

2 Read the introduction to the text. Are the sentences true (T) or false (F)?

1 You need lots of friends to be happy. _____
2 There are four different types of friends. _____
3 It is important to have different types of friends in your life. _____

3 A ▶ 1.3   Match the types of friends in the box with descriptions 1–4. Listen and check.

> The super planner   The party animal   The good listener   The straight talker

B Do you have any friends like these? What type of friend are you?

THE FOUR FRIENDS YOU NEED

We all know that friends are important … but do we have the "right" friends? Dr. Adam Greenberg, a psychologist, doesn't think we need lots of friends to be happy. Instead, he says it's more **important to have different types of friends**. He believes that there are four types of friends, and they all help us in different ways. So, what are these four friends like?

1 _____
You share everything with these friends and often tell them all your secrets. They're patient when you call them late at night with a problem and never complain when you tell them the same stories, over and over again!

2 _____
These friends know you very well, and they're honest … *really* honest. They always tell you the truth, even when you don't want to hear it. But this is because they care about you and don't want you to make a mistake and get hurt.

3 _____
These friends are very sociable, and you usually have a good time when you're with them. They're very funny and make you laugh when you're sad. All your friends and family love them, too. With friends like these, life is never boring!

4 _____
These friends are very organized, but they're sometimes a little serious. They hardly ever forget important dates, like your birthday! They're very busy and have lots of things to do every day, but they always find time to have coffee with you.

4 Choose the correct words to complete the sentences. Check your answers in the text.

1 *Do / Does* we have the "right" friends?
2 Dr. Greenberg *don't / doesn't* think we need lots of friends to be happy.
3 He *say / says* it's more important to have different types of friends.
4 They *don't / doesn't* want you to make a mistake and get hurt.
5 You usually have a good time when you *is / are* with them.
6 They hardly ever *forget / forgets* important dates.

5 **A** Complete the diagram with the adverbs of frequency in the box.

> hardly ever   never   often   usually

100% ────────────────────────────────────── 0%

always   1 _____   2 _____   sometimes   3 _____   4 _____

B Underline the adverbs of frequency in the text and complete the rule. Then read the Grammar box.

Adverbs of frequency go *before / after* most verbs, but they go *before / after* the verb *be*.

📖 **Grammar**   **simple present and adverbs and expressions of frequency**

Things that are always true:
Does Ahmet **live** in Ankara? No, he **lives** in Istanbul.
Do you **speak** Spanish? Yes, I **speak** a little.

Routines and habits:
How often do you **see** him? I **usually see** him on the weekends.
How often are you late? I**'m never** late!

Look! We also use expressions of frequency for regular routines e.g., *once a week*, *every month*

Personal Best

Go to Grammar practice: simple present with adverbs and expressions of frequency, page 112

6 **A** ▶1.5 **Pronunciation:** final *-s/-es* sound Listen and repeat the sentences. Then match the verb endings in **bold** with the sounds: /s/, /z/, or /əz/.

1 She like**s** Italian food. _____ **2** He teach**es** at the university. _____ **3** My brother know**s** him. _____

B ▶1.6 How do you say the verbs? Listen, check, and repeat.

believe**s** say**s** change**s** think**s** use**s** want**s** goe**s** watch**es** hope**s**

7 **A** Add adverbs and expressions of frequency to make sentences about your partner.

She usually takes the bus to work. He takes the bus to the university every day.

1 He/She takes the bus to work/college.
2 He/She goes to bed at 11:00 p.m.
3 He/She is patient.
4 He/She drinks coffee in the mornings.
5 He/She watches movies in English.
6 He/She is late for class.

B Read your sentences to your partner. He/She will tell you if you are correct.

Go to Communication practice: Student A, page 158; Student B, page 166

8 Read the text about two friends. Complete the text with the correct form of the verbs in the box.

> get   have   not have   invite   like   think

MY BEST FRIEND IS THE EXACT OPPOSITE OF ME

Lots of people ¹_____ I'm really serious, and that I never go out, but that's not true! I'm very hard-working, and my job at the bank is difficult, so I ²_____ much free time. I play the guitar in a jazz group, and we usually practice two or three times a week.

I ³_____ cooking, so I often ⁴_____ people over to my house for dinner. My best friend is Luca. He's the singer in the group, and he's completely different from me. He's a college student and, to be honest, he's a little lazy and hardly ever ⁵_____ to class on time. But he's funny and generous, and we always ⁶_____ a great time when we go out.

9 **A** Choose a friend and tell your partner his/her name.

B In pairs, use the prompts to ask and answer questions about your friends.

1 What / be / he/she / like?
2 Where / he/she / live?
3 What / he/she / do?
4 Where / he/she / work/study?
5 How often / you / talk to / him/her?
6 What / you / usually / talk about?
7 How often / you / see / him/her?
8 Where / you / meet / him/her?

Personal Best   Write a description of yourself and of someone you know who is the opposite of you.

Learning Curve

1B 21st century hobbies

1 Match the activities in the box with pictures a–h.

> get together with friends   go to concerts   bake cupcakes   play chess
> go on social media   collect records   get (some) exercise   shop online

2 In pairs, ask and answer the questions *Do you ...?* and *How often do you ...?* for the activities in exercise 1.

A *Do you collect records?*   **B** *No, I don't.*
A *How often do you get some exercise?*   **B** *I go to the gym once or* twice *a week.*

Personal Best

Go to Vocabulary practice: hobbies and socializing, page 137

> 🔧 **Skill**   **listening for the main idea**
>
> **It is important to understand the main idea when someone is speaking.**
> • Think about who is speaking and what he/she is talking about.
> • Don't worry if you don't understand all the words.
> • Remember that speakers often talk about the main ideas more than once.

3 ▶1.8   Read the Skill box. Watch or listen to the beginning of a webshow called *Learning Curve* and check (✔) the main idea.

1 People have less time for socializing today. ☐
2 Many popular hobbies are now online. ☐
3 Old hobbies are becoming popular again. ☐

4 A ▶1.8   Watch or listen again. Complete the chart with the online activities Kate mentions.

Traditional activity	Online activity
play team sports	
take cooking classes	
go to a shopping center	
go out to meet new people	

B In pairs, think of more traditional activities that you can now do online.

5 ▶1.9   Watch or listen to the second part of the show. Choose the correct options to complete the sentences about the main ideas.

 Viktor
 David
 Suzie
 Rebecca

1 Viktor …
  a plays chess a lot.   **b** does lots of activities online.   **c** meets up with friends every day.

2 David …
  a likes computers.   **b** exercises at home.   **c** prefers exercising at the gym.

3 Suzie …
  a downloads lots of music.   **b** prefers to relax at home.   **c** does her hobby with other people.

4 Rebecca …
  a does lots of activities online.   **b** doesn't like meeting new people.   **c** spends lots of time with her family.

6 ▶1.9   Watch or listen again. Are the sentences true (T) or false (F)?

1 Viktor plays chess with friends every day. ____
2 David goes to the gym five times a week or more. ____
3 Suzie loves music from the 1980s. ____
4 Rebecca makes videos of her cat. ____
5 Kate only likes traditional hobbies, like rock climbing. ____

7 **A** Ask your classmates the questions in the boxes and write down their answers.

> What do you do in your free time?   Do you have any online hobbies?

B Do you think online hobbies are more popular than traditional hobbies?

8 ▶1.10   In pairs, complete the sentences from the show with the contractions in the box. Listen and check.

> don't   I'm   he's   that's   what's   can't

1 _____ your name?
2 _____ really enjoying the game.
3 Computers _____ interest me.
4 You _____ do that online!
5 I use it when _____ not at the gym.
6 Wow, Suzie, _____ amazing!

🧩 **Listening builder**   **contractions**

When people speak, they usually make contractions:
We do not get together with friends. → *We do**n't** get together with friends.*
She is not very athletic. → *She**'s not** very athletic. /* *She **isn't** very athletic.*
I am ready to go rock climbing. → *I**'m** ready to go rock climbing.*

---

9 ▶1.11   Read the Listening builder. Listen and circle the contractions you hear.

1 *We're / We aren't / We can't*
2 *He's / He isn't / He doesn't*
3 *My teacher's / My teacher's not / My teacher isn't*
4 *It's / It isn't / It doesn't*
5 *They don't / They can't / They aren't*
6 *I'm / I'm not / I don't*

10 Discuss the questions in pairs.

1 Is it important to have a hobby? Why/Why not?
2 What hobbies are most popular in your country?
3 Do men and women usually like different hobbies?
4 Are your hobbies different now from when you were a child? If so, how?
5 Can you think of any dangerous hobbies? Would you like to try them? Why/Why not?

Personal Best   Write a paragraph about one of your partner's answers in exercise 10.

1C Famous families

1 Who are musicians a–c? In pairs, match them with their relatives: Anaïs, Skip, and Eve. Read the text and check.

THE NEXT GENERATION OF STARS

Anaïs

Skip

Eve

Their faces may look familiar, but if you're wondering who these cool young people are, the clue is in their names. Meet the children—and grandchildren—of some of music's biggest stars.

Anaïs Gallagher is the daughter of Noel Gallagher, former guitarist and songwriter with Oasis. In our photo, she's wearing a gold hat and already looks like a star! Anaïs, 16, goes to school in London and is currently hosting a music and fashion show on children's TV. She lives in London with her mom and, in the future, she wants to be a movie director.

Skip Marley wears his hair in dreadlocks and looks just like his famous grandfather, Bob. He's just 20, but he's also a musician who sings and plays the guitar, the piano, and the drums. He lives in Miami, where he's studying business administration in college. Right now, he's recording some new songs and planning to go on tour.

Eve Hewson is the daughter of Paul Hewson, better known as Bono, from the rock band U2. Eve, 25, is an actress and is living in New York right now, where she's playing the part of a nurse on a TV series. Does she miss her hometown of Dublin? Yes, but her sister and a lot of her friends from home live nearby, and her parents often visit.

With so much talent—never mind those famous connections—we can expect to see a lot more of Anaïs, Skip, and Eve in the future.

2 Read the text again. Complete the sentences with the correct name: *Anaïs, Skip, or Eve*.

1 _____ lives in Miami.
2 _____ is wearing a white hat in the photo.
3 _____ goes to school in London.
4 _____ is living in New York right now.
5 _____'s parents often visit.
6 _____ is recording some new songs right now.

3 **A** Underline the verbs in exercise 2. Which verbs are simple present and which are present continuous? What is the difference between them?

B Choose the correct tenses to complete the rules. Then read the Grammar box.

1 We use the *simple present / present continuous* to talk about actions that are happening now or actions that are temporary.
2 We use the *simple present / present continuous* to talk about things that happen regularly or things that are always true.

📖 **Grammar**	**present continuous and simple present**

Things that are happening now or are temporary:	Things that happen regularly or are always true:
*She's **living** in Lima right now.*	*He **lives** in Istanbul.*
*I'm **not wearing** my glasses.*	*They **don't wear** coats in the summer.*
***Is** she **working** in Paris today?*	***Do** you **work** as a teacher?*

Personal Best

Go to Grammar practice: present continuous and simple present, page 113

4 **A** ▶ 1.13 **Pronunciation:** -ng sound Listen and repeat the words. Pay attention to the /ŋ/ sound.

bringi**ng** meeti**ng** runni**ng** singi**ng** studyi**ng** so**ng** taki**ng** you**ng**

B ▶ 1.14 Practice saying the sentences. Listen, check, and repeat.

1 She's weari**ng** a lo**ng** coat.

2 She's carryi**ng** a lo**ng** coat.

3 He's bri**nging** me a stro**ng** cup of coffee.

4 He's taki**ng** a stro**ng** cup of coffee to the meeti**ng**.

5 Match the sentences in exercise 4B with pictures a–d.

 a
 b
 c
 d

Go to Vocabulary practice: useful verbs, page 138

6 **A** Choose the correct form of the verb to complete the questions.

1 What clothes *do you wear / are you wearing* today?

2 *Do you have / Are you having* a dictionary with you?

3 What *do you look forward to / are you looking forward to* this year?

4 *Do you think / Are you thinking* it will rain today?

5 What clothes *do you usually wear / are you usually wearing* if you go to a party?

6 What *do you do / are you doing* right now?

B In pairs, ask and answer the questions.

Go to Communication practice: Student A, page 158; Student B, page 166

7 ▶ 1.16 Complete the conversation with the simple present or present continuous forms of the verbs in the box. Listen and check.

> meet   work (x2)   be   do (x2)   write   not know   not join

Ruben Karen!

Karen Hi, Ruben. How [1] _____ you?

Ruben I'm fine, thanks. What [2] _____ you _____ here?

Karen I [3] _____ my sister for lunch at a café.

Ruben Oh, great. What [4] _____ she _____?

Karen She [5] _____ at a bank.

Ruben Here downtown?

Karen Not normally, but she [6] _____ at the main office this week. Hey, why [7] _____ you _____ us for lunch?

Ruben OK, but your sister [8] _____ me.

Karen Don't worry. It'll be fine. So, how's college?

Ruben Good, but I'm really busy. I [9] _____ my senior project right now, so ...

8 Imagine you meet your partner on the street. Ask and answer the questions in pairs.

1 How are you?

2 What are you doing here?

3 Where are you working/living right now?

4 How's it going?

5 How's your ...?

6 What does he/she do?

7 What's he/she like?

8 What's he/she doing now?

Personal Best Write about someone in your family with the simple present and present continuous.

1D Me in three objects

1 Read the blog and look at the pictures. Discuss the questions in pairs.

1 What can you find out about Sasha, Brady, and Julio?

2 Who do you think is the most interesting?

3 Who do you think is most similar to you?

4 Is it possible to know what someone is like by looking at the things he/she owns?

MSD COLLEGE — Learning for life

REPLIES: You in three objects . . . .

You in three objects . . .

POSTED:
November 5, 16:00

You can discover a lot about people by looking at the objects that are important to them. Post photos of three things that represent you, tell us why they are important, and, introduce yourself to the rest of the class!

Sasha — my laptop | coffee | my running shoes
POSTED: November 5, 18:26
SEE MORE ...

Brady — my paints | music | my backpack
POSTED: November 5, 18:44
SEE MORE ...

Julio — my cat | Mexican food | movie tickets
POSTED: November 6, 09:15
SEE MORE ...

2 Look at the mind map. Who drew it: Sasha, Brady, or Julio? Complete the diagram with the correct objects. Then read the Skill box.

work at movie theater on the weekends · college degree film studies · 1 _____ · cell phone · talk to my family · live alone · Me · cooking for my friends · 2 _____ · spicy food! · reminds me of home · 3 _____ · sitting on the sofa with Figaro

Skill | making notes

Making notes before you write is a good way to plan your work.

• Write as many ideas as you can about the main topics.

• Use diagrams like mind maps to see the ideas more clearly.

• Choose the best ideas and organize them into paragraphs.

3 A Look at the mind map again. Which idea doesn't Julio use? How many paragraphs do you think he'll write?

B Read Julio's blog post in exercise 4 and check your answers to the questions above.

4 ▶ 1.17 Complete Julio's blog post with the simple present or present continuous form of the verbs in the box. Listen and check.

> not agree   love   cook   work   live   sit   watch   study

Julio's blog

First, I chose a photo of Figaro, my cat, because he's very important to me. I ¹_____ alone right now, so it is good to see a friendly face when I come home. I ²_____ animals, especially cats. In the photo, he ³_____ on the sofa with me. He often sits with me, and we watch movies together.

I ⁴_____ at a college in the U.S. now, but I'm from Mexico. That's why I also chose Mexican food. I love spicy food, and I often ⁵_____ a big meal and invite all my friends over for dinner. It's great to get together with friends and, when I taste the food, I remember my friends and family back home.

I chose some movie tickets, because I work at a local movie theater on the weekends. I ⁶_____ on a degree in film studies, so movies are a really important part of my life. Some people say I ⁷_____ too many movies, but I ⁸_____ . I want to be a movie director, and I learn something new from every movie I watch.

5 Look at the phrases with the highlighted words in the text. Answer the questions.

1 What type of information comes after *because*? *a reason for something / a result*
2 What type of information comes after *That's why* and *so*? *a reason for something / a result*

Text builder **expressing reasons and results**

Reasons: *I chose a photo of my cat **because** he's very important to me.*
Results: *My cat is very important to me, **so** I chose a photo of him.*
              *My cat is very important to me. **That's why** I chose a photo of him.*

---

6 A Read the Text builder. Complete the sentences *with because, so, or That's why!*

1 I think it's really important to stay in shape, _____ I go running every morning.
2 I didn't choose my cell phone _____ everybody has one, and it's not very special.
3 I design websites and I'm always connected to the Internet. _____ I chose my laptop.
4 My backpack is important to me _____ it reminds me of my trips to lots of countries.
5 I love art, but I'm too shy to take a picture of one of my paintings. _____ I chose my paints, instead.

B Who wrote the sentences: Sasha, Brady, or Julio?

7 A Complete the sentences with your own ideas. Write three true sentences and three false sentences.

1 My favorite _____ is _____ because …
2 I think _____ is very _____ , so I …
3 I'm a very _____ person. That's why I never …
4 It's really important to _____ , so I always …
5 I am _____ right now because …
6 I'm terrified of _____ . That's why …

B Listen to your partner's sentences. Which sentences do you think are true?

8 A **PREPARE** Draw a mind map of some objects that represent you. Then add reasons why the things are special. Look at your diagram and choose three objects you want to include in your blog post.

B **PRACTICE** Write a blog post with the heading *Me in three objects*. Use your notes from Stage A to help you organize the paragraphs.

C **PERSONAL BEST** Exchange blog posts with your partner. Read his/her work and correct any mistakes. How could they improve it?

Personal Best | Write six sentences with *because, so,* and *That's why* about your friends, family and hobbies.   11

Stories and pictures

| LANGUAGE | simple past and time expressions ■ *-ed/-ing* adjectives |

2A That's me in the photo!

1 A Look at the photos in the text below and say what is happening. What do you call these types of photos?

B Read the text quickly. Match descriptions 1–3 with photos a–c.

the STORY OF SELFIES

The "age of selfies" began in the early 21st century when people started using smartphones with digital cameras. We now take over a million selfies every day! Here are three interesting selfies with their stories:

1 Robert Cornelius made the world's first "selfie" when he experimented with a camera in 1839. He tried to take a photo of himself, but early cameras worked very slowly, so Robert didn't move for one minute and he couldn't smile. That's why the final photo wasn't very exciting!

2 This terrifying selfie is of Alexander Remnev, from Russia. In May 2014, Alexander traveled to Dubai with a friend. They weren't interested in taking normal photos, so they decided to climb the Princess Tower, which is over 400 m. tall. They opened a door at the top of the building and climbed out … and they didn't use any safety equipment. Why did they do it? They said they were bored!

3 Teenager Jack Surgenor was very excited when he saw Queen Elizabeth II in Northern Ireland on June 24, 2014. He quickly took a selfie and sent it to all his friends. He was very pleased, but how did the Queen feel about being in someone else's photo? We don't know, but she looked a little annoyed!

 a
 b
 c

2 Read the text again. Complete the sentences with the names in the box.

| Alexander Remnev   Jack Surgenor   Queen Elizabeth II   Robert Cornelius |

1 _____ took a very dangerous photo.

2 _____ wasn't happy to be in a photo.

3 _____ waited a long time to take the photo.

4 _____ took a photo of a famous person.

3 A Write the simple past form of the verbs. Check your answers in the text.

1 begin _____
2 make _____
3 try _____
4 work _____
5 travel _____
6 decide_____
7 be ___ / ___
8 send _____

B Which verbs are regular and which are irregular?

4 <u>Underline</u> all the simple past negative sentences and questions in the text. Complete the rules, then read the Grammar box.

1 To form a negative in the simple past, we normally use _____ + the base form .
2 To form a question in the simple past, we normally use _____ + subject + the base form .
3 The negative of *was/were* is _____ /_____ and the negative of *could* is _____ .

📖 **Grammar**   **simple past and time expressions**

	Regular verbs	Irregular verbs
Positive:	Alexander **traveled** to Dubai.	He **took** a photo.
Negative:	Alexander **didn't travel** to Dubai.	He **didn't take** a photo.
Questions:	Why **did** he **travel** to Dubai?	Why **did** he **take** a photo?

Look! Time expressions go at the end or at the beginning of sentences:
Alexander traveled to Dubai **in May 2014**.   **In May 2014**, Alexander traveled to Dubai.

Go to Grammar practice: simple past and time expressions, page 114

5 **A** ▶2.3 **Pronunciation:** *-ed* endings Listen to three phrases from the text. Say how the *-ed* endings are pronounced: /t/, /əd/, or /d/.

1 People start**ed** using smartphones.   2 They open**ed** a door.   3 Early cameras work**ed** very slowly.

B ▶2.4 Say how the *-ed* endings of the verbs are pronounced: /t/, /d/ or /əd/. Listen, check, and repeat.

climb**ed**   decid**ed**   experiment**ed**   look**ed**   travel**ed**   watch**ed**

Go to Communication practice: Student A, page 158; Student B, page 166

6 **A** Choose the correct adjectives to complete the sentences. Check your answers in the text.

1 That's why the final photo wasn't very *excited / exciting*!
2 This *terrified / terrifying* selfie is of Alexander Remnev, from Russia.
3 They said they were *bored / boring*!
4 Teenager Jack Surgenor was very *excited / exciting* when he saw Queen Elizabeth II.

B Look at sentences 1–4 again and answer the questions.

1 Which adjectives describe people's feelings? _____ , _____
2 Which adjectives describe someone/something that causes a feeling? _____ , _____
3 How many more *-ed* and *-ing* adjectives can you find in the text? _____

Go to Vocabulary practice: *-ed/-ing* adjectives, page 139

7 **A** Complete the questions with the simple past of the verbs in parentheses.

When was the last time you …

1 _____ embarrassed? (feel)
2 _____ terrified? (be)
3 _____ something tiring? (do)
4 _____ something interesting? (eat)
5 _____ some surprising news? (receive)
6 _____ annoyed with your best friend? (get)

B In pairs, ask and answer the questions and explain what happened.

8 Think about a selfie or photo you took. Ask and answer the questions in pairs.

1 When did you take the photo?
2 Where were you?
3 What did you do?
4 Why did you take the photo?
5 How did you feel?
6 Did you send the photo to anyone?

Personal Best   Write down three important dates. Then write sentences explaining what happened and why they are important.

2B Party like it's 1829

1 Describe the picture of a party. Discuss the questions in pairs.

1 Why do people have parties?
2 What do you usually do when you go to a party?
3 Do you prefer to organize parties or to be a guest?
4 What's the worst thing about parties?

Skill   approaching a text

Before you read a text, predict as much information as you can.
• Read the title of the text. Can you guess what it means?
• Look at the pictures. What people, places, and things do they show?
• Read the headings of the different sections. What do you think they are about?

2 **A** Read the Skill box. Try to predict the answers to the questions about the text on page 15.

1 Who was Andrew Jackson?
2 Where did he live?
3 What did the guests do at the 1829 party?
4 What did the guests do at the 1837 party?

B Read the whole text quickly and check your answers to the questions.

3 Read the text in more detail. Look at the sentences and write: *1829 party*, *1837 party,* or *both*.

1 There was food at the party. _____
2 Some guests caused damage. _____
3 All the guests had a good time. _____
4 Jackson didn't stay until the end. _____
5 Jackson received a strange present. _____
6 The guests ate in the gardens. _____

4 Discuss the questions in pairs.

1 Were you surprised by the text? Why/Why not?
2 How would a party at the White House be different today?
3 What kind of person was Andrew Jackson?
4 Would you like to go to a party like one of Andrew Jackson's? Why/Why not?

5 Complete the sentences with the words in the box. Check your answers in the text.

after   after that   later   then

1 … they soon pushed their way inside. _____ , the party got out of control.
2 Eight years _____ , a farmer gave the president an enormous cheese.
3 Jackson didn't know what to do with it; he couldn't eat it himself, but _____ he had an idea.
4 _____ just two hours, he checked and it was gone.

Text builder   sequencers

To say one action happened after another:
*I went to the gym and **then** I went home.*   *I went to the gym. **After that**, I went home.*
To say one action happened after a period of time:
*Two hours **later**, I cooked dinner.*   ***After** two hours, I cooked dinner.*

6 Read the Text builder. In pairs, talk about an important party or celebration you went to. Use sequencers to explain what happened.

• What was the party or celebration?
• How many guests were there?
• What did you eat and drink?

• What did you do?
• Did you have a good time?
• Were there any problems?

PARTY LIKE A PRESIDENT

ANDREW JACKSON

Andrew Jackson was president of the United States from 1829 to 1837. He was the first president from the Democratic party and a very popular politician, but he's also famous for some surprising events that took place at the White House. The pictures below show two memorable parties held there when Jackson was president.

THE 1829 CELEBRATIONS

THE LAST PARTY, 1837

On March 4, 1829, when Jackson became president, he invited his supporters to visit the White House, and thousands of people followed him to his new home. At first, the crowd waited in the gardens, but they were very excited and soon pushed their way inside. After that, the party got out of control. People stood on tables and chairs, broke glasses, and some even fell down and hurt themselves. Jackson escaped through a window and went to a nearby hotel, but his staff stayed because they were worried about the building. In the end, they put lots of food on tables in the gardens and the hungry guests followed them outside to eat the food. The White House was safe ... for the moment!

Eight years later, a farmer gave the president an enormous cheese, which weighed over 600 kg. Jackson didn't know what to do with it; he couldn't eat it himself, but then he had an idea. He decided to have another party to celebrate the end of his presidency. In February 1837, thousands of guests arrived and started to eat the only thing on the menu—the cheese. After just two hours, he checked and it was gone. Everyone was very happy, but the expensive carpets in the White House were covered with smelly cheese. This time, Jackson wasn't worried about the mess. He left the White House two weeks later, and the next president, Martin van Buren, was very annoyed because the building still smelled of cheese!

Personal Best   Choose one of the parties from the text. Write a summary of what happened.   15

2C Behind the camera

1 In pairs, order the stages from 1 (birth) to 8 (death).

> start a career   get engaged   die   go to college
> be born   have children   finish school   get married

Go to Vocabulary practice: life stages, page 140

2 Read the radio guide about Mario Testino. What is his job? Why is he famous?

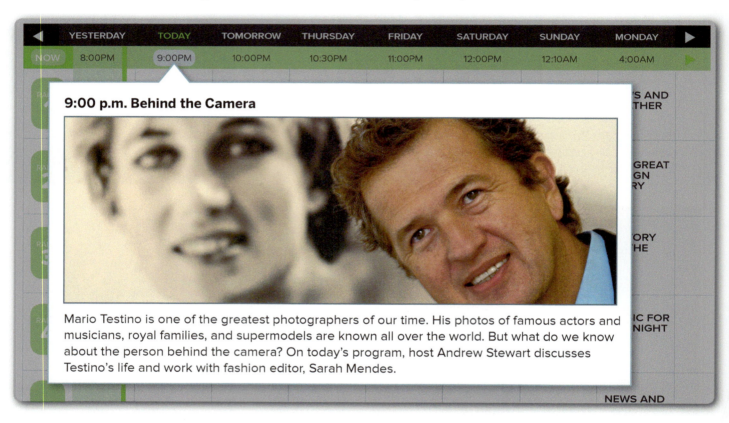

YESTERDAY	TODAY	TOMORROW	THURSDAY	FRIDAY	SATURDAY	SUNDAY	MONDAY
NOW 8:00PM	9:00PM	10:00PM	10:30PM	11:00PM	12:00PM	12:10AM	4:00AM

9:00 p.m. Behind the Camera

Mario Testino is one of the greatest photographers of our time. His photos of famous actors and musicians, royal families, and supermodels are known all over the world. But what do we know about the person behind the camera? On today's program, host Andrew Stewart discusses Testino's life and work with fashion editor, Sarah Mendes.

3 ▶ 2.7   Listen to the radio program. Choose the correct options to complete the sentences.

1 Mario was born in *Italy / Peru*.
2 He grew up in *Lima / New York*.
3 After high school, he *went to college / traveled around the world*.
4 In London, he got a job in a *restaurant / hospital*.
5 He started his career by photographing *models and actors / people he worked with*.
6 He became famous when he photographed *Madonna / Gianni Versace*.
7 He photographed Princess Diana in *1995 / 1997*.
8 In 2012, he opened a gallery in *London / Lima*.

4 ▶ 2.8   Complete the host's questions with the words in the box. Listen again and check.

> does   did   from   is   what   who

1 Where is he _____ ?
2 _____ did he do after he finished high school?
3 How _____ his career start?
4 _____ did he work with?
5 What _____ he doing today?
6 _____ he still live in London?

5 Look at exercise 4 again and answer the questions. Then read the Grammar box.

1 Which question doesn't have a question word? _____

2 In questions 1–6, which auxiliary verbs are used for:

  a the simple present? _____
  b the simple past? _____
  c the present continuous? _____

3 Which question doesn't have an auxiliary verb? _____

📖 | **Grammar** | **question forms**

Most verbs: **(question word) + auxiliary verb + subject + main verb**

Where do you live? *Does your brother live near here?* *What do we know about Mario Testino?*
When did you arrive? *Did you see him?* *How did his career start?*
What are you doing? *Is Mario working today?* *What am I doing?*

The verb *be*: **(question word) + *be* + subject**

Where is he from? *Was he late for work?*

Look! Prepositions don't usually come before the question word: *Who did he work with?* NOT *~~With who did he work?~~*

Go to Grammar practice: question forms, page 115

6 ▶ **2.11** **Pronunciation:** question intonation Listen to two of the questions from the radio program. Does the intonation go up ↗ or down ↘ at the end of the questions?

1 How did his career start? *up ↗ / down ↘*
2 Does he still live in London? *up ↗ / down ↘*

7 **A** Put the words in parentheses in the correct place in the questions.

1 Was Mario's father Peru? (from)
2 Why he take Mario to New York? (did)
3 When did move to London? (Mario)
4 Did Princess Diana in 1997? (die)
5 Does live in New York now? (he)
6 What does the radio host play? (song)

B ▶ **2.12** Say the questions with the correct intonation. Listen, check, and repeat. Then ask and answer the questions in pairs.

Go to Communication practice: Student A, page 159; Student B, page 167

8 In pairs, ask and answer questions with the words.

1 you / busy / right now?

2 what time / you / wake up / this morning?

3 you / have / a driver's license?

4 where / you / go on vacation / last year?

5 how often / you / take / photographs?

6 which TV series / you / watch / these days?

9 Write four sentences about you and your family. Read the sentences to your partner. He/She should ask questions to find out more information.

A *I went to college in São Paulo.* **B** *What did you study there?*
A *My father retired last year.* **B** *What was his job?*

Personal Best Write five quiz questions about a famous person.

2D That reminds me of …

1 ▶ 2.13 Look at the pictures. In pairs, predict what happened on Taylor's first day of work. Watch or listen to the first part of *Learning Curve* and check.

2 ▶ 2.13 Are the sentences true (T) or false (F)? Watch or listen again and check.

1 Taylor's new job is in a fitness center. _____
2 She was worried about being late. _____
3 She arrived at work fifteen minutes early. _____
4 A big car hit her car. _____
5 The man in the car shouted at her. _____
6 She was embarrassed. _____

✦✦ Conversation builder telling a personal story

Starting the story:
Something similar happened to me.
That reminds me of …
Let me tell you about …

Involving the listener:
You'll never guess … (who it was / what happened next / what she said)
Can you imagine?
But that's not all.

Saying how you felt:
It was so …
I felt really …
At first, I felt …

---

3 ▶ 2.14 Read the Conversation builder. Match the two parts to make sentences that Taylor used in her story. Listen, check, and repeat.

1 Let me tell you about
2 At first, I felt
3 I felt
4 But that's
5 You'll never guess
6 It was so

a embarrassing.
b not all.
c my first day.
d great.
e really angry.
f who took my parking spot.

4 In pairs, write three phrases that Taylor's new boss could use to tell the story of what happened.

5 A ▶ 2.15   In pairs, order phrases a–h from Penny's story. Watch or listen to the second part of the show, and check.

a ☐ I sent the message to him by mistake!

b ☐ My boss had the same name as my friend—Steve Jones.

c ☐ He thought it was funny, but can you imagine how I felt?

d ☐ Everyone in the office could hear him! It was quite embarrassing.

e ☐ Something similar happened to me at my last job.

f ☐ You'll never guess what he said. "I'm glad you think I'm handsome and amazing, but it isn't my birthday!"

g ☐ I worked at a radio station in London before I moved to New York.

h ☐ I sent my good friend Steve an e-mail message for his birthday. It said, "Happy birthday to my handsome, amazing friend!"

B ▶ 2.15   Watch or listen again. How are Taylor and Penny's stories similar?

6 ▶ 2.16   Listen and repeat the phrases when you hear the beeps. How do Taylor and Penny show they are interested in each other's stories?

🔧 **Skill**   **showing interest**

Good listeners show that they are interested in what someone else is saying.
- Use short response expressions, such as *Oh, no! Really?* etc.
- Ask questions about what happened.
- Use the correct intonation to show you are interested.

7   Read the Skill box. Put the phrases in the correct columns.

What happened?   That's amazing!   Really?   What did he do then?
Oh no!   You're kidding!   That's awful!   Lucky you!   You poor thing!   Great!

Responding to something positive	Responding to something negative	Showing interest or asking for more information

8 A ▶ 2.17   Listen to phrases 1–6. Which speaker sounds more interested: A or B?

1 What happened? _____

2 That's amazing! _____

3 Really? _____

4 Oh no, that's awful! _____

5 You're joking! _____

6 Lucky you! _____

B ▶ 2.18   In pairs, say phrases 1–6 to show you are interested. Listen, check, and repeat.

Go to Communication practice: Student A, page 158; Student B, page 166

9 A **PREPARE**   Choose one of the ideas. Make notes on what happened and how you felt.

your first day at work/school/college

a birthday or celebration

a time when you lost something important

a difficult day

B **PRACTICE**   In pairs, take turns telling your stories. Listen to your partner and show you are interested by responding to what he/she says or by asking questions.

C **PERSONAL BEST**   Find another partner and tell your story again. How is your storytelling better this time?

Personal Best   How well did you listen to your partner's story? Write about what happened and how he/she felt.

Grammar

1 Choose the correct options to complete the sentences.

1 _____ married?
 a You are
 b Are you
 c Is you

2 She _____ Japanese food.
 a 's liking
 b like
 c likes

3 _____ take a message?
 a I can
 b Can I
 c Do I can

4 In the summer I _____ .
 a every day go swimming
 b go swimming every day
 c go every day swimming

5 When _____ here?
 a do you got
 b did you get
 c are you get

6 We went to Brazil _____ year.
 a last
 b past
 c ago

7 The train _____ in the morning.
 a late is always
 b always is late
 c is always late

8 _____ time did you wake up yesterday?
 a Which
 b When
 c What

2 Rewrite the sentences using the tenses in parentheses.

1 I work in a restaurant.
 I *worked* in a *restaurant*. (simple past)

2 I don't wear dark clothes.
 I _____ dark clothes. (present continuous)

3 Where do you go to school?
 Where _____ to school? (simple past)

4 What do you do?
 What _____? (present continuous)

5 Did you take a lot of photos on your trip?
 _____ a lot of photos on your trip? (simple present)

6 I buy bread in the supermarket.
 I _____ bread in the supermarket. (simple past)

3 Complete the text with the correct forms of the verbs in parentheses.

Ishita Malaviya

Where ¹_____ (be) Ishita from?

She ²_____ (grow up) in Mumbai, India and now she ³_____ (live) in Manipal, in the state of Karnataka, 875 km. away.

What ⁴_____ she _____ (do)?

A few years ago, she ⁵_____ (become) India's first professional female surfer and now she ⁶_____ (have) a sufing school, where she ⁷_____ (teach) tourists and local people how to surf.

How ⁸_____ she _____ (start) surfing?

When she ⁹_____ (go) to college in 2007, she met a German student with a surfboard. At first, she ¹⁰_____ (not can) believe that people surfed in India, so she asked him about it and started to learn.

What ¹¹_____ she _____ (do) today?

She ¹²_____ (make) a movie about her story. She hopes it makes more people want to learn how to surf in India.

Vocabulary

1 Match the adjectives with the definitions.

shy embarrassed patient annoying confused disappointed lazy generous

Someone who ...

1 feels bad because he/she made a mistake. _____
2 doesn't want to work or try hard. _____
3 is happy to give money, help, or his/her time. _____
4 doesn't mind waiting a long time for something. _____
5 doesn't understand something. _____
6 feels sad because something bad happened. _____
7 doesn't like meeting lots of new people. _____
8 makes other people feel a little angry. _____

2 Circle the word that is different. Explain your answer.

1 wear   carry   bring   funny
2 rude   tired   honest   sociable
3 boring   excited   interesting   disappointing
4 retire   stay in shape   grow up   finish school
5 tell   expect   remind   nice
6 yoga   Pilates   swimming   exercise
7 get up   get married   get engaged   get a divorce
8 hope   relax   expect   look forward to

3 Choose the correct options to complete the sentences.

1 Thank you for eating at our restaurant. Please _____ soon!
   a go back   **b** grow up   **c** come back
2 She really _____ her mother. They have the same eyes.
   a looks   **b** looks like   **c** reminds
3 Hayley is really _____. She spends ten hours a day in the office.
   a hard-working   **b** serious   **c** patient
4 I _____ the meeting to finish at about 3:00.
   a wait   **b** expect   **c** look forward to
5 Can you _____ me your name please?
   a tell   **b** say   **c** remember
6 Raul _____ most weekends with his family.
   a joins   **b** spends   **c** keeps
7 When I was a child, I _____ swimming every Sunday.
   a went   **b** did   **c** played
8 My soccer team lost the game. I feel so _____!
   a excited   **b** relaxed   **c** disappointed

4 Complete the sentences with the verbs in the box.

| go on   lose   retire   wait   remember |
| learn   have   finish   miss   meet |

1 Most students _____ high school at the age of eighteen.
2 Sonia didn't _____ the train, but she arrived late.
3 All my friends _____ social media every day.
4 Did Alex _____ to buy some eggs?
5 My father is 62, and he wants to _____ next year.
6 When you are in college, you _____ lots of interesting people.
7 How often do you _____ your sunglasses?
8 I'm married, but I don't want to _____ any children.
9 This year, I want to _____ to play a musical instrument.
10 Can you _____ for me after class?

Personal Best

Lesson 1A
Describe two friends using personality adjectives.

Lesson 2A
Write two things you did last weekend.

Lesson 1A
Describe one thing you do every month and one thing you do every year.

Lesson 2B
Write a sentence about what you did yesterday using *after*.

Lesson 1B
Name five hobbies or activities you like doing.

Lesson 2C
Write two questions for an interview with a musician you like.

Lesson 1C
Write a sentence using the simple present and present continuous.

Lesson 2C
Think of a relative and describe two of his/her life stages.

Lesson 1D
Write a sentence about yourself using *because*.

Lesson 2D
Give an expression to start telling a story.

Lesson 1D
Write a sentence about someone you know using *so*.

Lesson 2D
Give an expression to show you are interested in a story.

Keep on traveling

| LANGUAGE | comparatives, superlatives, *(not) as ... as* ■ useful adjectives |

3A Tourist or traveler?

1 A Look at the title of the quiz. What is the difference between a "tourist" and a "traveler"?

B Match the speech bubbles with the people in the pictures.

2 Underline all the adjectives in the speech bubbles.

Go to Vocabulary practice: useful adjectives, page 141

3 A Take the quiz in pairs. Write down your partner's answers.

B Look at the results on page 174. Are you and your partner similar?

1
I want to go to different countries, try unusual food, and have an adventure.

2
I prefer to stay at nice hotels, visit famous sights, and have a good time.

1 What do you usually do on vacation?
a I try to see the most famous sights in a city or visit the big museums.
b I like to go somewhere unusual and discover new things.

2 Do you prefer to stay downtown or away from the center of town?
a Downtown can be more expensive, but it's the best place to be.
b I prefer to be farther away from the downtown area. It's cheaper and quieter.

3 Do you use a guidebook?
a Yes, I do. I like to plan my trip carefully before I go.
b Never! Reading guidebooks isn't as good as talking with local people.

4 Do you ever explore new places alone?
a No, I don't. Vacations are about spending time with friends and family.
b Yes, I do. You discover more about yourself when you're by yourself.

5 What time of year do you prefer to travel?
a In the summer, when the weather is hot and everyone is happier.
b The summer is the worst time! Places aren't as crowded at other times of the year.

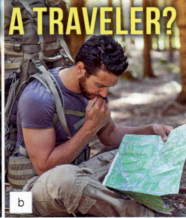

ARE YOU A TOURIST OR A TRAVELER?

a

b

4 Complete the chart with comparative and superlative adjectives from the quiz. Can you complete the other forms?

	famous	cheap	happy	far	good	bad
comparative						
superlative	*the most famous*					

5 Match sentences 1–2 with the correct meanings a–b. Then read the Grammar box.

1 Reading guidebooks isn't as good as talking with local people. ____
2 Reading guidebooks is as good as talking with local people. ____

a Reading guidebooks and talking with to local people are equally good.
b Reading guidebooks is worse than talking with local people.

📖 **Grammar** comparatives, superlatives, *(not) as … as*

Comparatives:	Superlatives:	*(not) as … as*:
Your hotel is **cheaper** than my hotel.	This is **the biggest** museum in the country.	The beaches **aren't as crowded as** they are in the summer.
The festival is **more exciting** than the castle.	The castle is **the most famous** building in the city.	

Go to Grammar practice: comparatives, superlatives, *(not) as … as*, page 116

6 ▶3.3 Listen to Michelle ask three friends for advice. Check (✔) the advice they recommend.

PARIS TRIP

Transportation:
roller skates ☐ bus ☐ metro/ subway ☐

Attractions:
the Eiffel ☐ the ☐ Buttes-Chaumont ☐
Tower Louvre Park

Food:
a restaurant ☐ a picnic ☐ fast food ☐

7 A ▶3.4 **Pronunciation:** sentence stress Listen to four sentences from the conversations in exercise 6. <u>Underline</u> the stressed words.

1 The metro is the quickest way.
2 The restaurants are much more expensive than I thought.
3 The ones downtown are the worst.
4 It's as cheap as fast food, but it's a lot better.

B ▶3.4 Listen again and repeat.

Go to Communication practice: Student A, page 159; Student B, page 167

8 A Complete the sentences to make recommendations for your town or city.

1 _____ is the most popular tourist attraction.
2 _____ isn't as famous as _____ , but I prefer it because _____.
3 _____ is the best way to travel because _____.
4 _____ is a great place to buy _____ , and it isn't as expensive as _____.
5 _____ is the most traditional food, and the best restaurant for it is _____.
6 _____ is the most interesting place for lunch because _____.

B Compare your recommendations in pairs. Say if you agree or disagree.

9 A Complete the questions with the correct form of the adjectives in parentheses.

1 In your opinion, is a trip to the city as _____ as a trip to the beach? (relaxing)
2 Do you think vacations in your country are _____ than going abroad? (good)
3 Where is _____ place in your country? (hot)
4 Do you think traveling by car is as _____ as traveling by train? (expensive)
5 Do you think vacations with friends are _____ than family vacations? (enjoyable)
6 In your opinion, what is _____ thing about a vacation? (bad)

B Ask and answer the questions in pairs. Try to give more information.

Personal Best Choose three places and make sentences about them with comparatives, superlatives, and *(not) as … as*.

Learning Curve

3B Staycation or vacation?

1 Match the activities in the box with the pictures. Which activities do you usually do on vacation?

> sunbathe   visit a museum   go sightseeing   buy souvenirs
> rent a car   eat out   go abroad   stay at a hotel

a
b
c
d
e
f
g
h

Personal Best

Go to Vocabulary practice: vacation activities, page 138

2 Discuss the questions in pairs.

1 How often do you take a vacation?
2 Do you ever go abroad? Why/Why not?
3 Where do you usually stay?
4 Who do you usually go with?
5 What do you enjoy doing most on vacation?
6 What is the worst thing about a vacation?

3 ▶ 3.8 Guess the correct definition of a "staycation". Watch or listen to the first part of *Learning Curve* and check.

A "staycation" is a vacation where you stay ...
a in your country.   **b** at your own home.   **c** at a friend's house.

🔧 **Skill** **Identifying key points**

When people speak, listen for the important things they say.
- They usually emphasize the most important ideas.
- After an important idea, they sometimes give an example or more information.
- Find the key words in the questions and listen very carefully when the speaker talks about them.

---

4 ▶ 3.7 Read the Skill box. Watch or listen again and check (✔) the key points Penny mentions.

1 Vacations need a lot of planning. ☐
2 They can be expensive. ☐
3 Hotels are great for relaxing. ☐
4 Travel can be tiring. ☐
5 You don't have to travel on a staycation. ☐
6 You can go to your favorite places. ☐
7 You can relax at home. ☐
8 You can continue your daily routine. ☐

5 ▶ 3.8 Watch or listen to the second part of the show. Check (✔) the type of vacation the people are having.

1 Terry and Carol   staycation ☐ vacation ☐
2 Ayoku   staycation ☐ vacation ☐
3 Lisa   staycation ☐ vacation ☐

Penny
Learning Cu

6 ▶ 3.8   Watch or listen again. Are the sentences true (T) or false (F)?

1 Terry and Carol are having a bad time on holiday. ____
2 They're in Ireland. ____
3 They think staycations can be boring. ____
4 Ayoku has two weeks off work. ____
5 He wants to spend the time relaxing in his apartment. ____
6 Last year he went on vacation, but didn't relax much. ____
7 Lisa's cousins have come to visit her in New York. ____
8 She prefers to show them popular tourist attractions. ____

Terry and Carol

Ayoku

Lisa

7 Discuss the questions about your last vacation in pairs.

> Where did you go?
> Where did you stay?
> What did you eat?
> What did you do?
> What was the weather like?
> Did you have a good time?
> Who did you go with?

🧩 **Listening builder**   sentence stress

English speakers usually stress the most important words in a sentence. You can usually understand the general idea if you only hear these words.
A **staycation** is a **vacation** where you **stay** at your **own home**.
You can **make time** to **eat out** at your **favorite restaurant** or **drive** to the **beach**.

8 **A** Read the Listening builder. Look at the words in the sentences 1–5 from the show. Can you understand the general ideas?

1 _____ hired _____ car _____ came _____ _____ lovely national park!
2 _____ usually stay _____ home _____ _____ often boring.
3 _____ doing all _____ things _____ don't usually _____ time _____ do.
4 _____ _____ actually _____ stressful _____ everything _____ planned.
5 _____ _____ family visits, _____ take _____ _____ places _____ many tourists never see.

B ▶ 3.9   In pairs, try to complete the sentences with the unstressed words. Listen and check.

9 Discuss the questions in pairs. Give reasons for your answers.
Which is better...

1 sunbathing or going sightseeing?

3 flying or traveling by train?

2 staying at a hotel or going camping?

4 packing a big suitcase or taking a small backpack?

Personal Best   Write a paragraph explaining to tourists what there is to do in your town or city.

3C A traveler's tale

1 A Read the introduction to the text and look at the pictures. Answer the questions in pairs.

1 How long do you think Alastair's trip took?
2 How many countries do you think he visited?
3 What type of problems do you think he had on the trip?
4 What kind of person do you think Alastair is?
5 Would you like to go on an adventure like this? Why/Why not?

B Read the rest of the text and check your answers.

Around the world by bike

In 2001, Alastair Humphreys was studying to become a teacher, but he really wanted to do something different. A few months later, he surprised his friends and family by beginning an amazing trip that took him around the world ... on his bike!

In all, Alastair visited 60 countries and, throughout the trip, he kept a blog to record all of his experiences. Although there were some special moments on the road, there was also disappointment and disaster. One disappointment came early. Alastair's dream was to ride his bike all the way, except for taking ships to cross the oceans. Unfortunately, this was impossible. The police stopped him while he was traveling through Egypt, and he had to ride in the back of a truck. He was angry, but there was no other way to continue.

The rest of the time, he rode, rode, rode. On one occasion, his bike broke down while he was crossing the Arizona desert. Help came from a surprising place. To his amazement, complete strangers bought him a new bike so that he could continue his incredible journey.

The trip was tough, and Alastair didn't have enough money to stay at nice hotels. While he was riding through Patagonia, he didn't take a shower for 24 days!

However, one of the hardest parts of his trip came when he traveled through Russia in the winter. Luckily, a friend joined him, so he wasn't traveling alone. But it was so cold that Alistair's beard froze while they were traveling through Siberia.

But none of these problems could stop him from completing the trip. Four years and 75,000 km. later, Alastair finally arrived back home in the U.K. with lots of stories to tell.

2 In pairs, answer the questions. Read the text again and check your answers.

1 Why didn't he ride his bike the whole time?
2 How did he get a new bike?
3 What were his accommodations like?
4 Where did he experience the worst weather?

3 A Complete the sentences with the correct verbs. Check your answers in the text.

1 He _____ the Arizona desert when his bike _____ down.
2 While they _____ their bikes through Siberia, Alastair's beard _____ .

B Look at the sentences again and answer the questions. Then read the Grammar box.

1 Which verbs describe completed actions in the past? _____ , _____
2 Which verbs describe actions happening at the time of the completed action? _____ , _____

Grammar — past continuous and simple past

Actions in progress at a time in the past:	Actions in progress when a completed action happened:
In 2001, Alastair Humphreys **was studying** to become a teacher.	The police **stopped** him **while** he **was traveling** through *Egypt*. He **was traveling** through *Egypt* **when** the police **stopped** him.

Go to Grammar practice: past continuous and simple past, page 117

4 A ▶ 3.11 **Pronunciation:** *was/were* Listen to the sentences and <u>underline</u> the stressed words. How do you pronounce *was* and *were*?

1 I was driving home at 6:00 yesterday evening.
2 They were working hard when I got to the office.
3 It didn't rain while Anita was staying in Seattle.
4 What were you doing at 8:00 this morning?

B Practice saying the sentences in pairs.

5 In pairs, ask and answer the question *What were you doing ...?* using the time in each of the boxes. Pay attention to how you say *was* and *were*.

> in 2014 | at 7:30 this morning | this time last week
> one hour ago | yesterday evening at 6:00 | last year

6 A Look at the pictures. Complete the sentences with your own ideas.

1 I was sleeping in bed when ...

3 While Barbara was cooking dinner, ...

2 They were running in the park when ...

4 My boss called me while ...

B Compare your answers in pairs.

Go to Communication practice: Student A, page 160; Student B, page 168

7 ▶ 3.12 Choose the correct form of the verbs to complete the conversation. Listen and check.

David Did I ever tell you about how I ¹*met / was meeting* a museum guide in Boston?
Emma No, I don't think so.
David It was in 2012. While I ²*traveled / was traveling* around the U.S., I ³*waited / was waiting* for a train to New York City, but I was hungry, so I ⁴*went / was going* to a café to buy a sandwich. While I ⁵*sat / was sitting* there, a man at another table ⁶*got up / was getting up* and ⁷*left / was leaving* his wallet.
Emma Oh no! What did you do?
David I ⁸*ran / was running* after him and ⁹*gave / was giving* him the wallet back. But the funny thing is, when I ¹⁰*got / was getting* to the platform later, the same man ¹¹*waited / was waiting* for the train.
Emma Really?
David Yes, and he ¹²*was / was being* a museum guide at the Museum of Natural History in New York City. He ¹³*offered / was offering* to show me around to thank me for returning my wallet. The museum was amazing!

8 Think about a vacation or travel experience you had. Discuss the questions in pairs.

1 Where and when did you go?
2 What were the best/worst moments?
3 What were you doing when the best/worst moments happened?

Personal Best Describe an important event in your life. Use the simple past and past continuous to explain what happened.

3D Travel problems

1 Discuss the questions in pairs.

    1 When was the last time you were at an airport?   **3** How do you usually feel when you are at an airport?

    2 Why were you there?   **4** What problems can happen at an airport?

2 ▶ 3.13 Look at pictures a–f and order them from 1–6. Listen and check.

3 ▶ 3.13 Complete the text with the correct form of the verbs in the box. Listen again and check.

arrive   book   buy   have   open   carry   receive   run   see   wait

In 2013, Martin Hendon was living in London. One morning, he ¹_____ a quick breakfast, when he ²_____ a letter from his best friend, Tony. It was an invitation to Tony's wedding … in Naples, Italy, in two weeks! So Martin quickly ³_____ a flight and ⁴_____ a new suit.

The day before the wedding didn't start well. Martin ⁵_____ patiently at the airport when he ⁶_____ that his flight was canceled. He caught a later flight that night and arrived in Naples early the next morning, but he was very tired and accidentally took the wrong suitcase. When he ⁷_____ it up in his hotel room, he found someone else's clothes!

He ⁸_____ down the street desperately looking for a new suit, but it was Sunday and the stores were still closed. Just then, he recognized a passenger from his plane walking slowly down the street. She ⁹_____ a suitcase the same color as Martin's. He asked her politely to open it, and there was Martin's new suit inside!

He changed his clothes and took a taxi to the wedding. When Martin ¹⁰_____ , he opened the door nervously. Inside, everyone was waiting for the wedding to begin. Tony looked at him and smiled. He was only a few minutes late.

4 Match the paragraphs from exercise 3 with descriptions a–d. Then read the Skill box.

Paragraph 1	**a** the problem (what happened)
Paragraph 2	**b** the resolution (how he solved the problem)
Paragraph 3	**c** the background (who, when, where)
Paragraph 4	**d** the ending (what happened in the end, how he felt)

🔧 **Skill** writing a narrative

When you write a story, make it easy to follow and interesting.

- Tell the story in chronological order.
- Organize your ideas into four paragraphs (the background, the problem, the resolution, the ending).
- Use adjectives and adverbs to make the text more interesting.

5 A Complete the sentences from Martin's story. Check your answers in the text.

1 One morning, he was having a _____ breakfast.   2 Martin _____ booked a flight.

B Answer the questions about sentences 1 and 2.

1 Which word is an adjective and describes a noun?   _____
2 Which word is an adverb and describes a verb?   _____
3 What letters do we add to most adjectives to make an adverb?   _____

6 <u>Underline</u> seven more adverbs that describe verbs in Martin's story.

Text builder   adverbs of manner

We use adverbs of manner to say how someone does an action:
*Martin was waiting **patiently** at the airport.*

Most adjectives:	*quiet → quietly, slow → slowly*
Adjectives ending in -y:	*happy → happily, angry → angrily*
Irregular adverbs:	*good → well, fast → fast, hard → hard*

Look! Adverbs of manner come at the end of the phrase:
*He speaks Spanish **well**.* NOT ~~*He speaks well Spanish.*~~

---

7 Read the Text builder. Choose the correct words to complete the first paragraph of another story.

Ana Carvalho is from Goiânia, Brazil, but in 2015, she was living in São Paulo where she was studying **¹**hard / hardly in college. After her exams, she was waiting **²**nervous / nervously for the results, but she was also very **³**happy / happily because it was her birthday in two days.

She planned to go home to celebrate with her friends and family in Goiânia. Ana was very **⁴**practical / practically, and the night before the flight she packed her suitcase **⁵**careful / carefully, checked to make sure she had her passport and tickets, and slept **⁶**good / well.

8 A **PREPARE** Match phrases 1–6 with pictures a–f. In pairs, discuss what happened to Ana Carvalho. Put your ideas into three groups for the next three paragraphs of the narrative.

1 apologize and give her a ticket to Goiânia   ____
2 begin to worry on the plane   ____
3 realize that the plane is flying to Guyana   ____
4 receive the exam results at her party   ____
5 not hear her correctly   ____
6 ask which gate is for Goiânia   ____

a

b

c

d

e

f

B **PRACTICE** Use your notes to help you write the rest of Ana's story. Remember to use adverbs.

C **PERSONAL BEST** Exchange stories with another pair. Check (✓) three sentences that are well-written.

Personal Best   Write five sentences about a vacation experience you had. Use a different adverb in each sentence.

The working world

| LANGUAGE | *will*, *may*, and *might* for predictions ■ jobs |

4A The future of work

1 **A** Look at the title of the text and the picture. What do you think it is about?

B In pairs, decide which jobs machines will do in the future and which jobs will always need people.

> accountant   fashion designer   farmer   journalist   model   police officer
> receptionist   salesperson   surgeon   tour guide   waiter/waitress

Go to Vocabulary practice: jobs, page 142

2 Read the text. Which jobs do experts think that machines will do?

WILL A ROBOT TAKE MY JOB?

I'm at the Henn-na Hotel in Japan. A well-dressed Japanese woman welcomes me and asks if I have a reservation. But this is no ordinary receptionist. She is, in fact, a robot—one of several at the hotel that can carry your bags to your room, and even give you travel tips.

Robots and computers are taking our jobs. According to experts, ninety years from now, machines will replace 70% of today's occupations. Accountants and telephone salespeople may be the first to lose their jobs. In restaurants, robots might replace waiters and waitresses. Models might also disappear; fashion designer, Ralph Lauren, is already experimenting with holographic models for his clothes. And in the future, when you go to the hospital for an operation, even the surgeon probably won't be real.

So, should we be worried? The answer is no. History shows us that as old jobs die, new jobs replace them. So, what jobs will exist for us in the future? Here are our top three predictions:

1 Drone controller
Drones will deliver our groceries, remove our trash, and may even act as police officers. But people will still need to control these flying devices from the ground.

2 Vertical farmer
Transporting food will probably become more expensive, and with crowded cities, there will only be one way to grow food and vegetables—upward! Supermarkets will grow all their food above them in special glass buildings.

3 Space tour guide
In the future, people won't want to travel around the world on vacation. Space tourism will create thousands of jobs for space pilots and tour guides to take tourists out of this world!

3 Match the two columns to make complete sentences. Check your answers in the text.

1 Ninety years from now, machines will
2 Accountants and telephone salespeople may
3 Models might
4 The surgeon probably won't
5 Transporting food will probably
6 People won't

a become more expensive.
b also disappear.
c want to travel around the world on vacation.
d replace 70% of today's occupations.
e be the first to lose their jobs.
f be real.

4 **A** Answer the questions about the predictions in exercise 3.

1 Which two sentences are about things that are likely? _____ , _____
2 Which two sentences are about things that are possible? _____ , _____
3 Which two sentences are about things that are unlikely? _____ , _____

B Choose the correct words to complete the rule. Then read the Grammar box.

When we use *probably*, it comes *before / after will* and *before / after won't*.

📖 **Grammar** *will, may,* and *might* for predictions

Predictions that are sure/very likely:	Predictions that are less sure/possible:	Predictions that are very unlikely:
The traffic **will** be very bad tonight.	It **might** rain tomorrow. The train **may** be late.	Chelsea **won't** win the FA cup next year.

Look! We can use *probably* with *will* and *won't*: **I'll probably** fail the exam / I **probably won't** pass the exam.

Go to Grammar practice: *will, may,* and *might* for predictions, page 118

5 A ▶ 4.4 **Pronunciation:** *want/won't* Listen and repeat the sentence from the text. Match the words in **bold** with the sounds /a/ and /o/.

In the future, people **won't want** to travel around the world on vacation.

B ▶ 4.5 How do you say the sentences? Pay attention to *want* and *won't*. Listen, check, and repeat.

1 He might **want** to look for a new job.
2 Robots **won't** replace politicians.
3 My boss will probably **want** to travel by boat.
4 In the future, you **won't** have to go to school.

Go to Communication practice: Student A, page 160; Student B, page 168

6 A Work in pairs and look at the topics below. What do you think will happen in the future? Make nine predictions.

Students won't go to school. Computers will probably replace teachers.

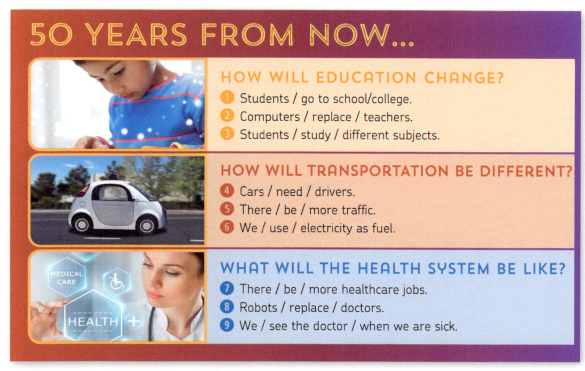

50 YEARS FROM NOW...

HOW WILL EDUCATION CHANGE?
1 Students / go to school/college.
2 Computers / replace / teachers.
3 Students / study / different subjects.

HOW WILL TRANSPORTATION BE DIFFERENT?
4 Cars / need / drivers.
5 There / be / more traffic.
6 We / use / electricity as fuel.

WHAT WILL THE HEALTH SYSTEM BE LIKE?
7 There / be / more healthcare jobs.
8 Robots / replace / doctors.
9 We / see the doctor / when we are sick.

B ▶ 4.6 Listen to an expert talking about the topics. What predictions does she make? How sure is she?

7 Did you agree with the expert? Can you think of any other predictions about these topics?

8 In pairs, make predictions about the topics. Say if you agree or disagree with your partner.

the weather tomorrow   your country winning the World Cup   your next English exam

the town or city where you live   your trip home tonight   tomorrow at work/school/college

Personal Best   Write predictions about how five different jobs will change in the future.

4B I'm so bored!

1 Look at the title and the pictures on page 33. Which jobs can you see? Discuss the questions in pairs.

1 How often do you feel bored?
2 What jobs do you think are boring?
3 Do you think boredom is a bad thing? Why/Why not?
4 What can you do to stop being bored at work?

Skill skimming a text

When we skim a text, we read it quickly to understand the main ideas.
- Look at the title, pictures, and any headings, and predict what the text is about.
- Read the first sentence in each paragraph carefully. These are "topic sentences" and are usually a summary of what the paragraph is about.
- Think about the ideas from all the topic sentences to understand the general meaning of the whole text.

2 Read the Skill box. Then read the <mark>highlighted</mark> topic sentences in the text and check (✔) the best description of the text.

1 Modern technology makes us feel bored more quickly. ☐
2 People can have better ideas after they do boring activities. ☐
3 Boredom in offices is a serious problem for companies. ☐

3 Answer the questions in pairs. Read the text again and check your answers.

1 What do most people do when they are bored?
2 How did the scientists use the plastic cups to test people's creativity?
3 What activity did some people do first to make themselves be bored?
4 Who was more creative in the experiment? What ideas did they have?
5 What does Jack White do to give himself ideas for new songs?
6 What kinds of activities make us more/less creative?

4 Has the text changed your opinion about being bored? Why/Why not?

5 A Look at the extract from the text. Who or what does *They* refer to?

Some scientists think we're making a mistake. **They** *believe that boring activities can be good for us.*

B Read the Text builder. Find pronouns 1–8 in the text and say what they refer to.

Text builder pronoun referencing

We use pronouns and possessive adjectives to avoid repeating nouns:
*Sharon had **a fantastic idea** yesterday. **It** was really creative.*
***Carlos** always works late. I saw **him** in the office at 8:00 last night.*
***My parents** earn a lot of money, but I think **their** jobs are very boring.*

6 A Complete the text with the pronouns in the box. What do the pronouns refer to?

his   it   he   them

Karl Duncker was a German psychologist. **1**_____ is most famous for developing a way to test creativity. In **2**_____ experiment, he gave students a candle, a book of matches, and a box of thumbtacks. He asked **3**_____ to stick the candle to a wall and light **4**_____ without dripping any wax on the table.

B In pairs, try to solve Duncker's problem. Explain your solution to the class.

THE TRUTH ABOUT BOREDOM

We all hate being bored, particularly at work. In fact, most of us try hard to avoid [1] **it** and, thanks to modern technology, there are now hundreds of ways to keep ourselves entertained. People watch videos or play games on the way to work, check their phones when they're in boring meetings, and talk with friends or listen to music while they do dull administrative tasks. But some scientists think we're making a mistake. They believe that boring activities can be good for us, and a recent psychology experiment tests this idea.

In 2013, Dr. Sandi Mann and Rebekah Cadman did an experiment to test people's creativity, i.e., how good we are at coming up with new ideas. [2] **Their** idea was to see if boredom had an effect on how creative we are. They gave 140 people some plastic cups and asked [3] **them** to think of different ways to use them. However, half of the people spent 15 minutes doing some very boring activities first. They had to read telephone numbers from a long list and copy [4] **them** on a piece of paper.

The results of the experiment were very interesting. The people who did the boring activities first were much more creative and thought of lots of ideas. Some people suggested wearing the cups as party hats or filling [5] **them** with fruit juice and freezing them to make popsicles. Whereas, the people who didn't do any boring tasks found it hard to think of many ways to use the cups.

Dr. Mann says a little boredom can be positive for us. [6] **She** doesn't think we should be afraid of "doing nothing." Many very successful people do "boring" activities in their free time. For example, rock musician Jack White, repairs furniture. [7] **His** hobby helps him relax and think of ideas for new songs. At work, some successful people do similar things to be more creative, like cleaning out their desk or deleting old e-mails.

However, there are good and bad ways to be bored. You should only do boring activities for a short time. And you should avoid physical activities that make you feel tired, as this can make you less creative. So, if you usually listen to music, read the news, and send messages to friends when you're bored at work, why not try doing less? Make yourself a cup of coffee, organize your paperwork, or look out the window—maybe [8] **it** will change your life … and you can always tell your boss that you're being creative.

Personal Best   Write about a time you thought of a creative solution to a problem.

4C The secret boss

1 Look at the two people in the pictures. What is the relationship between them? Read the text and check.

Carla Pine is the managing director of a chain of Italian restaurants. She works in Vancouver and is responsible for twenty restaurants in Canada. Next week, she's visiting two of her restaurants to find out what it's like to be a company employee, but she's going to do it in secret! She's going to dress like a member of the staff but, because people might recognize her, she's going to change her hair color and makeup, and become … Katie Rose.

She's going to Toronto and has a busy few days ahead of her. On Monday and Tuesday, she's working as a kitchen assistant with George Nowak.
On Wednesday and Thursday, she's working as a waitress in another restaurant in the city with Lucy Mendez … and on Friday, she's going to tell George and Lucy who she really is!

Carla Pine

Katie Rose

2 Choose the correct options to complete the sentences. Read the text again and check.

1 Carla is visiting *one / two / three* of her restaurants next week.
2 She is going to change her *appearance / opinion / voice* so people don't recognize her.
3 She's going to see what it's like to work as *a hair stylist / a boss / an employee*.
4 On Monday and Tuesday, she's working as a *managing director / waitress / kitchen assistant*.
5 On Wednesday and Thursday, she's working with *Lucy Mendez / George Nowak / Katie Rose*.

3 Answer the questions about the sentences in exercise 2. Then read the Grammar box.

1 Do the sentences refer to the past, the present, or the future? _____
2 Which sentences say *when* and/or *where* she will do things? _____
3 Which use the present continuous? _____ Which use *be going to*? _____

> 📖 **Grammar** *be going to* and present continuous
>
> **Future plans:**
> I**'m going to take** a training course.
> The company **isn't going to open** a new office.
>
> **Look!** We can also use *be going to* with arrangements:
> He**'s going to** travel to Seattle on Monday.
>
> **Future arrangements (with a fixed time and place):**
> He**'s working** in Seattle on Monday.
> What **are you doing** this evening?
>
> What **are** you **going to** do this evening?

Go to Grammar practice: *be going to* and present continuous, page 119

4 **A** ▶ 4.9 **Pronunciation:** *going to* and *want to* Listen to Carla speaking quickly. How are *going to* and *want to* pronounced?

I **want to** find out what it's like to work for my company, so I'm **going to** visit two of my restaurants … in secret.

B ▶ 4.10 In pairs, say the conversation quickly. Listen, check, and repeat.

A What are you **going to** do tonight?
B I'm **going to** try that new Chinese restaurant. Do you **want to** come?
A I can't. I'm **going to** work late tonight. I'm free tomorrow, if you **want to** get together.
B Yes, that's great. I **want to** hear all your news!

5 Check (✔) the things you have done from the box below. Tell your partner when and why.

> apply for a job ☐   take a training course ☐   get a promotion ☐   quit a job ☐   write a résumé ☐

When I was a student, I applied for a job as a DJ. I didn't get it.

Go to Vocabulary practice: phrases about work, page 143

6 A ▶ 4.13   Listen to the conversation between Carla, Lucy, and George. Complete the chart.

Name	Problems	Solutions
George Nowak, Head chef	*George's kitchen wasn't clean.*	
Lucy Mendez, Head waitress		

B Check your answers in pairs.

George's kitchen wasn't clean, so Carla is going to ...

7 A In pairs, look at the problems and think of the best way to solve them.

1 Your colleague is going on vacation, so you'll have to use a complicated new computer program at work.

2 Your boss does no work, but he wants you to work on the weekends to finish a project.

3 You want to buy a house, but your salary is the same as when you started work ten years ago!

B Tell the rest of the class your plans.

We're going to take a training course to learn about the new program.

Go to Communication practice: Student A, page 160; Student B, page 168

8 In pairs, ask and answer the question *What are you doing ...?* with the future times in the boxes below.

A *What are you doing tonight?*
B *I'm meeting some friends downtown. We're going to have dinner together.*

> tonight   tomorrow   next weekend   next summer   in two weeks   the day after tomorrow   next year

Personal Best   Write about your work plans for the future.

4D Can I leave a message?

1 Look at the reasons for making telephone calls. Can you think of any more?

call a taxi   speak to a colleague   call in sick to work   ask for technical help
reserve a table at a restaurant   make an appointment   call a store for information

2 Discuss the questions in pairs.

1 How often do you call people?
2 Who do you usually talk to on the phone?
3 How do you feel when you speak to someone you don't know on the phone?
4 What problems can you have when you speak in English on the phone?

3 ▶4.14 Watch or listen to the first part of *Learning Curve*. Who called these people, and why did they call?

Ethan

Receptionist

Penny

Mo

4 ▶4.14 Watch or listen again. Are the sentences true (T) or false (F)?

1 Penny thinks that communication is easier with modern technology. ____
2 Penny and Ethan have a video conference call with Simon and Kate at 10:00. ____
3 Ethan makes an appointment with the dentist for 9:50. ____
4 Mo says it will take ten minutes to fix the Internet connection. ____
5 Mo says he will bring Penny a telephone to call Simon and Kate. ____

Conversation builder   telephone language

Caller:
Hello, this is …
Could I speak to …?
Can you tell him/her that …?
Could you ask him/her to call me back, please?
Thank you, goodbye.

Person being called:
Good morning, … How can I help you?
Hello, this is … (speaking/calling).
I'm afraid he/she's not available at the moment.
Can I take a message?
I think you have the wrong number.
Thanks/Thank you for calling.

5 A ▶4.15 Read the Conversation builder. In pairs, order the conversation from 1–9. Listen and check.

a ☐ Thanks for calling.
b ☐ Yes, can you ask her to call Fiona when she can?
c ☐ Hello, Mo Bensallem speaking.
d ☐ Yes, of course.
e ☐ Hello, could I speak to Julia, please?
f ☐ I'm afraid she's not at her desk at the moment.
g ☐ Sorry, I don't know. Can I take a message?
h ☐ Do you know when she will be back?
i ☐ Thank you, goodbye.

Fiona   Mo

B In pairs, practice saying the conversation. You can change the names and any details.

6 ▶ **4.16** Watch or listen to the second part of the show. Does Penny speak to Kate and Simon?

7 ▶ **4.16** Check (✔) the problems Penny has. Watch or listen again and check.

Charlotte

1 She dials the wrong number. ☐
2 Simon forgot about the conference call. ☐
3 Kate doesn't answer the phone in time. ☐
4 Charlotte can't hear Penny very well. ☐
5 Charlotte doesn't understand English well. ☐
6 Penny forgot to leave her number. ☐

8 ▶ **4.17** Listen and repeat the phrases when you hear the beeps. How do the speakers deal with difficulties?

> 🔧 **Skill**   **dealing with difficulties**
>
> **It is sometimes difficult to understand people when they speak, especially on the telephone.**
> • Ask the speaker politely to speak louder or repeat what he/she said.
> • Ask the speaker to spell any difficult words.
> • Repeat what the speaker says to make sure it is correct.
> • Stress any words or phrases you want to check.

9 Read the Skill box. Put the phrases in the correct column.

> I'm afraid I didn't catch that.   Did you say ...?   And was that ... or ...?   Sorry, could you speak louder?
> Can you spell that for me, please?   Could you speak more slowly, please?   Could you repeat that, please?

You don't hear something	You need to check or confirm specific information

10 A ▶ **4.18** Listen to five conversations and <u>underline</u> the information the speaker wants to check.

1 Sorry, did you say you needed three blue shirts?
2 And you bought the product on June 5, 2010?
3 So your flight is at 5:00 p.m. on Wednesday of next week?
4 Sorry, did you say you wanted to reserve a double room for next week?
5 Was that vegetable soup for table 12?

B In pairs, repeat questions 1–5. Pay attention to the words you stress.

Go to Communication practice: Student A, page 159; Student B, page 167

11 A **PREPARE** In pairs, look at the situations below. Decide which role you will play and think about what you will say.

	Situation 1	**Situation 2**
Student A	You have arranged to meet with a colleague. Call to cancel the meeting.	You are going on vacation to Acapulco. Make a hotel reservation for your trip.
Student B	Answer the phone. The person the speaker wants to talk to is not in the office. Take a message.	You are a receptionist at a hotel. Write down details of the reservation. It is very noisy, and you can't hear the speaker well.

B **PRACTICE** Sit back to back with your partner so you can't see him/her. Practice the telephone conversation.

C **PERSONAL BEST** Are you more confident at speaking on the telephone in English? How could you improve? Change partners and practice the conversations again.

Personal Best   Write down one of the conversations from exercise 11.

Grammar

1 Put a (**X**) by the sentence that is NOT correct.

1   **a**   This hotel is more expensive than Hotel Atlanta. ☐
    b   This hotel is the most expensive as Hotel Atlanta. ☐
    c   Hotel Atlanta isn't as expensive as this one. ☐

2   **a**   Simon was cutting his finger while cooking. ☐
    b   Simon cut his finger while he was cooking. ☐
    c   Simon was cooking when he cut his finger. ☐

3   **a**   I don't think he'll win the race. ☐
    b   He might not win the race. ☐
    c   He might won't win the race. ☐

4   **a**   This phone is the smallest in the store. ☐
    b   This phone is smaller than the others. ☐
    c   This phone as small as in the store. ☐

5   **a**   It may be hot tomorrow. ☐
    b   It will be probably hot tomorrow. ☐
    c   It might be hot tomorrow. ☐

6   **a**   What do you do next week? ☐
    b   What are you doing next week? ☐
    c   What are you going to do next week? ☐

7   **a**   I met Jerry while I was studying in college in 2010. ☐
    b   In 2010, while I was studying in college, I met Jerry. ☐
    c   I was meeting Jerry in 2010, while I studied in college. ☐

8   **a**   She's not meeting her friend at the theater. ☐
    b   She's not going to meet her friend at the theater. ☐
    c   She doesn't meet with her friend tonight. ☐

2 Use the words in parentheses to complete the sentences so they mean the same as the first sentence.

1   London isn't as hot as Madrid.
    Madrid _____ London. (hotter)

2   I don't think I will pass the exam.
    I _____ the exam. (probably / pass)

3   Kelly is shorter than Nicki.
    Kelly _____ Nicki. (as / tall)

4   My phone rang while I was cooking dinner.
    _____ my phone rang. (when)

5   He's arriving at 6:00 p.m.
    He's _____ at 6:00 p.m. (going)

6   The store may be closed.
    The store _____ open. (might)

7   I was talking on the phone when I missed my train.
    I missed my train _____ . (while)

8   What are you going to do on Saturday?
    What _____ on Saturday? (doing)

3 Choose the correct options to complete the text.

The i-Aid

In 2009, Canadian Alex Deans [1]*watched / was watching* a blind person cross the street when he [2]*had / was having* a great idea. He realized that he could use sound to help blind people know where things are, like some animals do.

Even though he [3]*still studied / was still studying* in high school, he [4]*found / was finding* time to develop his idea. Four years later, he finished work on the i-Aid, a device that makes it [5]*easier / easiest* for blind people to move around objects.

In 2013, he won an award for the [6]*better / best* invention in Canada and gained a great deal of interest from tech companies. In fact, the Canadian Institute for the Blind was very impressed. The blind people at the institute immediately started testing the device, and the results were very positive.

Deans will [7]*might / probably* have to wait a couple of years to see the i-Aid in stores, but he is just as [8]*busy / busier* as before. Right now, he [9]*is studying / going to study* engineering in college, and whichever project he's working on, it [10]*will / may* definitely be just as exciting as the i-Aid.

Vocabulary

1 Match the words in the box with the definitions.

souvenir   modern   sunbathe   resort   famous   expensive   crowded   pack

1   to put things in a bag for a trip   _____
2   something that reminds you of a vacation   _____
3   known and recognized by many people   _____
4   to relax in the sun   _____
5   full of people   _____
6   up to date   _____
7   costing a lot of money   _____
8   an area where tourists stay and do activities   _____

2 Circle the word that is different. Explain your answer.

1	lively	busy	quiet	quickly
2	a hotel	a table	a museum	a double room
3	surgeon	model	firefighter	police officer
4	résumé	raise	salary	promotion
5	scientist	tour guide	travel agent	flight attendant
6	ad	apply	career	degree
7	lively	polluted	crowded	ugly
8	hire	abroad	eat out	pack

3 Complete the sentences with the words in the box.

> tour guide   movie director   fashion designer
> flight attendant   soccer coach   news reporter

1 He's my favorite _____ , but his clothes are really uncomfortable. You can't wear them for long.

2 The _____ was happy when the team won. It was a difficult game, though. They only won by one goal.

3 The _____ will meet you in the main square. It's very busy, so look for this sign.

4 My sister is a _____ . She flew to 50 different foreign countries last year.

5 My cousin is a _____ . He knows lots of famous actors.

6 I work as a _____ for my city's radio station. I talk about interesting events in the area.

4 Complete the conversation with the verbs in the box.

> write   get   go (x2)   start   see   book
> visit   quit   apply

Omar Did you [1]_____ the job ad in yesterday's newspaper?

Nuria No, I didn't.

Omar Royal Airlines is looking for new flight attendants. You said you wanted to [2]_____ your job.

Nuria Do you think I should [3]_____ for the job?

Omar Yes, it's perfect for you! Didn't you want to [4]_____ abroad more often?

Nuria Yes, but on vacation. I don't think you have much time to [5]_____ sightseeing or [6]_____ local attractions.

Omar Not when you're working, but you'll probably get a discount when you [7]_____ flights, so you can travel more on vacation!

Nuria Hmm, maybe. What's the salary?

Omar It's fairly low when you [8]_____ work, but you might [9]_____ a pay raise after a year or two. I'll help you [10]_____ a résumé, if you want.

Nuria OK, I'll do it!

Personal Best

Lesson 3A
Write two sentences about your friends using (not) as … as.

Lesson 4A
Write two predictions about next year.

Lesson 3A
Write two sentences about where you live using comparatives and superlatives.

Lesson 4B
Name three pronouns and three possessive adjectives.

Lesson 3B
Name five things you usually do on vacation.

Lesson 4C
Name three things an employee usually does.

Lesson 3C
Write what you were doing at this time yesterday.

Lesson 4C
Think of three plans or arrangements you have for tomorrow.

Lesson 3C
Write a sentence using the simple past and the past continuous.

Lesson 4D
Give three expressions you can use if someone calls you on the telephone.

Lesson 3D
Describe three things you did yesterday using adverbs of manner.

Lesson 4D
Give three expressions you can use when you have problems understanding something.

Mind and body

5A Should I see a doctor?

1 Match the speech bubbles with the pictures.

1 I have a headache.

2 I cut my finger.

3 I'm stressed.

4 I have the flu.

5 I have a cough.

Go to Vocabulary practice: health and medicine, page 144

2 Look at the title and the pictures in the text. In pairs, try to match the strange health tips with the problems in exercise 1. Read the text quickly and check.

Five strange health tips that you should know about

The Internet is full of websites that offer health tips, some serious and some strange. Here are our top five tips from the web … do they work? You can decide on that!

Do you have a temperature or the flu? Then you should put some onion in your socks and wear them at night. You'll feel much better the next morning. Remember though, you shouldn't eat the onion afterward!

You're chopping vegetables in the kitchen and you cut your thumb. What should you do? Put a little black pepper on the cut, of course! It stops the bleeding and helps the cut get better. But you should only do this for small cuts. For anything serious, you should see a doctor.

Do you have regular headaches? Then you should always have an apple nearby. Some studies have found that the smell of green apples can help with headaches and can also make you feel less anxious.

Are you stressed? You should call your mom. A study by the University of Wisconsin showed that people who had more contact with their mother had lower levels of stress. So you shouldn't delay—call her today!

If you have a cough that won't go away, then you should eat some chocolate. Scientists say that chocolate contains a chemical that is better at stopping coughs than many cough medicines. So you shouldn't go to a pharmacy—go to a candy store.

3 Discuss the questions in pairs.

1 Would you try any of the tips? Why/Why not?
2 Do you know any other strange health tips?
3 Do you ever use the Internet to look for health advice?
4 What are the advantages and disadvantages of using the Internet for this?

4 **A** Look at the question and sentence from the text. Check (✔) the correct meaning.

Are you stressed? You should call your mom.

1 It's necessary to call your mom if you are stressed. ☐
2 It's a good idea to call your mom if you are stressed. ☐
3 It's a bad idea to call your mom if you are stressed. ☐

B Complete the sentences with the words in the box. Check your answers in the text. Then read the Grammar box.

> do go put should (x2) shouldn't

1 What _____ you _____?
2 You _____ _____ some onion in your socks.
3 You _____ _____ to a pharmacy.

📖 **Grammar**   *should/shouldn't*

Ask for advice: *What **should** I do?*
Say something is a good idea: *You **should** see a doctor.   I think you **should** get help.*
Say something is a bad idea: *You **shouldn't** trust tips on the Internet.   I don't think you **should** go to work.*

Personal Best

Go to Grammar practice: *should/shouldn't*, page 120

5 **A** ▶5.3 **Pronunciation:** *should/shouldn't* How do you say *should* and *shouldn't?* Listen to the sentences and check.

1 What should we do?
2 Why shouldn't I speak to him?
3 I think you should talk to an expert.
4 You shouldn't believe him.

B ▶5.3 <u>Underline</u> the stressed words in each sentence. Listen, check, and repeat.

6 **A** Complete the conversation with *should* and *shouldn't* to give health advice.

Paul   I'm really stressed. I can't sleep. What ¹_____ I do?
Doctor Well, I don't think you ²_____ work so many hours, and you ³_____ go to bed so late. You ⁴_____ try to get more exercise. That will help you to sleep better.
Paul   ⁵_____ I drink less coffee?
Doctor Yes, you ⁶_____ ! And you ⁷_____ drink more water, too.
Paul   OK, thank you.
Doctor If that doesn't help, you ⁸_____ come to see me again.

B ▶5.4 Listen and check. Repeat the conversation in pairs.

Go to Communication practice: Student A, page 161; Student B, page 169

7 **A** Discuss these situations in pairs. What advice would you give?

I forgot my friend's birthday and now she's really angry with me. What do you think I should do?

Sara

My roommate is really messy. The kitchen is always dirty after he cooks, and he takes my food from the refrigerator without asking. I don't know what to do!

Enrique

My boss wants me to go to a work conference in New York. The only problem is that it's the same date as my wedding anniversary. What should I tell my wife?

Julio

B Tell the rest of the class your advice. Who had the best ideas?

Personal Best   Think of a common health problem and write down five examples of advice.

5B Modern life is stressful

1 Look at the pictures. In pairs, order them from 1 (most stressful) to 5 (least stressful).

a interviews

b presentations

c exams

d traffic

e moving

2 Read the text. Complete the tips with *do, make, have,* or *take*.

The best ways to deal with stress

Over 60% of adults say their lives are too stressful. So if you´re stressed right now, you should stop for a minute and read our tips—they might be very helpful!

1 First, _____ **a deep breath** and give yourself time to think.
2 Then _____ **a list** of everything you have to do.
3 Next, _____ **a decision** about what you can realistically do today.
4 Remember to _____ **a break** every two or three hours.
5 You should _____ **something** that makes you feel happy.
6 Try to _____ **a talk** with friends and family about the situation.
7 And finally, _____ **your best** to eat well, exercise, and get at least eight hours' sleep.

Go to Vocabulary practice: collocations with *do, make, have,* and *take*, page 145

3 Ask and answer the questions in pairs.

1 Do you think your life is stressful? Why/Why not?
2 What things make you feel stressed?
3 Do you think the tips are useful? Why/Why not?
4 Can you think of any other ways to deal with stress?

🔧 **Skill** listening in detail

It is often important to understand what someone says in detail.
• Read the questions carefully and think about the possible answers.
• Listen carefully to everything the speaker says before you answer the question.
• Pay attention to how the things the speaker says relate to each other.
• Be careful in case the speaker changes his/her mind or corrects himself/herself.

4 **A** ▶ 5.6 Read the Skill box. Watch or listen to the first part of *Learning Curve*. Choose the correct options to answer the questions.

1 How does Simon deal with stress?
   a He makes a list of jobs.   **b** He walks around.   **c** He talks to his brother.
2 How many people in the U.S. suffer from stress every day?
   a 77% of citizens   **b** 400,000 people   **c** only a small number of people
3 What do some scientists say about a small amount of stress?
   a It can make us sick.   **b** It makes us feel bored.   **c** It can help us work better.

B ▶ 5.6 Compare your answers in pairs. Watch or listen again and check.

5 A ▶5.7   Watch or listen to the second part of the show. Match the names of the speakers with the tips for dealing with stress.

1 running _____   **2** speaking to family _____   **3** doing yoga _____

Taylor

Edward

Maurice

B ▶5.7   Watch or listen again. Are the sentences true (T) or false (F)?

1 Taylor helps people who suffer from stress.   ____
2 She thinks complaining about stress can help.   ____
3 Edward's boss makes him feel stressed at work.   ____
4 He listens to music while he's running.   ____
5 Maurice had a stressful job.   ____
6 He uses his phone to deal with stress.   ____

6 Discuss the questions in pairs.

1 Do you think life today is more stressful than 50 years ago? Why/Why not?
2 Do you think a little stress can be good for us? Why/Why not?

Listening builder   linking consonants and vowels

When a word ends in a consonant sound and the next word begins with a vowel sound, we often link the words together:
Kate likes to take a break once an hour and walk around.

---

7 ▶5.8   Read the Listening builder. Look at the sentences from the program and mark where you think the words link. Listen, check, and repeat.

1 After a long day I take a hot shower.
2 Kate is on the street doing an interview.
3 After work, I run about five miles a day.
4 And we talk on the phone every day.

8 ▶5.9   Listen and complete the conversation.

> **Edward** I don't think I can _____ more.
> **Lara** What's wrong, Edward? Tell _____.
> **Edward** I _____ work to do ... and no time!
> **Lara** I can help. Let's _____ your jobs for today.

9 Discuss the questions in pairs.

1 What do you think the biggest cause of stress is for most people?
2 What do you think the most stressful stage of our lives is?
3 Think of three stressful jobs. Are there any advantages to these jobs?
4 Think of three low-stress jobs. What kind of job would you prefer? Why?

Personal Best   Write your own list of five tips to beat stress.

5C How to be happy

1 A How do you think the woman is feeling? Match the adjectives in the box with the pictures.

> calm delighted upset cheerful nervous

a b c d e

B In pairs, think of situations that make people feel these emotions.

An exam can make you feel nervous.

Go to Vocabulary practice: emotions and feelings, page 146

2 A Do you think money makes people happy? Why/Why not?

B Read the text. Check (✔) the sentence that best summarizes the main idea.

1 People with a lot of money often feel miserable. ☐
2 If people have less money, they often feel envious of others. ☐
3 Spending money on other people can make you feel good. ☐

CAN MONEY BUY YOU HAPPINESS?

The Beatles may have been right when they sang "money can't buy me love" but, according to a new study, it can buy you happiness—if you spend it in the right way. Many people think that they'll be happier if they earn more money. But Dr. Michael Norton from Harvard Business School believes that it's not about how much money you make, but about how you spend it.

Dr. Norton tried an experiment with people in different countries. At the start of the experiment, he asked people how happy they were. Then he gave them an envelope with some money and instructions on how to spend it. Some people had to spend the money on themselves, and others were told to spend it on someone else. At the end of the experiment, they measured how happy the people felt again.

The results show that if you spend money on other people, you'll feel happier. And if you only spend money on yourself, you won't feel any different. So the next time you want to buy a new TV or some new clothes, ask yourself, "If I buy this, will it make me happier?" According to Dr. Norton, we should think less about ourselves and more about others because, if we do that, we'll feel much better!

3 A Complete the sentence. Check your answers in the text.

If you _____ money on other people, you _____ feel happier.
　　　　　　　A　　　　　　　　　　　　　　B

B Answer the questions about the two parts of the sentence: A and B. Then read the Grammar box.

1 Which part of the sentence is a possible future action? ____ What tense is the verb? _____
2 Which part of the sentence is the result of that action? ____ What tense is the verb? _____
3 Can we rewrite the sentence so that part B comes first and part A comes second? _____

📖 **Grammar**	**first conditional**

Possible future action:	**Result of action:**
*If it **rains** tomorrow,*	*Laura **won't go** to the beach.*
*If the train **doesn't arrive**,*	*I'**ll be** late for the meeting.*
*If she **fails** the exam,*	***will** she **have** to do it again?*

Look! We can change the order of the clauses: *Laura won't go to the beach if it rains tomorrow.*

Go to Grammar practice: first conditional, page 121

4 **A** ▶ 5.12   Listen to the conversation. Why doesn't Sam accept the movie ticket? Do you think this is a good reason?

B Complete Sam's reason. Listen again and check.

If I ¹_____ to the movies, we ²_____ a scary movie. And if I ³_____ a scary movie, I ⁴_____ nervous. And if I ⁵_____ nervous, I ⁶_____ well tonight. And if I ⁷_____ well, I ⁸_____ late for work. And if I ⁹_____ late for work, my boss ¹⁰_____ angry. And if my boss ¹¹_____ angry, I ¹²_____ a pay raise. And if I ¹³_____ a pay raise, I ¹⁴_____ on vacation. And if I ¹⁵_____ on vacation, I ¹⁶_____ miserable. So, no thank you!

5 **A** ▶ 5.13   **Pronunciation:** *'ll* contraction How do you say *'ll*? Listen, check, and repeat.

I'll   you'll   he'll   she'll   it'll   we'll   they'll

B ▶ 5.14   Match the two columns to make sentences. In pairs, say the sentences. Pay attention to the *'ll* sound. Listen, check, and repeat.

1 I'll be really envious   a she'll call you later.
2 You'll miss your flight   b if your boss sends you to Jamaica.
3 If you give her your phone number,   c she'll be really upset.
4 If you can fix the computer now,   d if you can't take them to the station.
5 If she fails her exam,   e if you don't leave now.
6 They'll get a taxi   f it'll be very helpful.

Go to Communication practice: Student A, page 161; Student B, page 169

6 **A** Take the quiz in pairs. Write down your partner's answers.

B Go to page 174 and look at the results. Do you agree with them? Why/Why not?

How happy are you?

1 **If I wake up very early tomorrow morning, ...**
  a I'll be miserable all day.
  b I'll try to go back to sleep.
  c I'll get up and make a big breakfast.
  d I might go running or work out at the gym.

2 **If my best friend buys a new laptop, ...**
  a I might feel a little envious.
  b I'll buy an even better one.
  c I might look for a new one, too.
  d I'll be delighted for him/her.

3 **If I find some money on the street next week, ...**
  a I'll put it in my bank account.
  b I'll buy myself some new clothes.
  c I'll give it to the police.
  d I'll donate it to charity.

4 **If my boss asks to speak to me, ...**
  a I'll think he/she wants to fire me.
  b I'll probably feel very nervous.
  c I'll be calm and find out what he/she wants.
  d I'll think I'm going to get a promotion.

5 **If my parents give me a present that I don't really want, ...**
  a I'll ask for the receipt and exchange it for something I like.
  b I'll thank them, but say I don't want the present.
  c I'll say thanks, but use it as a present for someone else.
  d I'll tell them I love it and try to use it in some way.

7 **A** In pairs, complete the sentences.

1 If I make a lot of money, ...   3 I won't believe it if ...   5 If I don't come to class next week, ...
2 If I get a headache later, ...   4 I'll be delighted if ...   6 I'll have a big party if ...

B Tell the class what your partner said.

Personal Best   Write twelve first conditional sentences with all the emotions and feelings words from the Vocabulary practice on p. 146.

5D I need your advice

1 In pairs, order the work problems from 1 (most serious) to 6 (least serious).

> lazy colleagues   mean boss
> boring work   too many working hours
> low salary   long trip to work

2 Look at the picture of Tom, who works at a busy health club. Guess the answers to the questions in pairs.

1 How is he feeling?
2 What problems does he have at work?

3 Read the e-mail and check your answers to exercise 2.

1 _____ .... Catching up

2 _____ .... Hi Duncan,

3 _____ .... How's it going? Hope you're well. I'm still working at the health club, but I'm not very happy. That's why I'm writing. I wanted to ask you for some advice.

4 _____ .... One of my colleagues, Sebastian, is really lazy, and he's not very nice to me, either. Whenever there's a problem, our manager always blames me! I also think his friends use the gym without paying. What do you think I should do? If I tell the manager, it might cause even more problems with Sebastian!

5 _____ .... Anyway, I saw an ad for a job at a new gym the other day. If I start work there, the salary will be lower, but it's a large chain, so there might be more opportunities in the future. Do you think I should apply? Do you feel like getting together for coffee some time this week so we can talk about it? Let me know when you're free.

6 _____ .... See you later,
Tom

4 Label the sections of the e-mail with the words in the box.

> details   ending   subject   reason for writing   greeting   request for response

🔧 **Skill**   writing an informal e-mail

We write informal e-mails to people we know well, such as friends, family, and colleagues.
- Structure the e-mail with a subject, greeting, reason for writing, details, request for a response, and an ending.
- Use contractions like *I'm, he's,* and *don't.*
- Use informal words and phrases like *Hi, How's it going?,* and *anyway.*

5 Read the Skill box. Find the informal words and phrases in the e-mail for phrases 1–6.

1 Hello _____
2 How are you? _____
3 On another subject ... _____
4 Would you like to ... _____
5 Please tell me _____
6 Goodbye _____

6 Discuss the questions in pairs.

1 Do you ever have problems similar to Tom's?
2 Who do you talk to about problems at work?
3 What should Tom do about Sebastian?
4 What should Tom do about the job ad?

7 Read Duncan's reply. Do you agree with him? Why/Why not?

RE: Catching up

Hi Tom,
Good to hear from you! I'm OK, thanks, but I was **very** sorry to hear your news about work. Everyone has colleagues who are **a little** lazy like Sebastian, but the problem with his friends using the gym is serious. I think you should speak to him first. Explain that it's like stealing money from the company, and if he doesn't stop, you'll have to tell the manager. I know she's **not very** nice, but it's **really** important to tell her.
You also mentioned applying for another job. I think it's an **extremely** good idea. If you get the job, you can ask for the same salary as you earn now, and you might get a promotion **pretty** quickly in the future.
I'd love to get together. I'll be in town next Thursday evening. Let me know where and when you want to meet.

All the best,
Duncan

8 A Look at the modifiers in **bold** in Duncan's e-mail and complete the rules.

1 Modifiers make adjectives and adverbs *stronger / weaker / both stronger and weaker*.
2 Modifiers come *before / after* adjectives and adverbs.

B Put the words in **bold** in the correct places in the diagram.

1 *extremely*   2 _____   *fairly*   5 _____   *not at all*

3 _____   4 _____   6 _____

Text builder | **modifiers**

We use modifiers to make adjectives and adverbs stronger or weaker:
*Be careful, the soup is **extremely** hot.*
*She was driving **very** fast when the accident happened.*
*I'm **a little** nervous about the exam next week.*

Look! We usually use *a little* with negative adjectives:
*She's **a little** upset today* NOT ~~She's a little cheerful today~~.

---

9 Read the Text builder. Complete the sentences with a modifier and an adjective. Compare your answers in pairs.

1 Most of my friends are …
2 Learning English is …
3 Today, I'm feeling …
4 My job is …
5 The weather is …
6 Eating out is …

10 A **PREPARE** Choose one of the problems.

• Your parents want you to study medicine, but you don't want to. You would prefer to study music.
• You want to get in shape, but you only have a few hours a week free and don't have very much money.
• Your boss gives you too much work. You are worried that if you refuse to do it, you might lose your job.

B **PRACTICE** Write an e-mail to a friend asking for advice about the problem.

C **PERSONAL BEST** Exchange e-mails with a partner. Underline five things that you think are very good.

Personal Best Write a reply to your partner's e-mail. Try to use different modifiers.

Risks and experiences

LANGUAGE   present perfect with *ever* and *never* ■ phrasal verbs

6A Try something new!

1   Look at the pictures. Ask and answer the questions in pairs.

   1   Which activities are the most difficult, in your opinion?

   2   Which activities would you like to try? Why/Why not?

   3   What stopped you from doing these activities in the past?

learn to play an instrument

climb a mountain

ride your bike to work

read a book in a foreign language

do an extreme sport

2   Read the text. Which activities from exercise 1 has Matt Cutts done?

The 30-day Challenge

June

SUN	MON	TUE	WED	THU	FRI	SAT
			1	2	3	4
5	6	7	8	9	10	11
12	13	14	15	16	17	18
19	20	21	22	23	24	25
26	27	28	29	30		

Have you ever wanted to try something new? Perhaps you've wanted to take up a new hobby or learn a new skill. What stopped you? Not enough time? The fear of failure? Was it difficult to change your routine?

Matt Cutts is an American software engineer. A few years ago, he was bored with his life. That's when he decided to try the 30-day challenge. The idea is simple. You think of something you haven't done before, but you've always wanted to do, and you try it for 30 days. He started with small challenges, such as walking more, riding his bike to work, and giving up sugar for a month. Gradually, his challenges became bigger and more difficult. Now, Matt has written a novel, he's taught himself to play the ukulele, and he's even climbed Mount Kilimanjaro!

Trying something new can be kind of terrifying, but doing it for just 30 days doesn't seem so hard. At the end of the month, you can stop … or who knows? You might decide to go on with your new activity. For example, Matt gave up TV and did other things like reading books, instead. After 30 days, the first thing he did was turn on the TV. However, he found that he watched less TV than before because he enjoyed doing the other things, too.

Matt says that the challenges have made his life much more interesting. He's also become more confident. So, what about you? Is there something you've always wanted to do? What are you waiting for? **Try it for 30 days!**

3   Answer the questions in pairs.

   1   Why did Matt start doing 30-day challenges?

   2   Why is it easier to try something for 30 days?

   3   How have the challenges helped Matt?

   4   What challenge would you do for 30 days?

4   Choose the correct words to complete the sentences. Check your answers in the text.

   1   Maybe you've wanted to **take** *up* / *over* / *in* a new hobby or learn a new skill.

   2   You might decide to **go** *over* / *in* / *on* with your new activity.

   3   Matt **gave** *under* / *up* / *above* TV and did other things like reading books, instead.

   4   After 30 days, the first thing he did was **turn** *on* / *in* / *around* the TV.

Go to Vocabulary practice: phrasal verbs, page 145

5 **A** Complete the sentences about Matt from the text. Check your answers in the text.

1 A few years ago, he _____ bored with his life. 2 Matt has _____ a novel.

B Answer the questions about sentences 1 and 2 in exercise 5A.

1 Which sentence is about an event at a particular time in the past? ____
What is the tense? *simple past / present perfect*

2 Which sentence is about a general experience in Matt's life? ____
What is the tense? *simple past / present perfect*

3 How do we form the present perfect tense? the verb _____ + past participle

6 Underline a present perfect question and an example of the present perfect negative in the text.
Then read the Grammar box.

> 📖 **Grammar** | **present perfect with *ever* and *never***
>
> **Experiences in your life:**
> **Have** you **ever eaten** Japanese food? I**'ve been** to Australia, but I**'ve never seen** a kangaroo.
> She **hasn't seen** the new Star Wars movie.
>
> **Look!** We use the simple past to talk about **when** an event happened and to give more details:
> I've been to the U.S. I **went** to California in 2015. It **was** great!

Personal Best

Go to Grammar practice: present perfect with *ever* and *never*, page 122

7 ▶6.4 **Pronunciation:** irregular past participles Listen and repeat the words. Pay attention to
the /ən/ sound in the -*en* endings.

brok**en** chos**en** driv**en** eat**en** fall**en** forgott**en** giv**en** spok**en** tak**en** writt**en**

8 **A** ▶6.5 Practice saying the questions. Listen, check, and repeat.

1 Have you ever writt**en** a poem? 4 Have you ever brok**en** your arm or leg?
2 Have you ever eat**en** Japanese food? 5 Have you ever forgott**en** an important birthday?
3 Have you ever driv**en** a fast car? 6 Have you ever fall**en** asleep in class or at work?

B Ask and answer the questions in pairs. If you answer *Yes, I have*, give more information in the
simple past.

A *Have you ever written a poem?* **B** *Yes, I have. I had to write a poem when I was at school.*

Go to Communication practice: Student A, page 161; Student B, page 169

9 **A** ▶6.6 Complete the text with the present perfect form of the verbs in the box. Listen and check.

study give up write win work be

DID YOU KNOW ...?

Natalie Portman is a world-famous actress.
You probably know that she ¹_____ an
Oscar, but here are some facts you might
not know.

⭐ She ²_____ with Britney Spears.
⭐ She ³_____ two scientific papers that
⁴_____ published.
⭐ She ⁵_____ Japanese, German, and Arabic.
⭐ She ⁶_____ watching TV.

B ▶6.6 Listen again. Are the sentences true (T) or false (F)?

1 Natalie was the main character in a musical when she was 10 years old. ____
2 She studied psychology at Harvard University. ____
3 She started learning languages when she was a child. ____
4 She never watches any TV shows. ____

10 **A** Write down some of your experiences that not many people know about.

B In pairs, talk about your experiences and give more information.

Personal Best Write ten sentences about yourself using the phrasal verbs in the Vocabulary practice.

6B An amazing story

1 Look at the pictures on page 51. Discuss the questions in pairs.

1 Have you seen the movie *127 Hours?*
2 If you have seen it, what is it about? If you haven't, can you guess what happens in it?
3 Have you ever tried rock climbing?
4 What problems could you have doing this activity?

2 Read the safety advice and guess which three mistakes Aron made. Read the text quickly and check your answers.

BLUE JOHN CANYON: SAFETY ADVICE

1 Always tell someone where you are going to climb.
2 Only climb here if you are an experienced climber.
3 Pack at least three liters of water and lots of food.
4 Take a knife and a first-aid kit for emergencies.
5 Always take a cell phone to call for help.

3 Read the text again. Order the events from 1–8.

a ☐ He wrote a book.
b ☐ A helicopter rescued him.
c ☐ He cut off his hand.
d ☐ He ran out of food and water.
e ☐ A rock fell and trapped his hand.
f ☐ He started climbing in the canyon.
g ☐ In a dream, he saw a little boy.
h ☐ He had a son named Leo.

Skill   guessing the meaning of words from context

You can sometimes guess the meaning of a word you don't know without using a dictionary.
• Look at the words before and after it to identify what type of word it is (noun, adjective, verb, adverb, etc.).
• Read the whole sentence carefully and guess what the word means.

4 A Read the Skill box. Look at words 1–8 in the text and identify what type of words they are: *noun, adjective, verb,* or *adverb.* Can you guess what they mean?

1 remote _____
2 stuck _____
3 loudly _____
4 realized _____
5 dawn _____
6 wound _____
7 eventually _____
8 hurried _____

B Match definitions a–h with words 1–8 to check if you guessed correctly.

a a large cut or injury ☐
b far away ☐
c the first light of the day ☐
d moved quickly ☐
e with lots of sound ☐
f after some time ☐
g understood a fact ☐
h unable to move ☐

Text builder   linkers to add extra information

We use the linkers *and, also, as well,* and *too* to add extra information:
• *and* comes between two phrases: *It's a very beautiful place, **and** it's very remote.*
• *also* comes before the main verb: *He **also** gives talks about his adventure.*
• *as well* and *too* come at the end of a phrase: *... he was alone, **as well**. ... he pushed with his feet, **too**.*

5 Read the Text builder. Discuss the questions in pairs and add extra information with the linkers.

A *I think Aron was stupid because he didn't take a phone.*
B *Yes, but he was brave, as well.*

1 How would you describe Aron?
2 What would you do in Aron's situation?
3 What advice do you think he gives in his talks?
4 What would you pack on a trip to the desert?

ARON RALSTON'S
AMAZING STORY

A TRIUMPHANT TRUE STORY
FROM THE ACADEMY AWARD*-WINNING DIRECTOR OF
SLUMDOG MILLIONAIRE

JAMES FRANCO
127 HOURS

"DAZZLING
AND PERPETUALLY
SURPRISING..."
—The New York Times

THERE IS NO FORCE MORE POWERFUL THAN THE WILL TO LIVE

Aron Ralston is an experienced climber, but one day in 2003, he forgot a few basic rules, and a day in the desert turned into a nightmare that lasted nearly a week. That particular day, he went rock climbing in Blue John Canyon in Utah, U.S. It's a very beautiful place and it's very ¹**remote**, a long drive from the nearest town. The problems began when he didn't tell anyone where he was going, so nobody knew he was there.

A few hours later, he was climbing in the canyon when suddenly a big rock fell and trapped his right hand against the canyon wall. Trying not to panic, he pulled with his left arm and pushed with his feet, too, but he couldn't move the rock even one centimeter. He was ²**stuck** and alone, as well.

He had left his phone in his car, so he couldn't call for help. He tried shouting ³**loudly**, but there was nobody to hear him. In his bag, there was a small bottle of water, two burritos and some chocolate—enough food for a short walk. Waiting for help day after day, he ate his food and drank the water slowly, but no help came. He ⁴**realized** he was probably going to die and recorded video messages for his family on a camera. After five days, all of his food and water were gone. That night, he had a strange dream and saw a small boy who was his future son. He woke up at ⁵**dawn** the following morning and he knew what he had to do. The only way to escape was to cut off his hand.

First, he broke his arm, and then he used a small knife to remove his hand. It took an hour and was extremely painful. He used a small first-aid kit on the ⁶**wound**, but he was losing a lot of blood. He managed to climb down the canyon and walked slowly toward his car. ⁷**Eventually**, he met a Dutch family who gave him food and ⁸**hurried** to find help. Soon after, a helicopter arrived to rescue him.

Aron wrote a book about his experience, and director Danny Boyle made the story into a movie. Seven years after the accident, Aron had a son named Leo, and today he still goes climbing. He also gives talks about his adventure to help other people. ■

6C Into the wild

1 Read the text and answer the questions in pairs.

1 Would you like to have Gemma's job?
2 What are the best and worst things about it?
3 Do you think you could survive in the wild?
4 Which photo do you prefer? Why?

Gemma Tang is a professional photographer and survival specialist. She grew up in Guangzhou, China, but has spent years traveling around the world, taking amazing photos of wildlife and spectacular landscapes. She is currently living in Cuzco, Peru where she runs survival courses in the Amazon rainforest. A new exhibit of her photos just opened in London. Here are two of the best.

2 Match the words in the box with parts of the landscapes.

cliff   waves   peak   sunset   waterfall   rocks

1 _____ 2 _____ 3 _____ 4 _____ 5 _____ 6 _____

Go to Vocabulary practice: the natural world, page 147

Personal Best

3 A ▶ 6.8   In pairs, do the survival quiz. Listen to Gemma and check your answers.

B Look at page 174 and read the results. Do you agree? Why/Why not?

SURVIVAL QUIZ

1 If I were in the mountains and saw a bear outside its cave, …
  a I'd run away as fast as possible.
  b I'd climb the nearest tree.
  c I'd take a photo. What an opportunity!

2 If I were on a hike in the rainforest and ran out of food, …
  a I'd eat a small animal, like a tarantula.
  b I'd find some plants and eat them.
  c I wouldn't eat anything.

3 If I were swimming in the ocean and saw a shark in the water, …
  a I'd scream and swim in the opposite direction.
  b I'd move towards the shark and kick it in the nose.
  c I'd try to swim quickly and quietly away.

4 If I were hiking and needed to drink some water, …
  a I'd drink the water from a river or lake.
  b I'd find a stream to get water.
  c I wouldn't drink any water.

4 ▶ 6.8   Listen again and answer the questions.

1 Why should you climb up high in a tree?   _____
2 What do tarantulas taste like?   _____
3 What percentage of sharks don't attack humans?   _____
4 What can river water contain?   _____

5 **A** ▶ 6.9 Match the two parts to make sentences from the audio. Listen and check.

1 If you ran,
2 If I were in this situation,
3 If you needed water,

a I wouldn't take a photo.
b would you look for a stream?
c the bear would follow you.

B Answer the questions. Then read the Grammar box.

1 Which tense do we use after *if*? _____
2 Which auxiliary verb do we use with the base form in the second part of the sentence? _____
3 Are these situations impossible or unlikely? _____
4 What do you notice about the past tense of *be* in sentence 2? _____

📖 **Grammar** **second conditional**

Impossible or very unlikely situations:
If I **saw** a bear in the mountains, I'**d run**.
If he **ran out** of food in the rainforest, he **wouldn't eat** anything.
What **would** you **do** if you **saw** a shark in the ocean?

Look! We can use **were** instead of **was** in the second conditional:
*I wouldn't drink the river water if I **were** you.*

Go to Grammar practice: second conditional, page 123

6 **A** ▶ 6.11 **Pronunciation:** sentence stress Listen to the sentences from conversations 1–3. Underline the stressed words.

1 If I saw a bear, I'd run.
2 If you ate a poisonous one, it would make you sick.
3 I wouldn't eat a spider if it were the last food on earth.
4 I wouldn't survive five minutes in the wild!

B Practice saying the sentences in pairs.

7 In pairs, look at the situations and make sentences about what you would and wouldn't do. Pay attention to the sentence stress.

If I found a wallet on the street, I wouldn't spend the money. I'd try to find the owner.

1 If I found a wallet on the street, …	2 If I accidentally hit a parked car with my car, …	3 If I was invited to a costume party, …
a give it to the police	a leave my phone number	a make an excuse and not go
b spend the money	b drive away	b make an amazing costume
c try to find the owner	c wait for the owner to return	c wear a silly hat

Go to Communication practice: Student A, page 161; Student B, page 169

8 Discuss the questions in pairs.

What would you do if …

1 you didn't have to work?
2 a salesperson gave you too much change?
3 you saw a colleague stealing from work?
4 you found a spider in the bathtub?
5 your boss offered you a job in New York?
6 your parents forgot your birthday?
7 you couldn't use the Internet for a week?
8 you met a famous person in the supermarket?

Personal Best Write a paragraph about what you would do if you won a competition to go anywhere in the world.

6D Would you take the risk?

1 A Are you a risk-taker? In pairs, ask and answer the questions to find out.

B Look at the results on page 174. Do you agree? Why/Why not?

Would you ...

1 make reservations a few days before you go on vacation to get a better price?
2 buy something you love with a credit card even if you didn't have the money?
3 try an unusual foreign food or drink?
4 go to a party the night before an exam?
5 ride a motorcycle on a busy street?
6 do a parachute jump if you had the chance?

2 ▶ 6.12 Watch or listen to the first part of *Learning Curve*. Match the phrases in the box with the people.

has tried parachuting   works as a chef   went to college with Jack   left a job to travel and work

3 ▶ 6.12 Read the statements below. Who says each one: Simon or Kate? Watch or listen again and check.

1 We should see the world when we're young. ____
2 You should never leave a job without having another one. ____
3 There aren't that many jobs for vets at the zoo. ____
4 I can go for days without my cell phone. ____

⊣+→ **Conversation builder**	**agreeing and disagreeing**

Agreeing:
Exactly!   *You're right.*
I suppose so.   *True.*
Absolutely!

Disagreeing:
I don't think so.   *Oh, come on!*
I don't know.   *I'm not sure about that.*

4 A Read the Conversation builder. Which expressions did Simon and Kate use to agree/disagree?

B ▶ 6.13 Put the phrases in the correct columns from the Conversation builder. Listen, check, and repeat.

agree/disagree strongly	agree/disagree	agree/disagree with doubts

5 A Look at sentences 1–6. Check (✔) the box to show how much you agree or disagree.

	agree strongly	agree	not sure	disagree	disagree strongly
1 English is a difficult language to learn.	☐	☐	☐	☐	☐
2 We should all give up watching TV.	☐	☐	☐	☐	☐
3 People use cell phones too much.	☐	☐	☐	☐	☐
4 True love only exists in fairy tales.	☐	☐	☐	☐	☐
5 Music was better 20 years ago.	☐	☐	☐	☐	☐
6 Money doesn't make you happy.	☐	☐	☐	☐	☐

B In pairs, read the sentences to each other and agree or disagree using the phrases from the Conversation builder. Explain your reasons.

6 ▶ 6.14 Watch or listen to the second part of the show. What is Jack's news?

7 ▶ 6.14 Choose the correct options to answer the questions. Watch or listen again to check.

1 What does Jack think about Alyssa's plan to travel to Africa?
   a It's a good idea. **b** It could be dangerous. **c** It will be difficult without Wi-Fi.

2 What does Jack say about being on social media?
   a It's not expensive. **b** It's risky. **c** It will be good for his business.

3 What does Simon say about cooking?
   a He's bad at it. **b** He's good at it. **c** He can only cook eggs.

4 What do Kate and Simon offer to do?
   a help Jack cook **b** pay for the dessert **c** help Jack to make a video

🔧 **Skill** taking turns

When people talk in groups, they take turns.
- Wait until someone has finished their point before you start speaking.
- If you start speaking at the same time, stop and apologize.
- If someone isn't speaking much, encourage them to join in.

8 A ▶ 6.15 Read the Skill box. Listen and repeat the phrases when you hear the beep.

1 Sorry, go on. 3 Sorry, you were saying?
2 Don't you think, Jack? 4 What about you, Simon?

B Why do the speakers use phrases 1–4?

9 ▶ 6.16 Listen and check (✔) the conversation in which the speaker waits the right amount of time before speaking.

Conversation 1 ☐ Conversation 2 ☐ Conversation 3 ☐

Go to Communication practice: All students, page 174

10 A PREPARE Choose one of the statements and decide if you agree or disagree. Think of arguments and examples to support your opinion.

1 If you want a good job, you need to speak English. 3 There is a perfect partner for everyone.
2 Friends are more important than families. 4 Sugar is dangerous for our health.

B PRACTICE In groups of three, take turns talking about the statements you chose. Encourage other students to give their opinions and be polite.

C PERSONAL BEST Whose arguments did you agree with the most? Why?

Personal Best Write a conversation where two people disagree about something strongly.

Grammar

1 Choose the correct options to complete the sentences.

1 I'd get together with her if I _____ more time.
  a had
  b 'll have
  c have

2 Be careful! You _____ risks.
  a won't take
  b shouldn't take
  c wouldn't take

3 If it's cold tomorrow, I _____ a jacket.
  a 'd take
  b 'll take
  c take

4 If the bus _____ , I'll walk to work.
  a doesn't arrive
  b didn't arrive
  c won't arrive

5 A: I have an interview today. How do I look?
  B: I _____ wear those shoes.
  a don't think you should
  b think you should to
  c shouldn't think you

6 Have you _____ to Mexico?
  a ever been
  b ever go
  c went ever

7 What _____ if you saw an accident?
  a did you do
  b will you do
  c would you do

8 I _____ Turkish food.
  a never have eaten
  b have never eaten
  c have eaten never

2 Use the words in parentheses to write sentences that mean the same as the first sentence.

1 I haven't eaten sushi in my life.
  I _____ sushi. (never)

2 I don't have my phone, so I can't call him.
  If _____ my phone, I _____ him. (had / call)

3 It's a bad idea to go to the party.
  I _____ you _____ to the party. (think / should)

4 I think you should look for a new job.
  If _____ you, I _____ for a new job. (were / look)

5 They might lose the game. Mario will be upset if that happens.
  If _____ the game, Mario _____ happy. (lose / be)

6 Where's Julio? Is he in Paris for the meeting?
  Where's Julio? _____ to Paris for the meeting? (has / go)

3 Complete the text with the correct forms of the verbs in parentheses.

The truth about Murphy's Law

Have you ever [1]_____ (drop) a piece of toast and wondered why it always seems to land with the buttered side on the floor? Or, when you leave the house in the morning, have you ever [2]_____ (think), "If I [3]_____ (take) an umbrella, it [4]_____ (not rain), but if I [5]_____ (not take) one, it [6]_____ (rain)?" These are examples of Murphy's Law, the law that says, "If something can go wrong, it will." We've all [7]_____ (have) experiences like this, but what [8]_____ we _____ (should / do) about it?

Well, maybe we [9]_____ (not should / worry) too much. Professor Richard Dawkins, at the University of Oxford, doesn't think Murphy's Law is really true. He says that certain things happen all the time, but we only notice them when they cause us problems. Imagine if you [10]_____ (be) outside filming a video and a noisy plane [11]_____ (fly) by, you [12]_____ (think) it was Murphy's Law. However, planes fly by all the time. It's only when they cause us a problem that we notice them!

So next time something goes wrong, don't blame Murphy; think positively and try to remember the other times that things went well.

Vocabulary

1 Match the words in the box with the definitions.

ache	give up	take a break	make an excuse
lonely	miserable	run out of	roots	valley
have a talk				

1 low land between mountains _____
2 to finish, use, or sell all of something _____
3 to talk together in a friendly way _____
4 to rest for a moment before starting again _____
5 very unhappy _____
6 to stop _____
7 a pain somewhere in your body _____
8 sad because you are alone _____
9 the parts of a tree that are underground _____
10 to explain why something bad happened _____

2 Choose the correct words to complete the sentences.

1 When will you find _____ your results?
 a out   **b** about   **c** of

2 I _____ my best, and that's all I can do.
 a did   **b** made   **c** was

3 He's very _____ today. He's not worried at all.
 a calm   **b** guilty   **c** upset

4 I'll _____ bus schedules on the Internet.
 a fill out   **b** take care of   **c** look up

5 She broke my laptop. She feels really _____ .
 a guilty   **b** envious   **c** jealous

6 I _____ a big argument with my parents.
 a had   **b** did   **c** made

3 Circle the word that is different. Explain your answer.

1 backache   earache   sore throat   nosebleed
2 cliff   sunset   lightning   thunderstorm
3 flu   cold   cough   stressed
4 calm   upset   confident   cheerful
5 a mistake   a talk   a good time   an argument
6 lake   cave   river   stream
7 lonely   guilty   miserable   delighted
8 a break   an effort   a chance   your time

4 Complete the conversation with the words in the box.

| waves wildlife hurt made cut take |
| down have rainforest rocks |

Matt Hi, Kerry. Did you ¹_____ a good time on vacation?
Kerry Not really. In fact, it was a disaster.
Matt Oh no! What happened?
Kerry Well, I tried surfing for the first time, but the ²_____ were too big!
Matt Did you have an accident?
Kerry Yes, I hit some ³_____ that were under the water and I ⁴_____ my leg.
Matt Oh dear! Does it still ⁵_____ now?
Kerry Yes, it does. And another day, I went on a boat trip in the ⁶_____ to see the animals that live there, but the boat broke ⁷_____ , and we had to wait for hours for another one to rescue us.
Matt Did you see any ⁸_____ ?
Kerry Just mosquitoes!
Matt Oh no. That's too bad!
Kerry I think I ⁹_____ a mistake. Next year, I'm going to stay home and not ¹⁰_____ any chances.

Personal Best

Lesson 5A
Write three examples of advice to stay healthy.

Lesson 6A
Write a question with *ever*, and a sentence with *never*.

Lesson 5A
Name five reasons to see a doctor.

Lesson 6A
Name five phrasal verbs.

Lesson 5B
Name four verb collocations with *make*.

Lesson 6B
Write a sentence using *also*, and another using *as well*.

Lesson 5C
Name five feelings or emotions.

Lesson 6C
Name five natural features you could see in a rainforest.

Lesson 5C
Write a sentence using the first conditional.

Lesson 6C
Write a sentence beginning *If I were …*

Lesson 5D
Describe three things using adjectives and modifiers.

Lesson 6D
Give two expressions to agree with someone, and two to disagree.

City living

LANGUAGE present perfect with *yet* and *already* ■ city features

7A Life in the city

1 Discuss the questions in pairs.

1 Do you live in a city, a town, or a village?
2 Do you like where you live?
3 What are the good and bad things about it?

2 A Look at the picture. Which city is it?

B Match the words in the box with the things in the city.

sidewalk   traffic lights   bridge
bike lane   crosswalk   bench

1 _____   2 _____   3 _____   4 _____   5 _____   6 _____

Go to Vocabulary practice: city features, page 148

3 A Read the text. Who is more positive about the city: Alex or Megan? _____

B Read the text again and match the headings in the box with the paragraphs.

Cost of living   Job opportunities   The weather   The people   Transportation   Entertainment

Big City

San Francisco is one of the fastest growing cities in the U.S. Today, we speak to two people who recently moved here and find out their first impressions of living in the city.

Alex, 25, is an IT professional. He just moved to San Francisco from London.

1 _____
There are so many tech companies here; it's really exciting. I've joined a networking group to meet people from the industry, and I've already been to a couple of events. Have I found a job yet? No … but I'm sure I will soon! At least I have my visa!

2 _____
In my apartment building, there are people of all nationalities, as well as from other places in the U.S. I haven't met all my neighbors yet, but I love living in a city where everyone is different.

3 _____
Whatever you're interested in, there's always something going on. I've already been to the theater twice and I've seen a baseball game, and I only arrived two weeks ago!

Megan, 27, has moved to San Francisco from her hometown in Idaho to study engineering.

4 _____
San Francisco is expensive and you need a good salary to live here. I've rented a room in a shared house, but after I've paid the rent, it doesn't leave me with much money for other things.

5 _____
All my friends told me that the summers wouldn't be as hot as back home. It hasn't been too cold yet, but it can get really foggy, especially when you're near the ocean.

6 _____
The traffic here is terrible, so forget driving! Cable cars are fun, but public transportation can get really crowded, so I just bought myself a bike. It's one of the best ways to get around the city, and the bike lanes are great.

4 A Who said sentences 1–3: Alex or Megan?

1 Have I found a job _____?

2 It hasn't been too cold _____ .

3 I've _____ been to the theater twice.

B Complete the sentences with the words in the box. Check your answers in the text.

already   yet (x2)

5 Answer the questions about the sentences in exercise 4. Then read the Grammar box.

1 Which tense is used in the sentences? _____

2 Which word do we add in questions and negative sentences to talk about something we expected to happen before now? _____

3 Which word do we add to sentences to talk about something that happened earlier than we expected? _____

> **Grammar**   **present perfect with *yet* and *already***
>
> Something that happened earlier than we expected: ***He's already* finished his homework.**
> Something we expected to happen before now: ***Have* you *had* lunch *yet*? I *haven't seen* the movie *yet*.**

Personal Best

Go to Grammar practice: present perfect with *yet* and *already* page 124

6 A ▶ 7.3   **Pronunciation:** *just* and *yet* Listen and repeat the words. Pay attention to the /y/ sound *(yet)* and the /ǰ/ sound *(just)*.

1 /y/   **y**et   **y**oung   **y**ou   **u**sually

2 /ǰ/   **j**ust   **j**ob   **g**ym   bri**dge**

B ▶ 7.4   How do you say the sentences? Listen, check, and repeat.

1 Have **y**ou **j**oined a **g**ym **y**et?

2 She **j**ust **u**sed a **y**ellow pen.

3 I already have a **j**ob.

4 An**g**ela hasn't arrived **y**et.

Go to Communication practice: Student A, page 162; Student B, page 170

7 ▶ 7.5   Complete the phone conversation between Alex and his friend Josh. Use the present perfect form of the verbs in the box and *yet* or *already*. Listen and check.

find   make   meet   not see   go

Josh Hi Alex, this is Josh. How's it going in San Francisco?
Alex Great, thanks. I'm really enjoying it.
Josh Have you [1] _____ any friends [2] _____ ?
Alex Yes, I [3] _____ quite a few people. As a matter of fact, I just had lunch with two guys who work for an Internet company.
Josh Great! And [4] _____ you _____ a job [5] _____ ?
Alex No, not [6] _____ . But I [7] _____ on three interviews. I'm waiting to hear back from them.
Josh Well, good luck! Oh, what's Chinatown like?
Alex I [8] _____ it [9] _____ ! I've been too busy, but I might go this weekend.

8 A Make a list of things you have already done and things you still have to do this week.

B In pairs, ask and answer the question *Have you ... yet?* about your partner's list. Give more information in your answers.

A *Have you been to the supermarket yet?*
B *Not yet. I'm going shopping tonight, though.*
A *Have you called your parents yet?*
B *Yes, I've already called them twice this week.*

Things to do
– go to the supermarket
– call my parents
– get together with my friends

Personal Best   Write about the town or city you live in.

Learning Curve

7B The daily commute

1 Is traffic a problem in your town/city? How do most people get to work?

2 Look at the pictures in exercise 4. In pairs, use the words in the box to describe them.

> traffic jam   drive   rush hour   commuter   passenger   parking lot
> platform   take the train   parking space   public transportatiton

In picture a, people are driving to work, but there's a really bad traffic jam.

Personal Best

Go to Vocabulary practice: transportation, page 148

3 7.8   Look at exercise 4. Which cities do pictures a–c show? Watch or listen to the first part of *Learning Curve* and check.

a _____   b _____   c _____

Skill   listening for facts and figures

We often have to listen for specific information.
- Before you listen, focus on what type of information you need to listen for. For example, is it a number, a person, a time, a place, etc.?
- Listen for "clues." For example, if the information is an age, you might hear "old" or "years."
- Write the exact word(s) you hear. Then read the sentences to make sure they make sense.

---

4 **A** Read the Skill box. Match the types of information in the box with the blanks in the text.

> a specific time   a verb (x2)   a noun   an adjective (x2)   a period of time (x2)   a number (x2)

B 7.8   Watch or listen again and complete the text with the correct words.

Commuting around the world

The global average commuting time is ^{1}_____ , but it is much worse in some cities.

a

The average travel time is ^{2}_____.

Rush hour is between ^{3}_____ and 9:30 in the morning.

This city has a population of ^{4}_____ people.

b

Companies employ "pushers" to ^{5}_____ passengers onto trains.

They wear ^{6}_____ gloves as a sign of respect to passengers.

^{7}_____ passengers use the train system every day.

c

Seven million ^{8}_____ come into this city every day.

24% of people have ^{9}_____ about a parking space in the last year.

Parking lots are so ^{10}_____ that people can lose their cars.

5 ▶ 7.9 Watch or listen to the second part of the show. How do Mike, Sandra, and Lorena get to work/the university?

 Mike
 Sandra
 Lorena

6 A Read questions 1–8. What kind of information do you need to answer them?

1 How long does Mike's commute take in total? _a period of time_
2 What time does he usually leave the house? _____
3 What causes him problems on his commute? _____
4 Which city is Sandra in? _____
5 How often does she usually travel with Bonnie? _____
6 How far is it to Sandra's work? _____
7 How long does it take Lorena to walk to the university? _____
8 How much does she spend on public transportation? _____

B ▶ 7.9 Watch or listen again. Answer the questions.

7 Discuss the questions in pairs.

1 How do you get to work/college/class?
2 How long does it take you?
3 What time do you start out?
4 Do you ever have any problems?
5 Who do you travel with?
6 How does the trip make you feel?

8 ▶ 7.10 Listen to the sentences from the show. When are the /t/ sounds in **bold** pronounced?

1 What time do you se**t** off?
2 My bigges**t** problem is pedestrians.
3 I'm here in fron**t** of our building in New York.
4 Today, I'm jus**t** listening to my car radio.

✦ Listening builder final /t/ sound

English speakers don't often pronounce the /t/ sound at the end of a word when the next word begins with a consonant. If the next word begins with a vowel sound, they link the sounds together.

I get off the bus.   I ge(t) to talk with my good friend.
There's still a lot of traffic.   She doesn'(t) drive.

---

9 ▶ 7.11 Read the Listening builder. Listen and complete the sentences.

1 The _____ _____ to get to work is to drive, _____ _____ is impossible.
2 I _____ _____ at 8:00 and _____ _____ me over an hour.
3 The traffic _____ _____ completely, so we _____ _____ and walked.
4 It's the _____ _____ in the world for commuting, but they _____ _____ buy a car.
5 I _____ _____ taking the subway. I get _____ _____ _____ people come out of the station.

10 A In pairs, prepare a talk of 1–2 minutes about the transportation system in your city or country. Use the ideas in the boxes.

| the type of transportation people use | the cost and frequency of public transportation | the problems commuters have | suggestions for people visiting your city or country |

B Work with another pair. Take turns listening, then ask at least one question.

Personal Best Write a paragraph about the advantages and disadvantages of one type of transportation.

7C A life in three cities

1 A Look at the pictures. Try to answer the questions in pairs.

1 Who is the person?
2 What is her job?
3 What movies has she been in?
4 What nationality is she?

B Read the introduction in the text and check your answers.

A TALE OF THREE CITIES

She won an Oscar for her first movie, *12 Years a Slave*, in 2013. Since then, the Kenyan actress Lupita Nyong'o has become a Hollywood superstar and appeared on red carpets and magazine covers all over the world. We look at the three cities that have shaped this talented actress.

MEXICO CITY

Lupita was born in 1983 in Mexico City, where her father was working at a university. The family returned to Kenya when she was just a few months old, but at the age of 16, Lupita went back to Mexico for a year to learn Spanish. She's spoken Spanish since 1999, and has even given TV interviews in Spanish.

NAIROBI

Lupita went to school in Nairobi, and this is where she first started acting. Her first big performance was at the age of 14 when she played Juliet in *Romeo and Juliet*. One of her happiest memories is of climbing the mango trees in her grandmother's village and eating the fruit straight from the branches!

NEW YORK

Lupita has lived in Brooklyn, New York, since 2013, and this is now her home. When she's not working, she spends her time doing yoga and cooking her favorite dishes like *enchiladas verdes*. She also loves riding the subway into Manhattan to go shopping, just like anyone else in New York! The big question is: Where next for Lupita?

2 Read the rest of the text. Are the sentences true (T) or false (F)?

1 Lupita has been very famous since 2013. ____
2 She has had an interest in acting for over ten years. ____
3 She has spoken Spanish since she was a small child in Mexico. ____
4 She has lived in New York for most of her life. ____

3 Look at sentences 1–4 in exercise 2. Choose the correct options to answer the questions. Then read the Grammar box.

1 Are the situations in the sentences finished? *yes / no*
2 Which tense are the verbs in? *present continuous / present perfect*
3 When do we use the word *since*? *for a point in time / for a period of time*
4 When do we use the word *for*? *for a point in time / for a period of time*

📖 **Grammar** **present perfect with *for* and *since***

For situations that started in the past and continue in the present:
I*'ve worked* as an actress *for* twenty years.   She *hasn't seen* me *since* 2010.

Look! We use *for* for a period of time and *since* for a point in time:
I*'ve had* this car **for six months**.   I*'ve had* this car **since February**.

Go to Grammar practice: present perfect with *for* and *since*, page 125

4 **A** ▶ 7.13 **Pronunciation:** *for* and *since* Listen and repeat the sentences. Pay attention to the rhythm. Are *for* and *since* stressed or unstressed words?

1 She's lived in New York since 2013.   **2** She hasn't been to Mexico for a few years.

B ▶ 7.14 <u>Underline</u> the stressed words in the sentences. In pairs, practice saying them. Listen, check, and repeat.

1 I've lived in this house for six years.   **3** I haven't seen him for months.
2 She's known him since 1995.   **4** They've had the car since March.

Go to Communication practice: Student A, page 162; Student B, page 170

5 ▶ 7.15 Listen to the conversation and answer the questions.

1 Where do you think the people are?
2 How do Laura and Pete know each other?
3 What is Jess's job?
4 What do Laura and Jess discuss at the end?
5 Do you think connections are important for finding a good job?

6 **A** Complete the questions with the simple past or present perfect form of the verbs in parentheses.

1 Where _____ Laura and Pete _____? (meet)
2 How long _____ Jess _____ in L.A.? (be)
3 How long _____ Jess _____ in Toronto? (live)
4 How long _____ Jess _____ scripts for TV and movies? (write)
5 What _____ she _____ before she was a writer? (do)
6 How long _____ Laura and Pete _____ the idea for the TV comedy series? (have)

B ▶ 7.15 Listen to the conversation again. Ask and answer questions 1–6 in pairs.

7 **A** Complete the circles with information about you.

the name of an important friend

the name of your street

your occupation (job/student, etc.)

a hobby you enjoy

an important possession

a place you want to visit

something you use every day

something you are terrified of

B In pairs, ask and answer the question *How long have you ...?* with an appropriate verb and the information in the circles. Try to give more information.

A *How long have you known Martin?*
B *I've known him since we were in high school together. We were in the same class.*
A *How long have you had your phone?*
B *I've had it for six months. It was a birthday present from my brother.*

Personal Best   Think of someone you know well and write a paragraph about his/her life. Try to use the present perfect with *for* and *since*.

7D I think it's a great idea!

1 Look at the pictures in exercise 2. Discuss the questions in pairs.

1 How often do you use your cell phone each day?
2 Do you call people when you are on the street? If so, who?
3 Do you use your phone on public transportation? If so, what for?
4 Do you send messages when you go out with friends? If so, how often?
5 Do you think we use our phones too much? Why/Why not?

2 A Read the title of the essay. What does the verb *ban* mean?

a make something illegal ☐   **b** make something easier ☐

B Read the essay. Does Kai agree or disagree with the question?

Is it time to ban smartphones in public?
Kai Meng

Smartphones are amazing inventions and help us in lots of different ways, but I'm worried that we use them too much. Every day, I see hundreds of people using their phones in the city, and it's causing some serious problems.

First, I believe smartphones can be dangerous. When people are sending messages or listening to music with headphones while walking down the street, they don't concentrate on the traffic, and it's much easier for them to have an accident.

The second reason is that I think talking on phones in public is annoying. If you're on public transportation or in a restaurant, you don't want to hear someone else's conversation. In my opinion, people should wait to call their friends and colleagues in private, unless it's a real emergency.

Finally, banning smartphones in public is a good idea because it would make people more sociable and encourage them to talk more. Even when some people get together with their friends, they spend half the time checking their phones and going on social media. If they didn't have their phones, they'd talk to each other more, and they'd have a much better time.

In conclusion, although there are lots of advantages to smartphones, I think we should ban them in public. Personally, I think this would be safer for pedestrians, nicer for passengers on public transportation, and would help us communicate with each other more.

3 Answer the questions about the essay. Then read the Skill box.

1 How many reasons for banning smartphones does Kai give? What are they? Which paragraphs are they in?
2 What is the purpose of paragraph 1? *to introduce the topic / to summarize all his reasons*
3 What is the purpose of the final paragraph? *to introduce the topic / to summarize all his reasons*

Skill writing an essay

In essays, we discuss a topic and give our point of view.
- Organize your ideas into paragraphs (introduction, reasons, and conclusion).
- Explain the reasons for your opinions in separate paragraphs. Give examples or evidence to support them.
- Use sequencers, like *first, the second reason, finally,* and *in conclusion* to help readers.

4 Look at the pictures. In pairs, think of some reasons why we *shouldn't* ban smartphones in public.

a

b

c

5 **A** Match the two columns to make sentences. Did you have similar ideas?

1 We can check e-mails, read documents,
2 I believe this is very important
3 Personally, I love being able to watch
4 In my opinion, smartphones
5 They make our lives safer, more
6 Second, smartphones make
7 In conclusion, I don't think we should
8 The first reason is that phones help us
9 The last reason is that they are
10 Modern technology has changed

a the way we communicate.
b have made our lives better in three different ways.
c stay in touch with each other.
d for our safety.
e us work more efficiently.
f and organize meetings outside the office.
g lots of fun and keep us entertained.
h movies or play games when I'm on the subway or a bus.
i ban smartphones in public.
j efficient, and even more fun.

B Which sentences can be found in:
the introduction? _____   paragraph 3? _____   the conclusion? _____
paragraph 2? _____   paragraph 4? _____

6 **A** In pairs, use the sentences in 5A to help you write an essay against banning smartphones in public.

B Which essay is more convincing: Kai's or the one you wrote in exercise 6A? Do you think we should or shouldn't ban smartphones in public?

7 Read the essay in exercise 2 again. <u>Underline</u> any phrases Kai uses to give his opinion.

> **Text builder** | **giving opinions**
>
> **We use a variety of phrases to give our opinions:**
> *I (don't) think/believe (that) …*   *I'm worried/delighted (that) …*   *… is a good/bad idea.*
> *In my opinion/view, …*   *Personally, …*   *I would(n't) say (that) …*

8 Read the Text builder. In pairs, give your opinions about ideas 1–5. Explain your ideas.

1 I *think / don't think* public transportation should be free for everyone because …
2 Children playing computer games is a *good / bad* idea because …
3 In my opinion, learning English *is / isn't* very difficult because …
4 Personally, I *watch / don't watch* too much TV because …
5 I *would / wouldn't* say that we eat less healthily than our parents because …

9 **A** **PREPARE** Choose an essay title and decide if you agree or disagree with it. Give three reasons with examples and evidence to support them.

• Should universities be free for everyone?   • Should people who live in cities be allowed to have pets?
• Do we need to ban fast-food restaurants?   • Do we need stores now that we can buy everything online?

B **PRACTICE** Write an essay giving your opinion. Use the Skill box and Text builder to help you.

C **PERSONAL BEST** Exchange essays with another student and correct any mistakes. Is his/her essay convincing? How could he/she improve it?

Personal Best Write an essay with the opposite point of view from the one in exercise 9.

Food for thought

| LANGUAGE | *too, too many, too much,* and *(not) enough* ■ food and drink |

8A Sweet, but dangerous

1 Put the words in the box in the correct columns. Can you add two more words to each column?

| beef | cabbage | peach | salmon | strawberry | shrimp | lamb | eggplant |

fruit	vegetables	meat	fish and seafood

Go to Vocabulary practice: food and drink, page 149

2 Ask and answer the questions in pairs.

1 What did you have for breakfast?
2 What did you have for dinner last night?
3 What food do you eat if you want a snack?
4 What would you cook for a romantic dinner?
5 Are you allergic to any food?
6 Do you think you have a healthy diet? Why/Why not?

3 Look at the picture of the breakfast. Do you think it's healthy? How much added sugar do you think it contains? Read the text and check.

Most of us know that too much sugar isn't good for us. We know that we shouldn't eat a lot of chocolate or drink too many soft drinks. But how much do we really know about the other kinds of food we eat?

Australian moviemaker, Damon Gameau, decided to investigate the "hidden" sugar in food. He spent 60 days eating only products advertised as "healthy," such as low-fat yogurt, cereal bars, fruit juices, and sports drinks. But instead of feeling healthier, Damon gained 8 kg. and started to have health problems. The reason? The high levels of sugar that manufacturers add to many food products to make them taste better. The breakfast pictured here looks good, but the juice, cereal, and yogurt actually contain a total of fourteen teaspoons of extra sugar!

Damon says that food companies are not honest enough about the amount of sugar they add to their products. Their marketing makes us believe we're eating and drinking well, when we really aren't. The World Health Organization recommends a daily limit of 25 g. (about six teaspoons) of sugar. That means there's enough sugar in three quarters of a can of cola for one day.

After Damon's experiment finished, he returned to his usual diet of fresh fruit, vegetables, meat, and fish. His weight came down and his health problems disappeared. He still enjoys a little chocolate once in a while, but he finds that most processed food now tastes too sweet.

So next time you're in the supermarket, remember to check how much sugar is in that "healthy" cereal before you buy it!

4 Check (✓) the best title for the article. Explain your answer.

1 Is sugar good or bad for you? ☐
2 How to lose weight in 60 days ☐
3 The truth about sugar and processed food ☐
4 Five unhealthy foods to avoid ☐

5 Discuss the questions in pairs.

1 Did the text surprise you? Why/Why not?
2 Do you think people in your country eat too much sugar?
3 How often do you check how much sugar is in the products you buy?
4 Should the government do anything about sugar in food? If so, what?

6 **A** Complete the sentences with the words in the box. Check your answers in the text.

> too   too much   too many   not   enough

1 We shouldn't drink _____ soft drinks.
2 _____ sugar isn't good for us.
3 Food companies are _____ honest enough.
4 There's _____ sugar in three quarters of a can of cola for one day.
5 Most processed food tastes _____ sweet.

B Match the words from sentences 1–5 with the definitions. Then read the Grammar box.

1 *too / too much / too many*   a less than necessary
2 *enough*   b more than necessary
3 *not enough*   c the right amount

📖 **Grammar** **too, too many, too much, and (not) enough**

More than necessary:	The right amount:	Less than necessary:
It's **too** noisy. I can't concentrate.	We have **enough** eggs to bake a cake.	I *don't* have **enough** time.
You put **too much** milk in my coffee!	Is the room warm **enough** for you?	The car isn't fast **enough**.
There are **too many** people on the bus.		OR The car's **not** fast **enough**.

Go to Grammar practice: *too, too many, too much, and (not) enough*, page 126

7 **A** ▶8.3 **Pronunciation:** *too much sugar* Listen and repeat the sentence from the text. Pay attention to the sounds in **bold**: /u/, /ə/, and /ʊ/.

T**oo** m**u**ch s**u**gar isn't good for us.

B ▶8.4 How do you say the words? Listen, check, and repeat.

c**oo**k   s**ou**p   c**u**p   f**oo**d   en**ou**gh   p**u**t   bl**oo**d   sh**ou**ld   **u**se

8 ▶8.5 How do you say the questions? Listen, check, and repeat. Ask and answer the questions in pairs.

1 Do you have enough time to cook dinner every night?
2 Do you think good food is too expensive?
3 Do you spend too much time using social media sites?
4 Do you think you have too many clothes?
5 Is your Internet connection fast enough for you?
6 Do you know anyone who drinks too much coffee?

9 ▶8.6 Listen to a conversation. Check (✔) the food that the restaurant needs to buy.

Go to Communication practice: Student A, page 162; Student B, page 170

10 **A** Complete the sentences with your own ideas. Compare them in pairs.

1 I don't spend enough time on _____ .
2 I spend too much money on _____ .
3 I worry about _____ too much.
4 Sometimes, I'm too _____ .
5 I have too many _____ .
6 I don't think I'm _____ enough.

B Tell the rest of the class about your partner.

He doesn't spend enough time on his homework.

8B Ice cream university

1 Look at the title of the article and the pictures. Discuss the questions in pairs.

1 Where do you think the university is?
2 Who do you think takes courses here?
3 Would you like to learn how to make ice cream?
4 What's your favorite flavor of ice cream?

Skill scanning for specific information

To find a specific piece of information in a text quickly, you should scan for it.
- Identify the key word(s) in the question for the information you need.
- Quickly look for the key words in the text. You can use your finger to help you.
- Stop when you find the key word. If the information you need isn't there, continue scanning until the key word appears again.

2 Read the Skill box. Scan the text and answer the questions. The key words are <u>underlined</u>.

1 What is <u>gelato</u>?
2 When did the <u>museum</u> open?
3 How much does a <u>one-day course</u> cost?
4 When was the Gelato University <u>founded</u>?
5 What is the <u>average age</u> of students at the university?

3 <u>Underline</u> the key words in the questions. Scan the text again to answer them.

1 How many students attend the university every year?
2 What languages are classes taught in?
3 What happens if you make *gelato* using too much sugar?
4 What is the right temperature for *gelato?*
5 How much is a visit to the museum?

4 Read the text in detail. Match the headings in the box with the paragraphs A–E.

> The secret of good *gelato*   A city to study in   If you just want a taste
> A course for everyone   A mix of students

Text builder linkers to contrast information

but: *There are courses that last up to five weeks,* **but** *I'm going to try the one-day course.*
however: *There are courses that last up to five weeks.* **However,** *I'm going to try the one-day course.*
although: **Although** *there are courses that last up to five weeks, I'm going to try the one-day course.*
I'm going to try the one-day course, **although** *there are courses that last up to five weeks.*

5 A Read the Text builder. <u>Underline</u> examples of *but*, *however*, and *although* in the text. In pairs, discuss what information is contrasted.

B Complete the sentences with *but*, *however*, and *although*. Which paragraphs do they go with?

1 _____ *gelato* is Italian, it has an international reputation.
2 It's a complicated process, _____ after a few hours, I have a liter of pink ice cream.
3 It's only four euros for children under thirteen. _____ , they have to be accompanied by an adult.
4 I'm really looking forward to this course, _____ I've never been a "good student."
5 There's even a course to become a professional *gelato* taster. _____ it sounds like a dream job, I don't think I could eat ice cream 365 days a year!

6 Discuss the questions in pairs.

1 Apart from English, are you studying anything else right now?
2 What courses would you like to take if you had the time and the money?
3 If you could start your own business, what would it be?

ICE CREAM UNIVERSITY

A _____

The city of Bologna in Italy is home to the oldest university in the world. It was founded in 1088. The list of former students includes artists, politicians, poets, and even movie directors. However, what a lot of people don't realize is that Bologna is also home to another, much newer, university. I've signed up for a course, although I'm not going to study law or engineering. I'm going to learn how to make *gelato*, Italian ice cream. Welcome to Gelato University!

B _____

The Carpigiani Gelato University was founded in 2003, and every year it attracts more than 6,000 students who want to learn how to make perfect ice cream. However, it's not just about making ice cream. Students all have the same dream of starting their own *gelato* business, so classes include how to write a business plan, how to market your product, even how to design your own *gelateria*, or ice cream store. There are courses that last up to five weeks, but I'm going to try the one-day course, which costs about 100 euros.

C _____

In my class of 20, there are students from all over the world and, although my classes are in English, there are also classes in Italian, Spanish, Chinese, and other languages. The average age of the students is about 35, but company director Robert from L.A. is planning to go into the *gelato* business at the age of 72! "You're never too old to try new things," he says.

D _____

Back to the classroom, and today we're making strawberry *gelato*. However, before we start, there's a science class. There's a lot of chemistry and mathematics, and a calculator is essential. If there's too much sugar in the mixture, it won't freeze. If there's not enough air, it will be too heavy. And it has to be served at the right temperature (5–10° C), which is much warmer than normal ice cream.

E _____

If you're interested in *gelato*, but you don't have the time or money to take a course, the university also has its own Gelato Museum, opened in 2012. For five euros, you can visit the museum, discover the history of *gelato*, the technology behind it and, of course, taste some of the different flavors! And if you're wondering how my strawberry *gelato* tasted, it was delicious!

Personal Best   Write a paragraph about your school or college. Remember to use linkers to contrast information.

8C You have to eat your vegetables!

1 **A** ▶ 8.7 Look at the pictures of school lunches. Which countries do you think they are from? Listen and check.

B ▶ 8.7 Match the adjectives in the box with the pictures. Listen again and check.

healthy   crunchy   sweet   spicy   salty   tasty

Go to Vocabulary practice: adjectives to describe food, page 150

2 Discuss the questions in pairs.

1 Did you ever have school lunches? If so, what were they like?
2 Which dishes from your childhood did you love/hate? Why?

3 Look at the pictures. Do you recognize the man? In pairs, answer the questions. Read the text and check.

1 What is the man's job?
2 Which country was he in?

3 Why was he in this country?
4 Why does he look disappointed?

THE FOOD REVOLUTION THAT FAILED

British celebrity chef, Jamie Oliver, tasted failure for the first time with his American TV show, *Jamie's Food Revolution.* One of the biggest health problems in the U.S. is obesity, and Jamie thought he could help by changing what children ate … but he found that it wasn't so easy.

In the U.S., more than 32 million children eat in school cafeterias every day. Unfortunately, the meals aren't always very healthy, and some children don't have to eat fruit or vegetables. Instead, they can choose hamburgers and pizzas with sweet drinks, like chocolate milk.

In 2010 and 2011, Jamie conducted an experiment. He tried changing the menu at a school in Los Angeles. The cooks made different meals, including vegetarian curry, fresh salads, and spicy chicken noodles. However, Jamie's experiment failed, and most children threw his new recipes away. With hungry children and angry parents, hamburgers and pizzas were soon back on the menu.

However, it's not all bad news. Although Jamie's idea didn't work, things are changing. New laws say that all schools have to serve healthier food. School meals can't contain too much salt, and cafeterias have to offer two vegetables a day … but these things take time. According to some previous rules, tomato sauce on pizzas counted as "one vegetable"!

4 Discuss the questions in pairs.

1 What do you think about Jamie's experiment?
2 Why do you think it failed?
3 What would you think if he tried to change school meals in your country?

5 A Match the two parts to make sentences. Check your answers in the text.

1 Children **don't have to**
2 All schools **have to**
3 School meals **can't**

a serve healthier food.
b eat fruit or vegetables.
c contain too much salt.

B Answer the questions about the words in **bold** in sentences 1–4. Then read the Grammar box.

1 Which words mean "there is a rule to do this"?   _____
2 Which words mean "this is not necessary"?   _____
3 Which word means "this is not allowed'?   _____

📖 **Grammar**	*have to, not have to,* and *can't*	

Obligation:
You **have to** start school at 9:00 a.m.
Do they **have to** wear a uniform?

Not necessary:
You **don't have to** take the course, but you can if you want.

Prohibition:
Students **can't** use a calculator during the exam.

Go to Grammar practice: *have to, not have to,* and *can't,* page 127

6 Choose the correct options to complete the hotel rules. Would you like to stay at this hotel? Why/Why not?

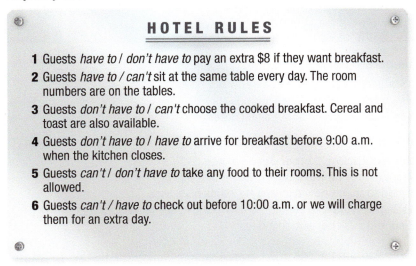

HOTEL RULES

1 Guests *have to / don't have to* pay an extra $8 if they want breakfast.
2 Guests *have to / can't* sit at the same table every day. The room numbers are on the tables.
3 Guests *don't have to / can't* choose the cooked breakfast. Cereal and toast are also available.
4 Guests *don't have to / have to* arrive for breakfast before 9:00 a.m. when the kitchen closes.
5 Guests *can't / don't have to* take any food to their rooms. This is not allowed.
6 Guests *can't / have to* check out before 10:00 a.m. or we will charge them for an extra day.

7 A ▶ 8.10   **Pronunciation:** sentence stress Listen to the sentences. <u>Underline</u> the stressed words.

1 People have to carry an identity card at all times.
2 You don't have to buy a ticket when you get on the bus.
3 People can't use their cell phones on public transportation.

4 Children have to stay in school until the age of 18.
5 Parents don't have to send their children to school. They can educate them at home.
6 Everyone has to vote in the national elections.

B ▶ 8.10   Say the sentences, paying attention to the stress in each one. Listen again, check, and repeat.

8 In pairs, decide if the sentences in exercise 7A are true in your country.

Go to Communication practice: Student A, page 163; Student B, page 171

9 A In pairs, imagine you are the managing director of a new company. Write a list of rules that will keep your employees happy and productive and make your company successful. Think about these factors:

working hours   meetings   food and drink   social activities   breaks during the day

days off / vacations   work clothes   communication

B Tell the rest of the class your rules.

Personal Best   Write a list of rules in your place of work or college. How could you change them to make them better?

8D First dates

1 In pairs, look at the pictures of restaurants. Decide which are the best places for the situations in the box.

a business meeting   a first date   getting together with friends
a birthday celebration   lunch by yourself   a family meal

2 Discuss the questions in pairs.

1 How would you feel if you had a first date?
2 Where would you go on a first date?
3 Who would you ask for advice about a first date?

3 ▶8.11 Watch or listen to the first part of *Learning Curve*. Are the sentences true (T) or false (F)?

1 Jack feels shy about asking Eleanor out on a date. ____
2 Jack met Eleanor while he was studying at the university. ____
3 He invites Simon to try his new dish and he wants his advice. ____
4 Simon thinks Jack should take Eleanor to a fish-and-chips restaurant. ____
5 Jack rings Eleanor to ask her out on a date. ____

4 ▶8.11 Use the words in the box to complete what Jack and Simon said. Watch or listen again and check.

dish   great   be   in   sounds
new   Would   that   interested
you   trying   a   Thanks   out

Conversation builder	making and responding to invitations

Inviting:
Would you like to ...?
Would you be interested in ...?
Do you want to ...?
Do you feel like ...?

Accepting:
I'd love to. Thank you.
Thanks, that sounds great!
That's very nice/kind of you.
That would be wonderful.
Fantastic.

Refusing:
That's really nice of you, but I'm sorry, I can't.
I'm afraid I already have plans.
I really appreciate the invitation, but ...
Sorry, I think I'm busy that evening.

5 Read the Conversation builder. In pairs, take turns inviting your partner for coffee one day this week. Refuse the first time, but when he/she invites you for coffee on a different day, accept.

6 A ▶ 8.12   Watch or listen to the second part of the show. Where do Jack and Eleanor decide to go for their date?

B ▶ 8.12   Complete the conversation with the words in the box. Watch or listen again and check.

appreciate   like   fancy   sorry   want   kind

Jack   I was wondering if you'd ¹_____ having dinner with me at my restaurant?
Eleanor   Oh, that's right, you're a chef. Thanks, that's very ²_____ of you.
Jack   Great. I know it's short notice, but would you ³_____ to come tonight? I have a new, special dish.
Eleanor   Did you say tonight? That's really nice of you, but I'm ⁴_____, I can't. I already have plans.
Jack   Well, do you ⁵_____ to go out on the weekend? Perhaps tomorrow?
Eleanor   Er, I would. I really ⁶_____ the invite, but, I'm going to go visit my granddad.

Eleanor

7 ▶ 8.13   Listen and repeat the phrases when you hear the beeps. Do Eleanor and Jack sound polite?

🔧 **Skill**   sounding polite

It's important to sound polite in English, especially when you say something negative.
- Use intonation to express yourself. Flat intonation can sound rude.
- Apologize before you say something negative.
- Use longer phrases and give explanations.

8 A ▶ 8.14   Read the Skill box. Listen to six conversations and check (✔) the response that sounds more polite: a or b.

1   Tom, could you help me with this box? It's really heavy.   a ☐   b ☐
2   Do you feel like going to the movies tonight?   a ☐   b ☐
3   So what did your boss think of the designs?   a ☐   b ☐
4   Would you like to go for coffee after class?   a ☐   b ☐
5   Wow! That new jacket looks great on you.   a ☐   b ☐
6   Would you be interested in seeing my band play tomorrow evening? a ☐   b ☐

B ▶ 8.15   Listen and repeat the polite responses. Explain why they are more polite.

Go to Communication practice: Student A, page 163; Student B, page 171

9 A PREPARE   In pairs, look at the diagram and discuss what you could say at each stage. You can make notes.

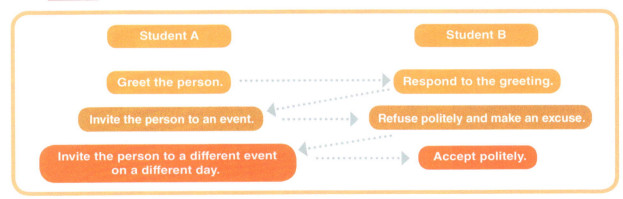

Student A   Student B

Greet the person. ⋯⋯⋯▶ Respond to the greeting.

Invite the person to an event. ◀⋯⋯ ⋯⋯▶ Refuse politely and make an excuse.

Invite the person to a different event on a different day. ◀⋯⋯ ⋯⋯▶ Accept politely.

B PRACTICE   Repeat your conversation until you can say it without looking at the diagram or your notes.

C PERSONAL BEST   Work with another pair. Listen to their conversation. Did they use the same language as you? Was their conversation polite? In what way?

Personal Best   Write another dialogue using the diagram in exercise 9A, but use different phrases.

Grammar

1 Put a (**X**) by the sentence that is NOT correct.

1 a I haven't called Claude yet. ☐
  b I've called Claude 10 minutes ago. ☐
  c I called Claude 10 minutes ago. ☐
2 a I have to wear a suit to work. ☐
  b I can wear a suit to work. ☐
  c I haven't to wear jeans to work. ☐
3 a I've worked here since January. ☐
  b I've worked here for five months. ☐
  c I've worked here since five months ago. ☐
4 a This restaurant is too crowded. ☐
  b This restaurant isn't quiet enough. ☐
  c This restaurant is too much crowded. ☐
5 a I've seen the movie yet. ☐
  b I saw the movie last week. ☐
  c I've already seen the movie. ☐
6 a You have too many clothes in your closet. ☐
  b You can't have space enough for your clothes. ☐
  c You don't have enough space in your closet. ☐
7 a I haven't seen my parents for a month. ☐
  b I didn't see my parents since last month. ☐
  c I haven't seen my parents since last month. ☐
8 a You can't walk on the grass. ☐
  b You have to walk on the path. ☐
  c You allowed to walk on the path. ☐

2 Use the words in parentheses to write sentences that mean the same as the first sentence.

1 It's not necessary for Sofia to take the train.
  Sofia _____ take the train. (have)
2 I didn't have breakfast this morning.
  I _____ breakfast _____ today. (yet)
3 I went to the grocery store this morning.
  I _____ to the grocery store. (already)
4 We've had the car since March.
  We _____ six months. (for)
5 We need more bread.
  We _____ bread. (enough)
6 She hasn't visited me for years.
  She _____ 2012. (visited)
7 The coffee has more milk than I wanted.
  There's _____ in my coffee. (too)
8 You're not allowed to use your phone in here.
  You _____ your phone in here. (use)

3 Choose the correct options to complete the text.

Don't look down!

The city of Dubai [1]*built / has built* over 200 skyscrapers [2]*for / since* 2000, and the Burj Khalifa is the tallest of these. It's 830 m. high, with 163 floors and has an incredible 24,000 windows … all of which [3]*have / have to* be cleaned! The tallest part of the building is [4]*too / too much* difficult for people to clean, and machines are used. However, a team of 36 men clean the rest of the building. Let's talk to Bibek Thapa from Nepal, who has [5]*already / yet* finished cleaning for the day.

What's the hardest part about the job?

I've climbed [6]*enough mountains / mountains enough* in Nepal not to be afraid of heights. The worst thing for me is the sun. Sometimes it's [7]*too / too much* hot, and we [8]*have to / can't* wear protective clothing.

What's it like in bad weather?

We don't work when there's [9]*too many / too much* wind or dust because it's very dangerous.

Do you need any special equipment?

We use lots of safety equipment, obviously, but we [10]*have to / don't have to* use any special cleaning chemicals. We just use soap and water, like when you clean windows at home. ●

Vocabulary

1 Match the words with the definitions.

> rush hour   fresh   start out   coconut
> raw   crosswalk   turkey
> give someone a ride   trash can   commuter

1 to take someone to a place in your car _____
2 a place for garbage when you're on the street _____
3 a person who travels to work _____
4 a large bird we can eat _____
5 a large fruit from a palm tree _____
6 to leave your house to go somewhere _____
7 food that is not cooked _____
8 a place where you can cross the street safely _____
9 the busiest time of day on the street _____
10 food that was prepared recently _____

2 Circle the word that is different. Explain your answer.

1 passenger   platform   pedestrian   commuter
2 sour   sweet   bitter   crunchy
3 drive   ride   go by   traffic
4 beef   lamb   shrimp   turkey
5 tunnel   bridge   bike lane   trash can
6 delayed   street sign statue   sidewalk
7 tuna   peach   pineapple   strawberry
8 tasty   burned   healthy   delicious

3 Choose the correct word to complete the sentences.

1 My bus never _____ on time.
   a arrives   b gets   c drives
2 Is the fish _____? It doesn't smell very good.
   a fresh   b tasty   c healthy
3 We _____ early on our hike at 9:00.
   a arrive   b started out   c drive
4 We're having _____ for dessert.
   a flour   b lettuce   c apple pie
5 My car is at the garage, so I can't _____ to work.
   a ride   b drive   c arrive
6 A: What's on the pizza?
   B: There's tomato sauce, peppers, and _____ .
   a flour   b cheese   c cereal
7 There are no _____ on this street; it's very dark!
   a traffic lights   b streetlights   c street signs
8 The doctor said I shouldn't eat _____ food.
   a fresh   b salty   c disgusting

4 Complete the conversations with the words in the boxes.

> parking space   benches   parking lot
> apartment building   public transportation

Jo   Is your new ¹ _____ near the city bridge?
Lee No, it's next to the square with the fountain and all the ² _____ to sit on.
Jo   That's a great area! Do you get a ³ _____ for your car?
Lee Yes, but I use ⁴ _____ to get to work because my office doesn't have a ⁵ _____ .

> fresh   delicious   seafood   spicy   vegetarian

Kim Don't forget you have to cook ⁶ _____ food for my parents. They don't eat meat.
Jon I know. I'm going to cook curry.
Kim Don't cook curry! It will be too ⁷ _____ for them! Why don't you cook the *paella* you made last week? It was ⁸ _____ ! I loved it.
Jon But that had ⁹ _____ in it!
Kim Oh, yeah. Can't you make it without it? Just add lots of ¹⁰ _____ vegetables.

Personal Best

Lesson 7A
Write a question with *yet*, and answer it.

Lesson 8A
Name five kinds of fruit.

Lesson 7A
Name five city features you usually see on the street.

Lesson 8A
Write one sentence using *enough*, and another with *too*.

Lesson 7B
Name four ways of going to work.

Lesson 8B
Write a sentence using *although*.

Lesson 7C
Write a question with *how long*, and an answer with *since*.

Lesson 8C
Name five adjectives to describe food.

Lesson 7C
Write three sentences about yourself or your family using *for*.

Lesson 8C
Write three rules you have at home.

Lesson 7D
Give three expressions for giving your opinion.

Lesson 8D
Give two expressions for accepting an invitation, and two for refusing.

Money and shopping

LANGUAGE | *used to* ■ money verbs

9A He used to be poor

1 A Look at the title of the text and the pictures. Discuss the questions in pairs.

1 Have you ever been to a Zara store?
2 What does Zara sell?
3 Who is the man?
4 What does the title of the text mean?

B Read the introduction and check your answers.

FROM ZERO TO ZARA

Today, he's one of the richest men in the world with a global business that is worth billions of dollars, but he used to be a poor boy from Galicia, in the north of Spain. This is the story of Amancio Ortega, the founder of the clothing company, Zara.

Amancio was born in 1936. His father was a railway worker and didn't earn much money. The family sometimes couldn't afford food. His mother used to ask for credit at the grocery store, but one day they said no. At that moment, Amancio decided to quit school and get a job. He was just 14.

Amancio's first job was at a shirt store. He used to fold the shirts and deliver them to customers on his bike. Then he moved to another store, where he learned a lot about the industry. Clothes used to be very expensive, and there wasn't much to choose from, so customers didn't use to buy many. Amancio realized that if he could produce more attractive clothes more cheaply, people would spend more money.

So, at the age of 27, and with just a little money that he'd saved, Amancio started his own business making pajamas, which he sold to local stores. After borrowing some money from the bank, he began making other types of clothing, and the business grew. In 1975, Amancio opened his first Zara store, and the company soon opened more stores in Spain.

Today, you can find Zara and the other fashion companies Amancio owns in 88 different countries around the world, but he still lives in Galicia, where he grew up.

2 Order the events from 1–8. Read the text and check.

a ☐ He worked in a shirt store.
b ☐ Zara expanded around the world.
c ☐ He quit school.
d ☐ The first Zara store opened.
e ☐ He started to produce other types of clothing.
f ☐ Amancio was born in northern Spain.
g ☐ He used his own money to start a business.
h ☐ He asked the bank for some money.

3 What do you think Amancio Ortega is like? Why?

4 A Match the two columns to make sentences. Check your answers in the text.

1 Amancio decided to
2 His mother used to
3 Customers didn't use to
4 He used to

a ask for credit.
b buy many clothes.
c quit school.
d be a poor boy from Galicia.

B Look at sentences 1–4 again and answer the questions. Then read the Grammar box.

1 Are the sentences about the past, the present, or the future? _____
2 Which sentence is an action that only happened once? _____ Which tense is it? _____
3 Which sentence is a situation that was true in the past, but isn't true now? _____
4 Which sentences are actions that happened more than once in the past? _____ _____

Grammar *used to*

Actions that happened regularly in the past, but don't happen now:	Situations that were true in the past, but aren't true now:
How **did** you **use to get** to school?	What **did** she **use to be** like?
We **used to walk** to school. We **didn't use to take** the bus.	She **used to be** really shy. She **didn't use to be** very confident.

Look! We use the simple past for an action that only happened once.
I **went** shopping yesterday. NOT *I used to go shopping yesterday.*

Go to Grammar practice: *used to*, page 128

5 **▶9.2** **Pronunciation:** *used to/use to* Listen to the sentences.
How do you say the words in **bold**? Do they sound different?
Listen again and repeat.

1 His family **used to** be poor.
2 He didn't **use to** earn much money.
3 Did he **use to** work from home?

Go to Communication practice: Student A, page 163; Student B, page 171

6 Match the words in the box with definitions 1–6. Look at the ==highlighted== words in the text on page 76 to help you.

> be worth   earn   can afford   spend   save   borrow

1 have enough money to buy something _____	4 have a value of a certain amount of money _____
2 not use money and keep it in a bank _____	5 take money from someone, but return it later _____
3 use money to buy something _____	6 make money from work _____

Go to Vocabulary practice: money verbs, page 151

7 Discuss the questions in pairs.

1 What do you spend your money on?
2 Do you find it difficult to save money?
3 Do you own your home or do you rent it?
4 Which professions earn the most money?
5 Have you ever borrowed money from a bank?
6 Do you have a car? How much is it worth?
7 Do you think athletes get paid too much money?
8 Do you ever waste money on things you don't need?

8 **A** **▶9.4** Listen to five people talking about their childhood. Match the topics in the box with the speakers.

> bedtime   money   toys   vacations   food

1 Rachel _____   2 Allan _____   3 Freddy _____   4 Lucy _____   5 Sam _____

B **▶9.4** Complete the sentences with the simple past or *used to* form of the verbs in parentheses. Listen again and check.

1 The first book I _____ was *Northern Lights*. (buy)
2 Our parents _____ about us. (not worry)
3 We _____ for dinner every Saturday night. (go out)
4 My grandpa always _____ me a story in bed at night. (read)
5 I _____ a Buzz Lightyear toy for my birthday one year. (get)

9 **A** In pairs, talk about your childhood. Use the topics in the boxes or your own ideas.

> bedtime   clothes   food   vacations   money   music   school   toys and games   TV

I used to go to bed at 7:00 p.m. every night. What time did you use to go to bed?

B Tell the class some things that you found out about your partner.

He/She used to ...   He/She didn't use to ...

Personal Best Write ten sentences about you, using the verbs from the Vocabulary practice.

9B What a bargain!

1 Match the options in the box with pictures a–f.

> discount   cash register   shopping center/mall   cash   line   receipt

Go to Vocabulary practice: shopping, page 151

2 Discuss the questions in pairs.

1 Do you prefer to shop in malls, department stores, small independent stores, or online? Why?
2 Have you ever found a bargain during a sale? If so, what was it?
3 Do you always try on clothes in the dressing rooms before buying them? Why/Why not?
4 How long do you keep a receipt after you have bought something? Why?
5 Do you ever go window shopping? Why/Why not?

3 ▶️ 9.7 Watch or listen to the first part of *Learning Curve*. Check (✔) the best summary of what Ethan says.

a Shopping in the past was very different. ☐
b Shopping centers have a long history. ☐
c Shopping centers or malls are the best place to find bargains. ☐

4 ▶️ 9.7 What do sentences 1–6 refer to: *Trajan's Market* (TM), or *Grand Bazaar* (GB)? Watch or listen again and check.

1 It is about 600 years old.   ____
2 Today it's a museum.   ____
3 It has about 5,000 stores.   ____
4 It has about 250,000 visitors per day.   ____
5 It's almost 2,000 years old.   ____
6 People used to live there.   ____

5 A Check (✔) Kate's opinion of the Grand Bazaar.

a She thinks it's an interesting place for tourists. ☐
b She thinks it's a good place to go shopping. ☐
c She prefers modern shopping malls. ☐

B Can you remember what words she used to give this opinion? Read the Skill box.

Ethan

🔧 **Skill**   **identifying attitude and opinion**

It's often important to understand what someone's personal opinion is.
- Listen for phrases that we use to give opinions: *I think ..., I'd say ..., to be honest ...,* etc.
- Listen for adjectives that describe feelings: *boring, excited, upset, annoyed, pleased,* etc.
- Listen for verbs that express attitude: *look forward to, prefer, love, have to,* etc.

6 ▶9.8   Watch or listen to the second part of the show. Match the reasons for going to a shopping center in the box with the three people.

> see a movie   return something to a store   meet up with friends

Andrea

Lohi

Joan

7 **A** ▶9.8   Watch or listen again. Are the sentences true (T) or false (F)?

1 Andrea is annoyed that her friends aren't coming.   ____
2 She doesn't like "queues" (lines).   ____
3 Lohi is surprised at the size of the mall.   ____
4 He thinks he made a mistake shopping there.   ____
5 Joan was angry because she couldn't exchange her jumper.   ____
6 She's happy with her new jumper.   ____

B Can you remember the words and phrases that helped you answer the questions?

8 Discuss the questions in pairs.

1 When did you last go to a shopping center?
2 Did you buy anything? If so, how did you pay?
3 What were the last clothes you bought?
4 Did you try them on?

9 ▶9.9   Read what Andrea said. Can you understand it without the missing words? Listen and complete the sentences.

> ¹_____ , I'm supposed to be meeting up with some friends, but ²_____ , they ³_____ , just texted me to say they're not coming. I'd say it's a bit rude really, but I can't do anything. So, I'm just ⁴_____ of looking around, window shopping, ⁵_____ ?

🔀 **Listening builder**   **filler expressions**

Fillers are words and phrases that speakers say to give themselves time to think. They don't really mean anything:
So, I bought this jacket, **like**, a week ago, **I mean**, I wanted to **kind of** return it and, **er**, get a refund.
Well, I don't have the receipt, **you see**, because I **I guess** I lost it.

10 ▶9.10   Read the Listening builder. Listen to the conversation and answer the questions.

1 What is Jason doing at the shopping center?   2 Which filler expressions do you hear?

11 In pairs, discuss how shopping has changed from the past. Use the topics in the boxes or your own ideas.

> size of stores   location   choice   ways to pay
> opening hours   customer service   quality of products   prices

I think the quality of clothes used to be much better.

 Personal Best   Use your ideas from exercise 11 to write a paragraph about how shopping has changed.

9C Going, going, gone!

1 Ask and answer the questions in pairs.

1 Have you ever been to an auction? Where was it?
2 Have you ever bought anything on an online auction website?
3 What did you buy? How much did you pay?

2 ▶ 9.11 Look at the pictures. In pairs, match four of the prices in the box with the items that were sold at auctions. Listen and check.

| $5,000 | $100,000 | $1.8M | $4.6M | $75M | $120M |

3 ▶ 9.11 In pairs, try to complete the sentences. Listen again and check.

1 *The Scream* **was painted** in _____ by Edvard Munch.
2 This version **is thought** to be _____ **by** many experts.
3 The jacket **was worn by** Michael Jackson in the music video for _____ .
4 It's **made** of red and black _____ .
5 The Aston Martin car **was driven by** Sean Connery in the _____ movies.
6 Another car from the movies **was stolen** in _____ .
7 Vegemite **is eaten by** millions of _____ every day.
8 This piece of toast **was given** to Niall Horan from _____ on an Australian TV show.

4 Look at the words in **bold** in exercise 3. Answer the questions. Then read the Grammar box.

1 Which grammar structure is used in the sentences? _____
2 Which sentences are in the simple present? _____ Which are in the simple past? _____
3 How do we make this structure? The verb _____ + the _____ of the main verb.
4 Which word do we use before the people who do/did the action? _____
5 What is more important in the passive: the people who do/did the action or the action? _____

📖 Grammar | the passive

Simple present passive
*Where **are** the cars **made**?*
*They **are made** in Italy.*
*They **aren't made** anywhere else.*

Simple past passive
*When **was** the book **written**?*
*It **was written** in 1957.*
*It **wasn't published** until 2015.*

Look! To say who does/did the action we use **by**.
*The cars are made **by factory workers**.*   *The book was written **by Harper Lee**.*

Go to Grammar practice: the passive, page 129

5 **A** ▶ 9.13 **Pronunciation:** sentence stress Listen and repeat the sentence. Pay attention to the <u>underlined</u> stressed words.

The <u>picture</u> was <u>painted</u> in <u>1945</u>.

B ▶ 9.14 <u>Underline</u> the stressed words. Listen, check, and repeat.

1 These clothes were worn by Lady Gaga.
2 These peaches are grown in Brazil.
3 The salmon is cooked with lemon.
4 The car was driven by Lewis Hamilton.
5 These watches are made in Switzerland.
6 The bridge was opened in 2010.

Go to Communication practice: Student A, page 163; Student B, page 171

6 Look at the picture and the title. What do you think the text is about? How much is the box worth? Read the text and check.

FAMILY FINDS "LOST" TREASURE IN FATHER'S HOME

This beautiful wood and gold box was made in Japan in 1640. It is one of ten boxes that were made in Kyoto by Kaomi Nagashige, a well-known Japanese artist. However, this box was thought to be lost. In fact, the Victoria and Albert Museum in London had spent over fifty years searching for it. Unknown to the museum, the box was just one kilometer away in a nearby house. It was bought by a French engineer for £100 in 1970, and amazingly, it was used as a table for his television! After he died, his family decided to sell it, and it was identified by art experts as one of the lost Japanese boxes from 1640. It went up for auction, and was sold to the Rijksmuseum in Amsterdam for 7.3 million euros, making the family millionaires. ■

7 **A** Use the words to make passive questions.

1 what / the box / make of ?
_____

2 where / the box / make ?
_____

3 when / the box / make ?
_____

4 who / the box / buy / by / in 1970 ?
_____

5 how much / the box / buy / for ?
_____

6 what / the box / use / for ?
_____

7 who / the box / identify / by ?
_____

8 who / the box / sell / to / for 7.3 million euros?
_____

B Ask and answer the questions in pairs.

8 Discuss the questions in pairs.

1 Do you think the box is really worth so much money?
2 How would you feel if you were the family of the French engineer?
3 What is your most important possession? Would you ever sell it?

9 Answer the quiz questions in pairs.

Quiz Time

① Where are roubles used as money?
② Who was *The Alchemist* written by?
③ When was penicillin discovered?
④ Which U.S. city is known as "The Big Apple"?
⑤ How many Harry Potter movies were made?
⑥ Which languages are spoken in Canada?

10 **A** In pairs, write five quiz questions with the passive form of the verbs in the boxes.

invent   make   sing   direct   wear   write   paint   record   know   discover   use   win

B Exchange quizzes with another pair and answer the questions.

Personal Best Write about an important possession and say how much it is worth to you.

9D I'd like a refund!

1 What are the advantages and disadvantages of online shopping? Discuss the questions in pairs.

  1 How often do you buy things online?

  2 What do you prefer to buy in stores? Why?

  3 Have you ever had a problem with something you bought online?

2 Match the problems in the box with pictures a–e.

> The wrong size was sent.   It was broken or damaged.   Part of the order was missing.
> The order arrived late / didn't arrive.   I was charged too much.

3 Read the e-mail and answer the questions.

  1 What are the three problems with Valerie's order?

  2 What did she pay extra for?

  3 What does she want the company to do?

  4 Would you use this company?

To: info@phonetastic.com
Subject: Problems with my order (P389746-D)

Dear Sir/Madam:
I am writing to complain about the problems I have had with my online order (P389746-D).
I ordered a red X3 smartphone from your website on January 14, and I paid $4.99 extra for next-day delivery. I waited for one week, but nothing arrived, so I contacted your customer service team. I was told that it was on its way. However, the phone was only delivered yesterday—two weeks after I ordered it. Apart from the late delivery, there are two other problems with the phone. First, it is the wrong color. The phone I was sent is black, not red. And second, the screen is cracked. I have attached a photo so you can see what I mean. Because of these problems, I wish to return the phone and I would like a full refund, including the extra delivery charge.
I look forward to hearing from you soon.
Regards,
Valerie Lemoir

---

4 A Is the style of the e-mail formal or informal? Why?

B Order the different parts of the e-mail. Then read the Skill box.

  a ☐ say what she wants the company to do

  b ☐ complain about the late delivery

  c ☐ give the reason for writing

  d ☐ end the e-mail

  e ☐ explain the other problems

  f ☐ include a short and accurate subject line

🔧 Skill   writing a formal e-mail

We often write formal e-mails to people who work for other companies and organizations.

- Use a formal greeting: *Dear Sir/Madam: Dear Mrs. Jones:*
- Order your paragraphs: reason for writing, explaining the situation, what you want to happen
- Avoid contractions: *I am writing* ... NOT ~~I'm writing~~ ...
- Use formal expressions: *I contacted* ... NOT ~~I called~~ ...
- Use passives to avoid being personal: *I was told* ... NOT ~~They told me~~ ...

5 Choose the correct options to complete the reply from Suleiman.

To: valerie.lemoir@mailshop.com
Subject: RE: Problems with my order (P389746-D)

[1]*Hi Valerie. / Dear Ms. Lemoir:*
I am writing [2]*in regard to / about* your e-mail of January 29.
First, [3]*I feel bad about / please accept my apologies for* the problems you experienced with our online ordering system, which were [4]*unacceptable / really bad*. Unfortunately, [5]*the wrong software was installed / they installed the wrong software* and this has caused some unexpected problems.
Therefore, I [6]*would be very happy to refund / don't mind refunding* the money, including all delivery costs that [7]*you were charged / they charged*. Please [8]*tell me / advise me of* a convenient date for our delivery team to pick up the phone. [9]*In addition to this / Also*, I would like to offer you a $50 gift certificate to spend on any product at Phonetastic. I hope this is satisfactory, and we look forward to you shopping with us in future.
[10]*Cheers! / Sincerely* yours,

Suleiman Malik
Customer Services Manager

6 How did Suleiman try to solve the problem? Do you think Valerie will use the company again?

7 A Complete the sentences from Valerie's e-mail with the words in the box. Check your answers in her e-mail.

> delivered   delivery   order   ordered

1 I am writing to complain about the problems I have had with my online _____ ...
2 I _____ a red X3 smartphone from your website on ...
3 However, the phone was only _____ yesterday—two weeks after I ordered it.
4 Apart from the late _____ , there are ...

B How does Valerie repeat her ideas without repeating the exact words?

Text builder	**noun forms of verbs**

No change:	*order → order*	**Noun ends in -*sion*:**	*decide → decision*
Noun ends in -*ment*:	*argue → argument*	**Noun ends in -*ation*:**	*inform → information*
Noun ends in -*y*:	*deliver → delivery*		

8 Read the Text builder. Complete the sentences with the noun form of the verbs in parentheses.

1 There's a problem with the _____ on this credit card. (pay)
2 We have received your _____ for the job. (apply)
3 In _____, this is a serious problem. (conclude)
4 I didn't receive an _____ for their mistakes. (apologize)
5 He hasn't given me an _____ yet. (answer)

9 A PREPARE Choose a problem with an online order. Make notes about the details of the problem and what you want the company to do (e.g., contact you/exchange/refund).

missing part | arrived 3 days late | wrong color | wrong product delivered

B PRACTICE Use the Skill box to write a formal e-mail complaining about the order. Repeat your ideas in different ways using noun and verb forms of words.

C PERSONAL BEST Exchange e-mails with your partner. Check (✔) three sentences you think are very good. Suggest three ways to improve his/her e-mail.

Personal Best | Write the company's reply to your partner's e-mail from exercise 9.

Sports and fitness

LANGUAGE past perfect ■ sports and competitions

10A Winning is everything!

1 ▶ **10.1** Listen and match the speakers with pictures a–c.

2 ▶ **10.1** Complete the sentences with the words in the box. Listen again and check.

> beat win game race umpire athlete medal trophy score crowd

1 The _____ is almost over. In one minute, Real Madrid will _____ the game and the _____.
But wait. What's this? Here comes Arsenal. The ball goes to Walcott. He has to _____ a goal, now. He does!

2 Serena Williams to serve. Was that out? She looks at the _____. You can hear the _____ cheering.
They're sure Serena is going to _____ her sister, Venus.

3 Here they come, the finish line of the 100-meter _____, and Bolt is going to win the gold _____ again.
Yes, he's done it. What an amazing _____!

Go to Vocabulary practice: sports and competitions, page 152

3 Discuss the questions in pairs.

1 Do you prefer to watch or take part in sports?
2 Have you ever won a medal or a trophy?
3 Would you like to be a professional athlete?
4 How have sports changed over the last 100 years?

4 Read the text. What are the names of the athletes in the pictures?

THE TOUGHEST RACE EVER?

There are some difficult events in the Olympic Games, but nothing compares with the 1904 Olympic Marathon. One athlete almost died, and the race ended in a public scandal.

The marathon started on an incredibly hot day in St. Louis, in the U.S., and there were lots of cars and horses on the dusty roads. One athlete, William Garcia, started coughing after he'd breathed in too much dust. It was so bad he had to quit the race and was taken to the hospital. Another runner, Len Tau from South Africa, eventually finished in ninth place, but he was disappointed because some wild dogs had chased him for over a mile in the opposite direction during the race!

Meanwhile, the first athlete to cross the finish line was an American, Fred Lorz. The crowd thought a local athlete had won, so they started celebrating, but actually, Lorz had cheated. He'd started feeling sick during the race and had ridden 11 miles in a car! Fortunately, a spectator had seen Lorz getting out of the car one mile before the finish line and told the referee, so Lorz didn't win the gold medal.

The next runner to finish was another American, Tom Hicks. Hicks hadn't felt well either, so his friends had given him a drink of eggs mixed with some chemicals to help him. However, this had made him feel even worse and, in the end, his friends had helped him walk the final part of the race. Even though he hadn't run the whole marathon on his own, the organizers presented Hicks with the gold medal after the hardest marathon of all time.

5 **A** Read the sentences. Check (✔) the action that happened first: **a** or **b**?

1 **a** ☐ William Garcia **started** coughing after
   b ☐ he**'d breathed** in too much dust.

2 **a** ☐ Len Tau **was** disappointed because
   b ☐ some wild dogs **had chased** him for over a mile.

3 **a** ☐ The crowd thought a local athlete **had won**, so
   b ☐ they **started** celebrating.

4 **a** ☐ Even though he **hadn't run** the whole marathon,
   b ☐ the organizers **presented** Hicks with the gold medal.

B Look at the verbs in **bold** in exercise 5A and answer the questions. Then read the Grammar box.

1 What tense are the actions that happened first? *simple past / past perfect*
2 What tense are the actions that happened later? *simple past / past perfect*
3 How do we form the past perfect? _____ + _____

> 📖 **Grammar** | **past perfect**
>
> **An action that happened before another action in the past:**
> *I **had forgotten** my keys, so I couldn't open the door.*   *I explained to my boss that I **hadn't finished** the report.*
> ***Had** you **eaten** anything before you went swimming?*   *When I got to the party, my friend **had gone** home.*

Go to Grammar practice: past perfect, page 130

6 ▶10.6 **Pronunciation:** *'d /hadn't* Listen to the sentences. How do you say *'d* and *hadn't*?
Listen again and repeat.

1 He**'d** breathed in too much dust.
2 He **hadn't** run the whole marathon by himself.

7 **A** Complete the sentences with the past perfect form of the verbs in parentheses.

1 They _____ before the game. (not warm up)
2 I knew they _____! (cheat)
3 She _____ a rugby game before. (not see)
4 We celebrated because he _____ a goal. (score)

B ▶10.7 In pairs, say the sentences. Pay attention to the *'d/hadn't* contractions. Listen, check, and repeat.

Go to Communication practice: Student A, page 164; Student B, page 172

8 ▶10.8 Complete the text with the correct form of the verbs in parentheses. Use the simple past or past perfect. Listen and check.

Who's the twelfth man?

There are eleven players on a soccer team, but in this team photo of Manchester United there are twelve–so who's the twelfth man? The team ¹_____ (be) very excited after they ²_____ (travel) to Germany for their Champions League game against Bayern Munich. The players ³_____ (line up) for a photo when suddenly Karl Power ⁴_____ (run) onto the playing field dressed in the Manchester United uniform and ⁵_____ (stand) next to them. Even though some of the players ⁶_____ (notice) Karl, the photographer still ⁷_____ (take) the photo. Karl then ⁸_____ (go) back to his seat to watch the game. Unfortunately, Manchester United ⁹_____ (lose), but Karl was happy because he ¹⁰_____ (meet) his heroes!

9 **A** In pairs, write as many sentences as you can about the pictures. Use the simple past and past perfect.

He was very disappointed because he'd lost the game.

B Tell the class your most interesting sentence. Who has the most original explanation?

Personal Best Write about an occasion when you did something that you had never done before.

10B Rock 'n' roll on wheels

1 Look at the pictures and the title of the text on page 87. Answer the questions.

1 What are the Paralympic Games?
2 Have you ever seen a wheelchair rugby game?
3 Would you like to take part in a game?
4 What kind of person do you think Laura is?

> **Skill** **finding information in a text**
>
> When we want to find information in a longer text, we need to know where to look.
> • Read the text quickly and understand the general topic of each paragraph.
> • Read the question carefully and underline any key words.
> • Match the question with the paragraph that has the information you need.
> • Read this paragraph in detail to answer the question.

2 Read the Skill box. Then read the text quickly and match paragraphs A–G with topics 1–7.

1 how it feels to play wheelchair rugby ____
2 how to find out more about the sport ____
3 creating interest in disabled sports ____
4 Laura's physical appearance ____

5 media interest in wheelchair rugby ____
6 the origins of the sport ____
7 the rules of wheelchair rugby ____

3 **A** Read the questions. Underline the key words and match them with paragraphs A–G.

		Paragraph	Answer
1	How long does it take Tim to cross the court?	____	_____
2	Which movie did wheelchair rugby appear in?	____	_____
3	What other wheelchair sports are there?	____	_____
4	When was wheelchair rugby invented?	____	_____
5	What is the official wheelchair rugby organization?	____	_____
6	Where does Laura have a bandage?	____	_____
7	How many players are on a wheelchair rugby team?	____	_____

B Read the paragraphs and answer the questions.

4 Did you know anything about wheelchair rugby before you read the article? Would you like to watch a game?

5 Find the highlighted words in the text.

1 Which words come before nouns?
2 Which words come at the start of a sentence?

> **Text builder** **giving examples**
>
> Listing examples:
> *I'd like to visit countries in south-east Asia, **like** Thailand and Vietnam.*
> *You shouldn't eat unhealthy food, **such as** pizzas or hamburgers.*
>
> Giving an example phrase:
> *She's had problems at work. **For example,** she arrived late every day last week.*
>
> **Look!** We can also use **for instance** instead of *for example* with no change in meaning:
> *She's had problems at work. **For instance,** she arrived late every day last week.*

6 Read the Text builder. Complete the sentences with your own ideas. Compare your sentences in pairs.

1 Cheating has become very common in some sports. For example, …
2 My country has produced some famous athletes, like …
3 Some sports can be very dangerous, such as …

7 **A** In pairs, choose an interesting sport. Prepare a short talk about it. Use the ideas in the boxes.

where it is played the rules how popular it is famous players how it feels to play media interest

B Tell another pair about your sport. Would you like to try this sport?

Sports interview:
Tim White meets wheelchair rugby player, Laura Sabetta

A

The first thing I notice about Laura Sabetta is her arms. They're almost as big as my legs. The next thing I notice is a bandage on her arm. "I get injuries fairly often because we play to win," the Argentinian athlete explains,"… it's rugby, after all."

B

Wheelchair rugby has always been a tough, physical sport. Invented in Canada in 1977, it was first called "murderball." As the sport's popularity grew, the name changed to the more serious "wheelchair rugby." It was a new name, but the game was just as violent.

C

People who have never played the sport might think of it as a fun way to spend an afternoon, but it's exhausting. Laura gives me a special wheelchair, and I move slowly onto the court. I wear gloves, but it's very hard work pushing the chair using only my arms. Wheelchair rugby is played on a basketball court that measures 28 x 15 meters, and it takes me over three minutes to cross it. Meanwhile, Laura has already finished warming up.

D

I'm soon happy to join the spectators and watch the game. Wheelchair rugby is a mix of basketball, rugby, and hockey. Two teams of four players throw and carry a volleyball, trying to score goals. Players score when their wheels cross the line at the end of the court while they are holding the ball in their hands.

E

Wheelchair rugby's popularity exploded after it featured in the 2005 movie *Murderball*. Many of its players are now big names in Paralympic sports, like the star of the movie, Mark Zupan. The sport is now played in more than 25 countries, such as Japan and the U.S. So, however you look at it, wheelchair rugby is big news.

F

This places lots of responsibility on the players, as Laura explains. "There are lots of sports opportunities out there for people who need a wheelchair, such as skiing, tennis, and sailing. The important thing is making sure people know about them, so they can take part. We also need fans. We want big crowds watching the game. That's why I'm doing this interview!"

G

Getting involved is easy. There's plenty of information online. For example, there's the website of the International Wheelchair Rugby Federation at www.iwrf.com. It's also fairly easy to find a game in most large towns if you just want to watch. Many people only watch the sport once every four years at the Paralympic Games, but as Laura tells me, "For people like me, this isn't a hobby. Since I lost the use of my legs, it's been my life."

10C   He said it had changed his life

1   Match the words in the box with the parts of the body.

| chest | knee | shoulder | elbow | neck | wrist |

1 _____   3 _____   5 _____

2 _____   4 _____   6 _____

Go to Vocabulary practice: parts of the body, page 153

2 A   Look at the poster. Discuss the questions in pairs.

1   How much exercise do doctors recommend you get each week?
2   Is it possible to get in shape with three minutes of exercise a week?
3   What do you think "high-intensity interval training (HIIT)" is?

B ▶ **10.10**   Listen to an interview and check your answers.

3   Discuss the questions in pairs.

1   How much exercise do you get a week? What do you do?
2   Do you believe that high-intensity training works? Why/Why not?
3   Would you like to try high-intensity training? Why/Why not?

4 A ▶ **10.10**   Complete the sentences about what Carlos and Vicky said. Listen again and check.

1   Carlos said that in HIIT you used almost all your _____.
2   Carlos said two years ago he had weighed almost _____ kg.
3   Carlos said he was eating more _____ and _____ now.
4   Carlos said that he had lost _____ kg.
5   Carlos told Vicky that first she would do some gentle cycling to _____.
6   Vicky told Carlos she was going to try _____ seconds of high-intensity cycling.

HIGH-INTENSITY TRAINING

GET IN SHAPE WITH THREE MINUTES OF EXERCISE PER WEEK

B   Look at the sentences 1–6 again and answer the questions.

1   Which two verbs do we use to report what someone says in the past? _____ _____
2   Which verb do we use when we say who the person is talking to? _____
3   Is it always necessary to use *that* with these verbs? *Yes / No*

5 A ▶ **10.11**   Listen carefully to what Carlos and Vicky said. Write the verbs they used.

1   In HIIT, you _____ almost all your muscles.

2   Well, two years ago I _____ almost 100 kg.

3   Oh, and I _____ more fruit and vegetables now.

4   Of course–75 kg. I _____ 25 kg.

5   OK, so first you _____ some gentle cycling to warm up.

6   Thanks, Carlos. Well, I _____ 20 seconds of high-intensity cycling now.

B   Compare the verbs in exercise 5A with the verbs in exercise 4A. How have they changed? Then read the Grammar box.

1   simple present →   *simple past*
2   simple past →   _____
3   present continuous →   _____
4   present perfect →   _____
5   *will* →   _____
6   *am/are/is going to* →   _____

📖 **Grammar**   **reported speech**

Direct speech:	Reported speech:
"I **play** tennis."	She said (that) she **played** tennis.
"Vicky **tried** HIIT."	He said (that) Vicky **had tried** HIIT.
"It's **raining**."	They said (that) it **was raining**.
"She **hasn't arrived** yet.'"	You said (that) she **hadn't arrived** yet.
"I'**ll help** you."	You said (that) you **would help** me.
"We'**re going to call** you."	They said (that) they **were going to call** me.
"Ravi **can't come** to work."	She said (that) Ravi **couldn't come** to work.

Look!   We use **told** to say who the person talked to: She **told me** (that) she played tennis.

Personal Best

Go to Grammar practice: reported speech, page 131

6 ▶10.13   Match the sentences in the box with the people. Listen and check.

> I go to the gym to meet my friends.   I'll tell my husband because he needs to lose weight.
> I can't do HIIT at my age!   I've tried it, but I hurt my shoulder.

Rosa   Kurt   Barry   Jessica

7 ▶10.14   **Pronunciation:** weak form of *that* Listen to the sentences. Underline the stressed words. How do we pronounce *that*? Listen again, check, and repeat.

1 Carlos said that HIIT was very popular.
2 He told me that I should ask some other people what they think.

8 **A** Complete the sentences using the information from exercise 6.

1 Rosa said that _____ .
2 Kurt told Vicky that _____ .
3 Barry told her that _____ .
4 Jessica said that _____ .

B ▶10.15   In pairs, practice saying sentences 1–4. Pay attention to the pronunciation of *that*. Listen, check, and repeat.

9 In pairs, ask and answer the question *What did … say?* Use reported speech to answer the questions.
A *What did José say?*   **B** *He said that he …*

1
> I can't go running because I've hurt my ankle.

José

2
Sara
> My bus is late, so I'm not going to be on time.

3
> Our teacher is wearing a leather jacket.

Laura

4
David
> If you're tired, I'll make you coffee.

Go to Communication practice: Student A, page 164; Student B, page 172

10 **A** In pairs, ask and answer the questions. Make notes of your partner's answers.

1 Have you ever run a long distance?
2 What was the first movie you saw at a movie theater?
3 What are you going to do this weekend?
4 Can you play any unusual sports?
5 What series are you watching on TV right now?
6 What are you doing after today's class?

B Work with another student. Report what your first partner said about questions 1–6.

Personal Best   Think of a news story or an interview with an athlete. Write what the person said.

10D Could you tell me …?

1 Discuss the questions in pairs.

1 What are the best ways to stay in shape? 3 What would be important for you if you joined a gym?

2 Have you ever thought about joining a gym? 4 Look at the web page. Would you join this gym? Why/Why no

2 ▶10.16 Watch or listen to the first part of *Learning Curve*. Why does Marc want to join the gym?

3 ▶10.16 Watch or listen again and complete the web page with the correct information.

OUR CENTERS | GYM FACILITIES | SWIMMING POOL | FITNESS CLASSES | MEMBERSHIP | SCHEDULE

CITY FITNESS

June offer
First month
FREE

Join today or speak to one of our advisers   JOIN NOW   CONTACT US

Standard membership fee: ¹_____ per month (minimum 12-month contract)
Access to all facilities while the center is open.

Off-peak hours membership fee: ²_____ per month (no contract, pay as you go)
Access to facilities: Mon–Fri ³_____ and ⁴_____ , on weekends closes at 2:00 p.m.
Additional $15 fee for access to swimming pool, sauna, and steam room.

Swimming-only membership fee: ⁵_____ per month
Access to the swimming pool only: Mon–Sun, 9:00 a.m.–5:00 p.m.

Opening hours: 6.00 a.m.–9.00 p.m.   Student discount available: 15%

4 ▶10.17 Match the two columns to complete Marc's inquiries. Listen and check.

1 Could I speak to someone   a the cost, please?
2 Could you tell   b information about that?
3 Could you give me some   c thing.
4 I'd also like to ask about   d off-peak membership.
5 Just one more   e about joining the gym?
6 So can I just double check   f me the cost?

| ◈↦ | **Conversation builder** | **making inquiries** |

Starting inquiries politely:
Could I speak to someone about …?
Could you give me some information about …, please?
Excuse me, I was hoping you could help me.

Asking for additional information:
I'd also like to ask about …
I was told … Is that true?
Just one more thing. Do you …?
Can I double check? Do you …?

5 Read the Conversation builder. Choose three subjects in the boxes. In pairs, make inquiries about City Fitness. Use the information on the web page to answer.

student discount   opening hours   swimming-only membership
June offer   how to join

6 A ▶10.18 Watch or listen to the second part of the show. Does Marc decide to join the gym?

B ▶10.18 Are the sentences true (T) or false (F)? Watch or listen again and check.

1 Marc thought Taylor worked at a different center. _____
2 Taylor likes this center because it's small. _____
3 The receptionist told Marc about all the facilities. _____
4 Taylor offers Marc a free training session as a special offer. _____
5 Marc wants to start training slowly. _____

7 ▶10.19 Listen and repeat the receptionist and Taylor's phrases when you hear the beeps. How are they helpful to Marc?

🔧 **Skill**   **being helpful**

There are different ways to be helpful in English, especially with colleagues and customers.
- Use friendly intonation to show you are happy to help.
- Make offers and suggestions: *Would you like me to …?   Shall I …?   I'll … if you want.*
- Check to make sure the person is satisfied: *Does that sound OK?   Is there anything else I can help you with?*

---

8 A Read the Skill box. Are phrases 1–6 answers to questions (A), offers and suggestions (O), or checking to make sure the customer is satisfied (C)?

1 The nearest one is on the corner of Sutton Street. _____
2 Do you have any other questions? _____
3 I think it costs about $20 to go downtown. _____
4 I'll just print out a map of the area for you. _____
5 Would you like me to write that down for you? _____
6 Is there anything else you'd like to know? _____

B ▶10.20 Listen and repeat phrases 1–6. Pay attention to the intonation.

Go to Communication practice: Student A, page 164; Student B, page 172

9 Discuss the questions in pairs.

1 Have you ever worked with customers or the public? What did you do?
2 What's the most difficult thing about working with customers or the public?
3 Have you ever had a bad experience with customer service? What happened?
4 Can you think of a good experience with customer service? What happened?

10 A PREPARE Choose one of the situations. Use the phrases and your own ideas to prepare questions.

Travel agent

Vacations in the U.S.
Best city to visit
Cost of flights

Pharmacist

Medicine for the flu
How often to take it
Other advice to feel better

Sports store salesperson

Running shoes
Best type for long distance
Colors and sizes

B PRACTICE In pairs, make inquiries using your questions. Your partner should try to answer your questions and be as helpful as possible.

C PERSONAL BEST Were you a satisfied customer? What could your partner do differently to be more helpful? Choose another situation and make more inquiries.

Personal Best   Write down five questions you could ask in a restaurant.

Grammar

1 Put an (**X**) by the sentence that is NOT correct.

1 a I used to have a bike, but then I sold it. ☐
   b I had a bike, but then I sold it. ☐
   c I used to have a bike, but then I used to sell it. ☐

2 a Cervantes wrote *Don Quixote*. ☐
   b *Don Quixote* was written by Cervantes. ☐
   c Cervantes was written *Don Quixote*. ☐

3 a He'd gone home because he'd forgotten his wallet. ☐
   b He went home because he'd forgotten his wallet. ☐
   c He'd forgotten his wallet, so he went home. ☐

4 a Emma said, "I'll be on time." ☐
   b Emma told me she would be on time. ☐
   c Emma said me she would be on time. ☐

5 a She didn't used to get much exercise. ☐
   b She didn't get much exercise. ☐
   c She didn't use to get much exercise. ☐

6 a The radio was invented by Marconi. ☐
   b The radio is invented by Marconi. ☐
   c Marconi invented the radio. ☐

7 a He was late because he had missed the bus. ☐
   b He missed the bus, so he was late. ☐
   c He had been late so he had missed the bus. ☐

8 a Pete said he was seeing the movie before. ☐
   b Pete said he had seen the move before. ☐
   c Pete said, "I've seen the movie before." ☐

2 Use the words in parentheses to write sentences that mean the same as the first sentence.

1 Someone stole my car last week.
   My car _____ someone last week. (stolen)

2 Neil said, "I haven't been to Greece."
   Neil said that _____ to Greece. (been)

3 When I was young I played the piano.
   I _____ the piano. (used)

4 They make Vespas in Italy.
   Vespas _____ in Italy. (are)

5 We ate our soup. Then he brought the drinks.
   When he brought the drinks, we _____ our soup. (had)

6 Kelly said, "I don't need any help."
   Kelly _____ any help. (me)

7 I didn't take an umbrella and I got wet.
   I got wet because I _____ an umbrella. (took)

8 I wasn't a very shy child.
   When I was a child, I _____ very shy. (be)

3 Complete the text with the correct form of the verbs in parentheses.

HOW NOT TO LOSE YOUR PET

Fumie Takahashi, a 64-year-old woman from Japan, was very happy when the police ¹_____ (tell) her that they ²_____ (find) her pet parakeet, Piko Chan. But the amazing thing was that the bird ³_____ (tell) the police its own address!

Mrs. Takahashi ⁴_____ (use / have) another parakeet, but it escaped and flew away. So, when she bought Piko Chan, she taught it to repeat her street name and house number. Last Sunday, Piko Chan also escaped, when the door to its cage ⁵_____ (leave) open. It flew to a nearby hotel and, after a few hours, it ⁶_____ (take) to the police station by a guest.

The police ⁷_____ (say) that the bird ⁸_____ (be) silent for two days, and they hadn't known what to do with it. Eventually, however, Piko Chan surprised them all when it ⁹_____ (tell) them where it ¹⁰_____ (live).

If Piko Chan escapes again, it'll probably be found even more quickly. Its photo has appeared in newspapers all over Tokyo, and Mrs. Takahashi recently took the bird to a press conference, where it told journalists its address again.

Vocabulary

1 Put the words in the box in the correct columns.

| receipt   cash register   ankle   crowd   knee   refund |
| medal   sales   referee   cheek   beat   chin |

the body	sports	shopping

2 Complete the conversation with the correct words.

Lena	These jeans look amazing! Where is the [1]d _ressing_ r _oom_ ?
Peter	Over there, but can you [2]a _____ to buy them? I didn't think you had much money right now.
Lena	Probably not. I don't [3]g _____ p _____ until the end of the month. Can I [4]b _____ some money from you?
Peter	You already [5]o _____ me 50 dollars!
Lena	I'll [6]p _____ you b _____ all the money at the end of the month. I promise.
Peter	OK, [7]t _____ o _____ the jeans. If they [8]f _____ you, I'll think about it.
Lena	Thanks, Peter! There's a 70% [9]d _____ on them today; they're a real [10]b _____ .
Peter	OK, Lena.

3 Circle the word that is different. Explain your answer.

1	win	tie	lose	score
2	earn	borrow	lend	pay back
3	bargain	game	discount	a sale
4	return	exchange	deliver	refund
5	finger	thumb	chest	hand
6	medal	umpire	trophy	race
7	knee	elbow	shoulder	forehead
8	shopping center	department store	supermarket	dressing room

4 Choose the correct word to complete the sentences.

1 I _____ my parents $100.
   a refund **b** owe **c** pay back

2 We _____ them 2–1.
   a won **b** scored **c** beat

3 I'm not buying anything. I'm just _____ .
   a spending **b** getting paid **c** window shopping

4 You can only use your _____ to move the ball.
   a brain **b** heart **c** foot

5 Here's your change and here's your _____ .
   a cash **b** refund **c** receipt

6 There was a _____ of 60,000 at the game today.
   a spectator **b** crowd **c** athlete

7 How much do you _____ in your job?
   a earn **b** be worth **c** borrow

8 You need to _____ before a game.
   a cheat **b** give up **c** warm up

9 Look how long the _____ is!
   a line **b** bargain **c** cash register

10 The day after the marathon, my _____ ached!
   a cheek **b** chin **c** muscles

11 When I was younger, it was easy to touch my _____ , but now I can't.
   a toes **b** fingers **c** thumb

Personal Best

Lesson 9A
Name five things you can do with money.

Lesson 10A
Write a sentence using the past perfect.

Lesson 9A
Write two sentences about your grandparents using _used to_.

Lesson 10A
Name three things you can win.

Lesson 9B
Name five things you usually see in a shopping mall.

Lesson 10B
Write a sentence with _for example_, and another with _such as_.

Lesson 9C
Write two sentences in the passive: simple present and simple past.

Lesson 10C
Name five parts of the body that we have two of.

Lesson 9D
Name five nouns ending in _-ion_.

Lesson 10D
Give a phrase to start an inquiry, and another to ask for additional information.

Lesson 9D
Write an expression to start a formal e-mail, and another to end it.

Lesson 10D
Give an expression to check to make sure someone is satisfied.

| LANGUAGE | *-ing*/infinitive verb patterns ■ household items |

11A Dream home

1 Look at the picture. Would you like to live somewhere like this? Why/Why not?

2 Read the text and answer the questions.

   1 Where is the house?
   2 Who are the people in the picture?
   3 Why do they live there?

Living the dream

Have you ever imagined escaping city life and moving to a desert island? Well, meet the family who did just that.

Karyn von Engelbrechten wanted to travel the world after she became tired of her three-hour commute to London, where she worked as an IT manager. She left her job and her home and, with husband Boris and their three children, decided to start a new adventure.

They bought some land on a tiny island in the South Pacific and started to build a house with materials they found on the island. Everything was done by hand. They learned how to cut down trees to make floors and doors. Electricity was generated using solar panels, and rainwater was collected so the family had water in the bathrooms and kitchen. They even started growing their own fruit and vegetables.

Now the family runs their home as a guesthouse for other travelers. If you don't feel like swimming in the beautiful clear ocean, you can sit on the balcony and enjoy watching whales and turtles. The kitchen is basic, but it has most things you'd need, like a refrigerator and oven.

There's no air-conditioning, but the bedrooms are cool and comfortable, and there are extra blankets and comforters in the closet for the colder months. From the house, steps go down to your own private beach, or if you're feeling brave, you can explore the island.

It sounds like paradise, but there are some disadvantages. Apart from the fruit and vegetables that Karyn and Boris grow, they need to buy other things, and the nearest store is a three-hour boat trip away. The island is also very near a volcano, and they often have earthquakes and tropical storms. And their eldest son, Jack, has gone away to school in New Zealand because he missed being with other children his own age.

However, if you're tired of your daily routine, the message is clear—follow your dreams!

3 Which of these things does the house have? *Yes* (✔), *No* (**X**) or *Don't know* (**?**). Read the text again and check.

   1 air-conditioning ☐   **3** central heating ☐   **5** refrigerator ☐   **7** washing machine ☐   **9** oven ☐
   2 blankets ☐   **4** dishwasher ☐   **6** closet ☐   **8** comforters ☐   **10** faucets ☐

Go to Vocabulary practice: household items, page 154

4 **A** Ask and answer the questions in pairs.

   1 Do you have a refrigerator or dishwasher at home?
   2 How often do you use your washing machine?
   3 How often do you use your iron? Do you like ironing?
   4 Do you have a carpet or rugs in your home? What color are they?
   5 Do you have a big closet? Is it well-organized or messy?
   6 Do you sleep with a blanket or a comforter?
   7 Do you have a microwave oven? How often do you use it?
   8 Do you have central heating or air-conditioning in your home? How often do you turn it on?

B Tell the class some things you found out about your partner.

5 **A** Choose the correct form of the verbs to complete the sentences. Check your answers in the text.

1 Have you ever **imagined** *to escape / escaping* city life?
2 Karyn von Engelbrechten **wanted** *to travel / traveling* the world.
3 She **decided** *to start / starting* a new adventure.
4 You can sit on the balcony and **enjoy** *to watch / watching* whales and turtles.

B Answer the questions about the verbs in **bold** in sentences 1–4.

1 Which form of the verb comes after *imagine* and *enjoy*? Infinitive / -*ing* form
2 Which form of the verb comes after *want* and *decide?* Infinitive / -*ing* form

6 **A** Find examples of the verbs in the box in the text. Put them in the correct column.

manage   start   learn   feel like   need   miss

Verbs followed by *-ing*	Verbs followed by the infinitive

B Which verb can be followed by both the infinitive and the *-ing* form? _____
Now read the Grammar box.

> 📖 **Grammar**   **-ing/infinitive verb patterns**
>
> Verbs followed by the **-ing** form: *She **enjoys living** in the city.*
> Verbs followed by the infinitive: *I **want to live** in a bigger house.*
>
> **Look!** Some verbs can be followed by both the infinitive and *-ing* forms:
>   *It started **to rain**. = It started **raining**.*

Go to Grammar practice: *-ing/infinitive verb patterns, page 132*

7 ▶11.4   **Pronunciation:** sentence stress Listen and <u>underline</u> the stressed words in the sentences. How is *to* pronounced? Listen, check, and repeat.

1 Karyn wanted to travel the world.
2 She enjoys watching whales and turtles.

8 **A** Complete the sentences with the correct form of the verbs in parentheses.

1 She's planning _____ science. (study)
2 My doctor suggested _____ less coffee. (drink)
3 I haven't forgotten _____ the customer. (call)
4 Do you feel like _____ for pizza tonight? (go out)
5 We can't afford _____ on vacation. (go)
6 We should spend more time _____ . (study)

B ▶11.5   In pairs, practice saying the sentences. Pay attention to the sentence stress. Listen, check, and repeat.

Go to Communication practice: page 174

9 **A** Complete the questions with the correct form of the verbs in parentheses.

1 Imagine _____ (design) your dream house. What would you want it _____ (be) like?
2 Do you expect _____ (work) in the same job all your life? Are you planning _____ (change) jobs soon? What do you hope _____ (do) in the future?
3 Do you enjoy _____ (travel)? Are you planning _____ (go) anywhere soon?
4 Do you like _____ (live) in your house? What would you like _____ (change) about it?
5 Would you like _____ (live) abroad in the future? Where do feel like _____ (live)?
6 At what age do you think you will stop _____ (work)? What will you spend your time _____ (do) when you retire? Do you think you will miss _____ (work)?

B Ask and answer the questions in pairs.

Personal Best   Write a description of a room in your house or apartment, including all the things in it.

11B The truth about housework

1 Look at the picture. Have you ever seen a kitchen like this? If so, where?

2 Complete the man's list of chores with the words in the box.

> do (x3)   clear   take out   load   mop   water   wash

1 _____ the dishes   3 _____ the ironing   5 _____ the table   7 _____ the trash
2 _____ the dishwasher 4 _____ the laundry   6 _____ the plants   8 _____ the floor

Go to Vocabulary practice: housework, page 155

3 Complete the chart about you. In pairs, compare your charts and explain your answers.

Housework I hate doing	Housework I don't mind doing	Housework I enjoy doing

4 A ▶11.7   In pairs, decide if the sentences are true (T) or false (F). Watch or listen to the first part of *Learning Curve* and check.

1 It's a fact that everyone hates doing housework.   ____
2 The majority of us usually prefer to do other activities in our free time.   ____
3 Today, robots that can do the housework for us really exist.   ____
4 Robots will never have arms and legs.   ____
5 In Japan, there's a robot that can pick up heavy things.   ____

B ▶11.7   Watch or listen again. Write down the key words that Simon or Kate use that helped you check the answers.

 Skill **understanding and interpreting information**

It's helpful to notice key words and phrases before you listen.
• Look at the questions and underline any key words or phrases.
• Think about other words or phrases that speakers could use to give this information.
• As you listen, pay attention to all the words and phrases you have noticed or thought of.

5 A Look at the <u>underlined</u> key words in questions 1 and 2 and think about what words and phrases Julie might use. <u>Underline</u> the key words in questions 3-6.

B ▶11.8 Watch or listen to the second part of the show. Choose the correct options.

1 What does Julie prefer doing on the weekend?
   a She prefers <u>spending time</u> with her <u>children</u>.
   b She prefers going <u>shopping</u>.
   c She prefers doing <u>housework</u>.

2 Why does she want her children to do housework?
   a She has <u>too much work</u>.
   b So they <u>learn</u> to do things <u>on their own</u>.
   c Because it's <u>healthier</u> than <u>video games</u>.

3 Why did Axel buy a cleaning robot?
   a He wants more time for himself.
   b The salesperson offered him a good price.
   c He injured his back.

4 What does he say about his dishwasher?
   a It's broken.
   b He prefers washing the dishes by hand.
   c It works very well.

5 Why does Roberta buy the "Mop It" robot?
   a It's better at cleaning than she is.
   b Her friend has one.
   c There was a discount.

6 How does housework help her?
   a It's a way to get exercise.
   b It helps her relax.
   c She saves money.

Julie

Axel

Roberta

6 Discuss the questions in pairs.
   1 Do you share the housework equally at home?
   2 Who does the most housework? Why?
   3 Did you do housework when you were a child?
   4 Do you think doing housework is good for you?

7 ▶11.9 Read and listen to the phrases from the show. Which words are missing? Why didn't the speakers use them?
   1 Just doing a bit of dusting in the studio.
   2 Anyone there with an opinion?
   3 Makes the floor look good.
   4 It does a better job than I can. So exciting!

▶◀► **Listening builder** omission of words

Speakers sometimes don't say all the words in a sentence because they think the meaning is obvious without them, or because they don't want to repeat words or phrases.

Pronouns: *No, (I) don't really like cleaning.*
Articles: *(The) Dishwasher's broken.*
be **and auxiliary verbs:** *(It's) Time for spring cleaning.*

There is/are: *(Is there) Anyone there with an opinion?*
Avoid repeating words: *It does a better job than I can (do).*
Phrases: *Anyway, (let's go) back to Kate.*

---

8 A ▶11.10 Read the Listening builder. Read and listen to the conversation. Which words are missing?

> **Mario** Hi, Maya. ¹_____ You there?
> **Maya** ²_____ In the living room. ³_____ Just clearing the table.
> **Mario** ⁴_____ Coffee's ready. ⁵_____ Want some?
> **Maya** No, thanks. ⁶_____ Already had three ⁷_____ today.

B ▶11.11 Listen and check.

9 In pairs, discuss the statement: "People only notice housework when it isn't done."

11C Technology you can wear

1 Discuss the questions in pairs.

1 Do you find it difficult to decide what to wear each day?
2 How often do you buy new clothes?
3 What are your favorite clothes in your closet?

2 Label the picture with the materials in the box.

cotton   leather   wood   denim   wool   metal

Go to Vocabulary practice: words to describe materials and clothes, page 156

1 _____
2 _____
3 _____
4 _____
5 _____
6 _____

3 In pairs, describe the different types of clothes.

what you're wearing now

what you wear on the weekend

what you'd wear to a wedding

what you'd wear to a party

what you'd wear to a job interview

what you'd wear on a first date

4 Look at pictures a–c. What do they show? Read the text and match them with descriptions 1–3.

WEARABLE TECHNOLOGY

a   b   c

Our houses are full of technology, but how much do we have in our closets? You might think you don't have any, but get ready for that to change. Experts predict that the amount of money we spend on wearable technology will reach $74 billion a year by 2025. You're probably already familiar with smart watches and fitness bracelets, but what are some of the other things coming our way?

1 MATERIAL THAT CAN COMMUNICATE

In the U.S., Google and Levi's® are developing a new kind of material that is touch sensitive, like the screen on a smartphone. The material is made by running thin metal wires through cotton, denim, or silk. Designers can then use this material to create interactive areas on clothes and furniture. Soon people will be able to control machines just by touching their pants legs!

2 ACCESSORIES THAT CONTROL YOUR TEMPERATURE

Have you ever been in a place where half the people are complaining about the cold, and the other half are too hot? The solution is *Wristify*, a bracelet that can heat or cool your skin at the touch of a button. It's perfect for a trip to the gym, a day at the beach, or for keeping you warm at home. In fact, the bracelet could also save you money on energy bills. The design isn't finished yet, but here's what the final product might look like.

3 CLOTHES THAT CHARGE YOUR PHONE

Pauline van Dongen is an exciting new designer who specializes in wearable technology, and uses both traditional and new materials to create amazing clothes. Her stylish T-shirts and jackets have solar panels that can charge a cell phone in just a few hours ... when the sun is shining, of course.

5 Discuss the questions in pairs.

1 Which idea do you think is the most useful? Why?
2 Would you buy any of these inventions? Why/Why not?
3 Can you think of other types of wearable technology?

6 Complete the sentences with the articles *a*, *an*, *the*, or – (no article). Check your answers in the text.

1 The amount of money we spend on wearable technology will reach $74 billion _____ year.
2 People will be able to control _____ machines just by touching their pants legs!
3 The solution is *Wristify*, _____ bracelet that can heat or cool your skin.
4 Perfect for a trip to _____ gym...
5 ... or for keeping you warm at _____ home.
6 _____ bracelet could also save you money on energy bills.
7 Pauline van Dongen is _____ exciting new designer.
8 ... when _____ sun is shining, of course.

7 Match sentences 1–8 in exercise 6 with rules a–h. Then read the Grammar box.

a We use *a/an* to talk about a person or thing for the first time. _____
b We use *the* when we have already mentioned the person or thing before. _____
c We don't use an article to talk about things in general (plural or uncountable nouns). _____
d We use *a/an* to talk about a person's job. _____
e We use *a/an* in some measurement expressions. _____
f We use *the* if there is only one of the thing. _____
g We use *the* with specific places in a town. _____
h We don't use an article with some places we go to regularly. _____

📖 **Grammar** **articles**

a/an	*the*	No article
*I live in **a** tall apartment building.*	*I live in a modern apartment. **The** apartment is in ...*	*They're interested in sports cars.*
*Eric is **an** architect.*	*The address is on **the** Internet.*	*I leave for work at about 9:00 a.m.*
*We go sailing twice **a** month.*	*I'll meet you in **the** park.*	*We go on vacation every summer.*

Go to Grammar practice: articles, page 133

8 **A** ▶ 11.15 **Pronunciation:** *the* Listen and repeat the phrases. Match the words in **bold** with the sounds /ðə/ and /ði/. Why does the pronunciation change?

1 **the** amount of money we spend on technology _____ 2 **the** screen on a smartphone _____

B ▶ 11.16 Practice saying the words in pairs. Pay attention to the pronunciation of *the*. Listen, check, and repeat.

the solution   the answer   the office   the U.S.   the Internet   the sun   the hour   the gym

Go to Communication practice: Student A, page 165; Student B, page 173

9 ▶ 11.17 Complete the text with *a*, *an*, *the*, or – (no article). Listen and check.

A BRIGHT IDEA

Christina Mercando is ¹____ businesswoman and ²____ inventor. She started ³____ company in ⁴____ U.S. named Ringly. Her first product was ⁵____ ring that connects to your smartphone. When ⁶____ phone receives ⁷____ text or e-mail, ⁸____ ring lights up. ⁹____ idea came to Christina when she was having ¹⁰____ dinner with friends. She didn't want to miss any important calls on her phone, but she didn't want to put her phone on ¹¹____ dinner table. It's ¹²____ common problem for ¹³____ women who keep ¹⁴____ phones in their handbags or purses, where they may not hear them. ¹⁵____ rings are made in China, and Christina talks with the factory once ¹⁶____ week. It's ¹⁷____ exciting time for Christina, and ¹⁸____ future is definitely bright!

10 In pairs, take turns talking about these things. Remember to use the correct articles.

| kinds of food and drink you hate | a machine that you couldn't live without | the places you went to yesterday |
| what you have in your bedroom | some clothes you want to buy, but can't afford | how often you charge your cell phone |

Personal Best Think of an idea for another piece of wearable technology. Write about how it could work.

11D House exchange

1 Discuss the questions in pairs.

  1 Have you ever done a house exchange or stayed at someone else's house on vacation?
  2 What are the advantages and disadvantages of a house exchange?
  3 How would you feel about letting strangers stay in your home?

2 Describe the pictures. Which home would you prefer to stay in? Why?

3 Read the description on a house exchange website. Which home from exercise 2 does it describe?

 Homes away from home   🔍 | Two-bedroom apartment in downtown Chicago

About our home

Our home is an attractive two-bedroom apartment, very near downtown Chicago. It's a 20-minute walk from the Willis Tower, where there is an amazing view of the city.

The main bedroom has its own bathroom and a double bed with plain white cotton sheets. Although the second bedroom is slightly smaller, it's bright and has two comfortable single beds. There's a fashionable leather sofa and two large armchairs in the modern living room. The spacious, up-to-date kitchen includes everything you'll need, including an electric oven, refrigerator, freezer, dishwasher, and a new Italian coffeemaker. Glass doors open from the kitchen onto a gorgeous, sunny balcony, where you can have a relaxing breakfast.

The apartment is on a peaceful street, but it's just a few minutes away from Chicago's famous Miracle Mile, known for it stores, hotels, and some excellent restaurants. The train station is also close by, so this is an ideal place if you want to explore all of Chicago's attractions.

7 reviews
★ ★ ★ ★

2 bedrooms

Sleeps 4

2 bathrooms

4 A Read the text again. Find words that mean the same as adjectives 1–6.

  1 big _____ _____
  2 beautiful _____ _____
  3 quiet _____ _____
  4 very good _____ _____
  5 light _____ _____
  6 modern _____ _____

B How does the writer make the text interesting? Read the Skill box.

 Skill   making writing interesting

We can use different techniques to make our writing more interesting.
- Use a variety of adjectives to describe things: *a **gorgeous**, **sunny** balcony*
- Use synonyms to avoid repeating words: *two **large** armchairs, the **spacious** kitchen*
- Use linkers to give reasons and results (*so, because, that's why*), to contrast information (*but, although, however*) or add information (*and, also, too, as well*).
- When you describe a place, use *where* and an example of what you can do: *a balcony, where you can have a relaxing breakfast*

5 In pairs, rewrite the sentences to make them more interesting.

  1 The house is very pretty. It has a pretty yard.
  The house is very pretty, and it has a gorgeous yard.

  2 The apartment is fairly small. It's a good place to stay. It's right downtown.
  _____

  3 There's an old living room. It has an old fireplace. You can stay warm in the winter.
  _____

  4 The building has a quiet roof terrace. You can enjoy nice views of the countryside.
  _____

  5 If the weather is nice, you can sit in the big yard.
  _____

6 Complete the phrases with the adjectives in parentheses in the correct order. Check your answers in the text.

  1 an _____ _____ apartment (two-bedroom, attractive)
  2 _____ _____ _____ sheets (cotton, plain, white)
  3 a _____ _____ sofa (fashionable, leather)
  4 a _____ _____ coffeemaker (Italian, new)

⊹ **Text builder**   **adjective order**

When we use more than one adjective to describe a noun, they go in a specific order:
opinion   size   shape   age   color   nationality   material   (noun)
She has long blond hair. NOT ~~She has blond long hair.~~
It's an interesting Chinese painting. NOT ~~It's a Chinese interesting painting.~~

---

7 Read the Text builder. Put the words in the box in the correct columns.

blue Dutch glass green large leather Mexican old
round small square stylish unusual young

opinion	size	shape	age	color	nationality	material

8 Complete the sentences with the adjectives in parentheses in the correct order.

  1 We live in a _____ _____ _____ house in the country. (stone, beautiful, old)
  2 It has _____ _____ floors, and is warm and cozy. (wood, attractive)
  3 There's a _____ _____ rug on the floor. (square, wool)
  4 You can relax on one of our _____ _____ _____ armchairs. (leather, old, comfortable)
  5 Outside, there's a _____ _____ garden. (Japanese, beautiful)
  6 Near the house, there's a _____ _____ restaurant. (Indian, fantastic)

9 Write descriptions of three items you own, using as many adjectives as possible. Compare with a partner.

  I have a beautiful old brown leather armchair.

10 **A** PREPARE Plan a description of your home or apartment for a home exchange website. Write notes for three paragraphs:

  Paragraph 1: the type of home it is and where it is
  Paragraph 2: description of the rooms and what is in the rooms
  Paragraph 3: description of the local area and what is nearby

  B PRACTICE Write your description. Remember to order adjectives correctly.

  C PERSONAL BEST Exchange texts with a partner. After reading the description, would you like to stay there? How could he/she make the description more interesting?

Personal Best   Write a short description of a place you know well, such as where you work or study, a restaurant, or a store.

People and relationships

12A Bring your parents to work

1 Match the words in the box with the definitions.

> colleague   neighbor   in-laws   boss   roommate
> employee   business partner   relative

1 someone who manages you at work _____
2 your husband's/wife's mother and father _____
3 someone who works for you _____
4 someone in your family _____
5 someone who works with you _____
6 someone who lives near you _____
7 someone who shares an apartment with you _____
8 someone who owns a company with you _____

Go to Vocabulary practice: relationships, page 157

2 Choose three of the relationships from exercise 1 and write down the names of people you know. Tell your partner about them.

3 Read the text and answer the questions.

1 Which company introduced the idea of a *Bring Your Parents to Work Day*?
2 How many people in the U.S. take part in the *Take Your Child to Work Day*?
3 What does the company say the benefits of the day are?
4 How many companies now have a similar day?
5 What does Martin Richards' daughter do at work?

Would you bring your parents to work?

How would you feel about bringing your mom or dad to work with you? Would you be worried about the things that they might say to your boss? Or nervous that they might start showing embarrassing photos of you as a child to the co-worker who sits next to you? Well, get ready for *Bring Your Parents to Work Day*, an event that is already becoming popular in some U.S. companies and that could be coming your way soon!

The company where it all started, LinkedIn, realized that there are a lot of parents who don't understand what their children's jobs involve. There is already a national *Take Your Child to Work Day* for workers who want to take their sons and daughters to their places of work, and more than 37 million Americans take part every year. So why not do the same thing for parents? LinkedIn's argument is that employees who feel supported by their family are happier and more productive. Now, there are more than 80 companies in 18 countries that organize an annual event for parents to get to know how their kids spend their time at work.

So what do the parents think of it? Martin Richards has just spent a day at the office where his daughter and son-in-law work. "For me, it was a great opportunity to see how digital marketing works, to meet some of Imogen's co-workers, and, best of all, to spend a day with my eldest daughter!"

4 Discuss the questions in pairs.

1 As a child, did you ever visit the place where your parents worked? Was it a useful experience?
2 How would you feel if you brought your parents to your place of work? Why?
3 Do you think people's jobs have changed a lot in the last thirty years? If so, how?

5 **A** Complete the sentences with *who*, *that*, or *where*. Check your answers in the text.

1 Get ready for *Bring Your Parents to Work Day*, an event _____ is already becoming popular in some U.S. companies.
2 There is already a national *Take Your Child to Work Day* for workers _____ want to take their sons and daughters to their places of work.
3 Martin Richards has just spent a day at the office _____ his daughter and son-in-law work.

B Look at sentences 1–3 and answer the questions. Then read the Grammar box.

1 Which word do we use to give information about: people? _____ things? _____ places? _____
2 In which sentence can we use *that* instead? ____

> 📖 **Grammar** | **defining relative clauses**
>
> **To give information about people**: *I'm going to see my cousin **who** lives in Greece.*
> *All employees **that** work in the sales department have a meeting.*
>
> **To give information about things**: *The company sells machines **that** are made in Japan.*
> *It looks like the shirt **(that)** my roommate bought last week.*
>
> **To give information about places**: *That's the restaurant **where** my brother-in-law works.*

Go to Grammar practice: defining relative clauses, page 134

Personal Best

6 **A** ▶12.3 **Pronunciation:** sentence stress Listen to the sentences and underline the stressed words. When do we stress *who*?

1 Who do you live with?
2 The man who works at the bank.

B ▶12.4 Match the halves to make sentences. Listen, check, and repeat. Pay attention to the sentence stress.

1 A remote control is something that
2 A flight attendant is someone who
3 A kindergarten is a place where

a young children go.
b you use to turn on the TV.
c works on a plane.

7 **A** Write definitions with *who*, *where*, or *that*.

1 something / use to see small things
_____

2 a place / buy newspapers and magazines
_____

3 someone / collects the garbage
_____

4 an animal / very slow and lives in trees
_____

5 a person / plays an instrument on the street
_____

6 a building / horses sleep and eat
_____

B In pairs, match definitions 1–6 with pictures a–f. Do you know the names of these things in English?

Go to Communication practice: Student A, page 165; Student B, page 173

8 Complete the sentences so that they are true for you. Compare your sentences in pairs.

1 I like going on vacation to places where ...
2 Most of my friends are people who ...
3 I like TV shows that ...
4 I wouldn't want to live in an area where ...
5 The worst kind of boss is someone who ...
6 I don't like food that ...

Personal Best Write about a friend, a relative, or a co-worker. Use relative clauses to describe him/her.

12B In our lifetime

1 In pairs, write down five activities that take up the most time on a typical day.

sleeping, working ...

2 Look at Chart 1 on page 105. Answer the questions.

1 What are the top five activities in the pie chart?

2 Are they similar to your list in exercise 1?

3 What information does the pie chart show?

4 Does anything surprise you?

 Skill interpreting data

Many texts include graphs and charts to show information more clearly.

• Read any words on the graphs like the title, the key, and the horizontal and vertical axes.

• Look at the data and think about the information it shows.

• When you read a paragraph, look at the graph or chart it describes again and see how the words relate to the data.

• Use information in the text and the graphs and charts to answer the questions.

3 A Read the Skill box. Look at Graphs 1 and 2. What do they show?

B Choose the correct options to complete the information about Graphs 2 and 3.

1 We spend *more / less* time at work than in the past.

2 Over the last twenty years, there *has / hasn't* been a big change.

3 The total time spent on housework by men and women has *decreased / increased*.

4 Men do *more / less* housework now than in 1965.

4 Read the text and look at Chart 1 and Graphs 1 and 2. Check (✔) the best summary of the text.

1 We have a lot more time to spend with friends and family than in the past. ☐

2 We worked more in the past, but we were happier. ☐

3 We have very busy lives and not much time to do the important things. ☐

5 Read the text and look at Chart 1 and Graphs 1 and 2 again. Are the sentences true (T) or false (F)?

1 On average, people live to be 76 years old. ____

2 In 1900, people worked 60 hours a week. ____

3 We spend about a third of our lives sleeping. ____

4 We spend two and a half years in the shower. ____

5 People who work in big cities spend less than a year in their cars. ____

6 We spend a lot of free time using technology. ____

6 Do you think the information is correct for people in your country? Why/Why not? Discuss in pairs.

Text builder expressing approximate quantities

Approximately:	*During a typical lifetime, we spend **around** 91,000 hours at work.*
	*People sleep for **about** eight hours a day.*
	*That means we spend **roughly** three and a half years of our lives studying.*
More than:	*... just **over** two years to spend with family and friends.*
The same/more:	*You can say goodbye to **at least** another year of your life.*
Less than:	*... which is **nearly** ten and a half years. We spend **almost** four years using our phones.*

7 Read the Text builder. Write sentences about how much time you spend doing the activities in the boxes. Use words to express approximate quantities.

sleeping   working   studying   watching TV   going on social media

driving/riding   talking on the phone   getting exercise   eating and drinking

Where does the time go?

We live for 78 years

6 years	(vacuum)
3.8 years	(phone)
10.5 years	(briefcase)
2.5 years	(shower)
11 years	(TV)
2.5 years	(shopping)

1 year	(car)
5 years	(laptop)
4 years	(eating)
3.5 years	(studying)
?	
26 years	(bed)

Chart 1 How we spend our lives

We have more free time than ever before. In many countries, the average working week is now under 40 hours, far shorter than it was for our parents and grandparents before us. So why do our lives feel so busy, and where does our time go?

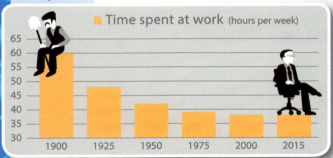

Graph 1
Time spent at work (hours per week)

(bar chart with years 1900, 1925, 1950, 1975, 2000, 2015 on x-axis; values in hours per week from 30 to 65)

People sleep for about eight hours a day, which means we spend 26 years in our beds, in an average lifetime of 78 years. We spend another eleven years watching TV and, depending on where you live, two years of that can be spent just watching the commercials!

In a typical lifetime, we spend around 91,000 hours at work, which is nearly ten and a half years. And do you drive to work? If so, you can say goodbye to at least another year of your life—even more if you work in a big city like Istanbul or Rio de Janeiro and have to sit in traffic jams every day.

In many countries, the law requires young people to stay in school until they're at least 16 years old. Many go on to higher education at a university or college. That means we spend, on average, 31,000 hours—roughly three and a half years of our lives—studying. Two and a half years of our lives are spent in the bathroom, brushing our teeth, using the toilet, taking a shower, and getting ready to go out. Shopping uses up another two and a half years, and we spend at least another four years eating.

The introduction of modern appliances, such as dishwashers, washing machines, and microwaves, means that, overall, we spend less time cooking and cleaning than our parents did. Women still do most of the housework, but men are sharing domestic tasks more than they used to.

Graph 2
Time spent on housework (hours per week)   ■ Men   ■ Women

(area chart with years 1965, 1975, 1985, 1995, 2005, 2015 on x-axis; values from 0 to 40)

In recent years, the biggest change in how we spend our time is technology. We spend an average of five years online and almost four years using our phones, and those numbers are increasing every year.

If you add up all that time, it leaves you with just over two years on average to spend with family and friends, to see the world, and to achieve your dreams. So, what are you waiting for? The clock is ticking!

12C Long-distance love

1 Look at the pictures and the title. Answer the questions in pairs. Then read the text and check.

1 What do you think the text is about?
2 Where do you think the man is?

3 Where do you think the woman is?
4 How do you think they stay in touch?

The *ultimate* long-distance relationship

Having a long-distance relationship isn't easy. Staying in touch takes extra effort, and not having your partner around when you need support can be difficult. So it's hard to imagine what life is like for Amiko Kauderer, whose boyfriend, Scott Kelly, is often not even on the planet with her. That's because Scott is an astronaut who spends months floating 400 km. above the Earth on the International Space Station!

Amiko works at NASA, which is how she got to know Scott. They met a few times, and after talking "for hours and hours" one evening, Scott finally asked her out. They've now been together for several years. However, Scott's job means he is often away. His first trip to the Space Station lasted six months. After that, he lived in space for a whole year to find out what would happen to the human body on a journey to Mars.

On his first trip, it wasn't easy for Amiko to stay in touch. E-mailing involved a six-hour delay, but now it's almost instant, and it's also possible to videochat once a week. But there are some things that can't be done. "One of the things I

miss most is holding hands," says Amiko. "We can connect by phone. I can upload pictures, but you can't upload human touch."

Other couples might have broken up in such a situation, but not Scott and Amiko. "We really appreciate a challenge because we know that in the end, we will be able to say, 'Yeah, we did that'."

So, whenever you think your love life is difficult, just think of Amiko and Scott!

2 A Match sentences 1–5 with pictures a–e.

1 Amiko **got to know** Scott at a friend's house. ____
2 They **fell in love** at first sight. ____
3 Scott **asked** Amiko **out** on a date. ____

4 **Staying in touch** now is easier than it was. ____
5 They **broke up**, but **got back together** in the end. ____

B Are the sentences true (T) or false (F)? Check your answers in the text.

Go to Vocabulary practice: relationship verbs, page 157

3 Choose the correct words to complete the sentences. Check your answers in the text.

1 *Have / Having* a long-distance relationship isn't easy.
2 ... after *to talk / talking* "for hours and hours" one evening, Scott finally asked her out.
3 He lived in space for a whole year *to find out / finding out* what would happen to the human body.
4 It's also possible *to videochat / videochatting* once a week.

4 Look at sentences 1–4 from exercise 3 again. Complete the rules with the -*ing* form or infinitive. Then read the Grammar box.

1 We use _____ after an adjective.
2 We usually use _____ as the subject/object of a sentence.
3 We use _____ after a preposition.
4 We use _____ to say why we did something.

> 📖 **Grammar** uses of the -*ing* form and the infinitive
>
> -*ing* form of the verb:
> After a preposition: I'm interested **in learning** languages.
> Subject/object of a sentence: **Breaking up** with someone is hard.   I hate **breaking up** with someone.
> Infinitive:
> After an adjective: It's **difficult to meet** new people in this city.   It's **important to stay** in touch.
> To express a purpose: I went to Juan's house **to talk** to him.

Personal Best

Go to Grammar practice: uses of the -*ing* form and the infinitive, page 135

5 **A** ▶12.7   **Pronunciation:** word stress Listen to the words and underline the stressed syllables. Listen again, check, and repeat.

1 distance   2 relationship   3 imagine   4 happen

B ▶12.8   Underline the stressed syllables in the words below. Listen, check, and repeat.

important   colleagues   impossible   except   technology   better   afraid   probably

6 **A** ▶12.9   Write the infinitive or the -*ing* form of the verbs in parentheses. Listen and check.

1 It's very important _____ with your colleagues at work. (get along)
2 _____ in love at first sight is impossible, except in the movies. (fall)
3 You can use technology _____ in touch, but meeting face to face is better. (stay)
4 You shouldn't be afraid of _____ someone out. He or she will probably say yes! (ask)

B In pairs, practice saying sentences 1–4. Say if you agree or disagree with the sentences.

Go to Communication practice: Student A, page 165; Student B, page 173

7 Complete the text with the infinitive or the -*ing* form of the verbs in the box.

arrive   choose   say   make   show

HOW TO SUCCEED ON A FIRST DATE

1 _____ a nice place to meet is the first thing you need to think about.
2 You should wear nice clothes _____ a good impression.
3 It's important _____ on time.
4 Don't be afraid of _____ the real you.
5 Before _____ good night, tell him/her that you enjoyed the date.

8 In pairs, think of more advice for how to succeed on a first date. Use the ideas in the boxes.

be polite   don't talk too much   ask questions   make eye contact   laugh   listen   smile   tell a joke   relax

A *I think it's important to be polite.*   **B** *Yes, but being polite isn't the most important thing ...*

Personal Best   Write a paragraph about a couple you know. Explain how they met and their relationship.

12D Thumbs Thanks a million!

1 A Look at the pictures. How are the people celebrating their birthday?

B Answer the questions.

1 How important are birthdays to you? Why?
2 How did you celebrate your last birthday?
3 What's the best birthday present you've ever received? Why?
4 Have you ever had a surprise birthday party? Did you enjoy it?

2 ▶ **12.10**   Watch or listen to the first part of *Learning Curve*. Are the sentences true (T) or false (F)?

1 Today is Simon's birthday.   ____
2 Everyone has forgotten about his birthday.   ____
3 Simon has a tennis match today.   ____
4 Kate gives Simon a present.   ____
5 Simon will pay to post the parcel.   ____
6 Simon's parents always call him in the morning.   ____

3 A ▶ **12.10**   Watch or listen again. Match the phrases 1–5 with the reasons a–e.

1 That's very kind of you.
2 Thanks a lot.
3 Thanks so much!
4 Thanks a million!
5 I will, thanks.

a Kate gives Simon a cup of tea.
b Kate offers to make Simon tea.
c Simon says he'll pay at the post office.
d Simon agrees to post a parcel.
e Kate wants Simon to say hello to his parents for her.

B Look at phrases 1–5 again. Answer the questions.

1 Which phrases are polite responses to something small?   ____ ____
2 Which phrases are used to say thanks for something special or a big effort?   ____ ____ ____
3 Can you think of any other ways to thank someone?

Conversation builder	**saying thanks**	
To be polite:	**For a special favor:**	**To be more formal:**
Thanks a lot.	*That's very nice/kind of you.*	*I can't thank you enough.*
Thanks very much.	*Thanks a million.*	*I'm so grateful to you.*
Thanks.	*Thank you so much.*	*We really appreciate it.*

---

4 ▶ **12.11**   Read the Conversation builder. In pairs, read the sentences out loud and thank your partner in an appropriate way. Listen and compare your answers.

1 Here's your T-shirt and $1 change.

2 We've decided to give you a 30% pay raise.

3 Here are some flowers. I know you've been sick.

4 The bus station? It's right across the street.

5 I've done all the shopping for you.

6 I cooked spaghetti. It's your favorite.

5 ▶12.12 Watch or listen to the second part of the show. What other ways of thanking people do you hear?

6 ▶12.12 Answer the questions. Watch or listen again and check.

1 Who cooked the food for the party? _____
2 Who sent flowers, chocolate, and biscuits? _____
3 Did Kate organize the party on her own? _____
4 Whose parents arrive at the party? _____

7 ▶12.13 Complete the sentences with the phrases in the box. Listen, check, and repeat after the beeps.

> it was easy   Glad you noticed   You're welcome   I had help   it isn't a problem

1	**Kate**	Oh, and thanks again for taking this parcel.
	Simon	Really, _____ .
2	**Simon**	You look great, Pen. Is that a new dress?
	Penny	Thanks. _____ !
3	**Penny**	Jack, you really made a fantastic meal!
	Jack	Oh, come on, _____ . I make this all the time.
4	**Simon**	Lovely. I'm so grateful to you both!
	Penny	It was nothing. _____ .
5	**Simon**	That was a fantastic surprise. Kate, did you do all this by yourself?
	Kate	No, _____ !

🔧 **Skill**   **responding modestly**

We often respond to congratulations, thanks, and compliments in a modest way.
- For congratulations, you can say it wasn't important or hard work, e.g., *It was nothing, I was just lucky.*
- For thanks, you can say it was something small or you enjoyed doing it, e.g., *No problem. It was a pleasure. You're welcome.*
- For a compliment, you can thank the person and say you are pleased, e.g., *Thanks. I'm glad you like it.* You can also say it's not as good as the person thinks, e.g., *This old thing? I've had it for years.*

8 ▶12.14 Read the Skill box. Match phrases 1–6 with responses a–f. Listen and check.

1 I can't thank you enough.
2 I love your new hairstyle.
3 This chicken is delicious.
4 You passed! Congratulations.
5 Thanks for taking care of my children.
6 Congratulations on your promotion.

a Really? I thought it was too spicy.
b Oh, it's just an small one.
c Thanks. I'm glad you noticed.
d It was a pleasure. They're lots of fun!
e Thanks. The exam wasn't that difficult.
f It's no problem.

Go to Communication practice: Student A, page 165; Student B, page 173

9 **A** PREPARE In pairs, look at the pictures and choose a situation. Prepare a short conversation between the people.

B PRACTICE Act out your conversation to another pair.

C PERSONAL BEST What was good about the other pair's conversation? What could they do better? Change partners and prepare a conversation for another situation.

 Personal Best Make a list of people you have thanked this week and explain why you thanked them.

Grammar

1 Choose the correct options to complete the sentences.

1 Kevin has decided _____ his job.
   a quit
   b to quit
   c quitting

2 I usually go to _____ bed at 11:00 p.m.
   a a
   b the
   c – (no article)

3 Do you want _____ out tonight?
   a go
   b to go
   c going

4 My sister is _____ lawyer.
   a a
   b the
   c – (no article)

5 I'm getting together with a colleague _____ just left the company.
   a where
   b what
   c who

6 I called him _____ a meeting.
   a arrange
   b to arrange
   c arranging

7 This is the café _____ we said we would meet.
   a where
   b who
   c that

8 I'm crazy about _____ to other countries.
   a travel
   b to travel
   c traveling

2 Complete the sentences with the correct form of the verbs in the box.

| remember   take   buy   find |
| go   work   meet   write |

1 I went to the library _____ a book about pets.

2 I'm not happy about _____ late this week.

3 He forgot _____ his girlfriend a birthday present.

4 I've finally finished _____ my essay.

5 I can't stand _____ the subway. It's so crowded!

6 She's suggested _____ to the movies tonight.

7 It's important _____ to turn off this machine when you leave.

8 _____ you is the best thing that has happened to me!

3 Choose the correct options to complete the text.

Stephanie is [1]*a / - / the* wedding planner and she is [2]*an / - / the* owner of *Blissful Days*, [3]*a / - / the* company based in Sydney, Australia.

How did you become a wedding planner?

I've always loved [4]*go / to go / going* to weddings. It's so exciting [5]*see / to see / seeing* everyone dressed up and enjoying such a wonderful day. But I noticed that some people couldn't enjoy it because they were worried about [6]*organize / to organize / organizing* everything. That's when I realized that I could start a company [7]*that / who / where* helps people plan their weddings.

What advice can you give to couples planning a wedding?

First of all, you should agree on the guests [8]*what / – / where* you're going to invite. Once you know how many people will be there, you can find a place [9]*who / that / where* everyone will be comfortable. Send out invitations at least six months before the wedding, but expect that about 20% of people won't be able to attend. There could be more if the date of your wedding is on or near [10]*a / - / the* legal holiday, so always check your dates carefully.

Vocabulary

1 Match the words in the box with the definitions.

| oven   get back together   plain   do the laundry |
| hang out the clothes   groom   stylish   iron |
| go out together   roommate |

1 a machine you use to make clothes flat _____

2 a man who is going to get married _____

3 to start a relationship with someone _____

4 simple, with no pattern or design _____

5 someone who you live with _____

6 a machine you use to cook food _____

7 to dry clothes after you wash them _____

8 to wash your clothes _____

9 fashionable and elegant _____

10 to return to a relationship with someone _____

2 Circle the words that are different. Explain your answers.

1	employer	classmate	colleague	business partner
2	break up	fall in love	go on a date	go out together
3	oven	dishwasher	sink	washing machine
4	mop	sweep	iron	vacuum
5	loose	wool	tight	casual
6	bride	girlfriend	stepsister	father-in-law
7	formal	cotton	denim	silk
8	sheets	pillow	comforter	iron
9	along well	married	in love	back together
10	wash the dishes	set the table	make the bed	load the dishwasher

3 Choose the correct word to complete the sentences.

1 My uncle's daughter is my _____ .
   a niece   **b** cousin   **c** stepsister

2 I am _____ . I don't have any brothers or sisters.
   a an only child   **b** a single parent   **c** a relative

3 I quit my job because I _____ badly with my boss.
   a got back   **b** got along   **c** went along

4 He _____ on a date!
   a introduced   **b** asked me out   **c** stayed in touch

5 The _____ is broken. Can you call a plumber?
   a oven   **b** faucet   **c** refrigerator

6 We need new _____ for the bed.
   a rugs   **b** carpets   **c** sheets

7 I don't know him. He's a complete _____ .
   a twin   **b** enemy   **c** stranger

8 It's really hot today. Can you _____ the plants?
   a sweep   **b** dust   **c** water

4 Complete the conversation with the words in the box.

> get to know   break up   vacuum
> introduce   nice   do   silk   mop

Sue When did you ¹ _____ with Harry?
Jo Two months ago.
Sue Let me ² _____ you to Lee. I'm meeting him tonight.
Jo I can't. I have to ³ _____ the carpets and ⁴ _____ the floor.
Sue You can do that any time!
Jo But I don't have anything to wear. I need to ⁵ _____ the laundry!
Sue Is your ⁶ _____ dress clean?
Jo Yes, it is.
Sue Well, that's really ⁷ _____ . Wear that! Come on, you should ⁸ _____ him. He's wonderful!
Jo OK, I'll come with you.

Personal Best

Lesson 11A
Name five objects you can find in a kitchen.

Lesson 12A
Write down five people, and say how you are related to each of them.

Lesson 11A
Name five verbs that are followed by the *-ing* form.

Lesson 12A
Write three sentences with relative clauses and *who, that,* and *where*.

Lesson 11B
Name five household chores you do at home.

Lesson 12B
Write three sentences using *roughly, at least,* and *almost*.

Lesson 11C
Write a sentence with *a/an*, and another with *the*.

Lesson 12C
Write a sentence with the infinitive.

Lesson 11C
Use adjectives to describe two things you are wearing now.

Lesson 12D
Give three expressions to thank someone.

Lesson 11D
Describe a noun using three adjectives in the correct order.

Lesson 12D
Give an expression for responding modestly when someone thanks you.

1A Simple present

We use the simple present to talk about things that are always true.

My best friend is from Argentina.   *He doesn't like tomatoes.*

We also use the simple present to talk about regular routines and habits.

I talk to my best friend every day.   *We go for coffee once a week.*

We form negatives and questions with *don't/doesn't* and *do/does* + the base form of the verb.

▶ 1.4	I / you / we / they	he / she / it
+	We **live** in Istanbul.	Carlos **lives** in Santiago.
−	They **don't live** in Quebec.	Megan **doesn't live** in Sydney.
?	**Do** you **live** in Shanghai?	**Does** she **live** in Cairo?
Y/N	Yes, I **do**. / No, I **don't**.	Yes, she **does**. / No, she **doesn't**.

We usually add **s** to the base form to make the third person singular (*he/she/it*) form.

Spelling rules for third person singular (*he / she / it*)

We usually add **-s** to the base form. *live* ⇨ *lives*

When the base form ends in consonant + **y**, we change the **y** to **i** and then add **-es**. *study* ⇨ *studies*

When the base form ends in **-sh**, **-ch**, **-x**, **-s** we add **-es**.
finish ⇨ *finishes*   *watch* ⇨ *watches*

Some verbs are irregular. *go* ⇨ *goes*   *do* ⇨ *does*   *have* ⇨ *has*

Look! The verbs *be* and *can* are irregular in the simple present.
I'm a generous person.   *David can swim well.*
You aren't late today.   *You can't use this computer.*
Are they good friends?   *Can you help us?*
Yes, they are.   *No, we can't.*

Adverbs and expressions of frequency

We use adverbs of frequency with the simple present to talk about habits and routines.

100% ————————————————————→ 0%

always   usually   often   sometimes   hardly ever   never

We put adverbs of frequency before the main verb.
I always see my friends after classes. NOT ~~Always I see my friends after classes.~~
But we put them after the verb *be*.
They're never late. NOT ~~They never are late.~~
We use *How often ...?* to ask questions about how frequently actions happen.
How often do you see your friends?
We can also use expressions of frequency, such as *every day/week/month* or *once a week/month/year* to talk about regular routines.

We usually use expressions of frequency at the end of sentences.
I meet Julia once a week. NOT ~~I meet once a week Julia.~~
I talk to her every day. NOT ~~I talk every day to her.~~

1 Complete the sentences with the correct form of the verbs in parentheses.

1 I _____ coffee. (not like)
2 _____ they _____ computer games with you? (play)
3 Luca _____ work at 6:00 p.m. (finish)
4 We _____ fun together. (have)
5 You _____ my best friend. (not know)
6 _____ Robert _____ with you? (work)
7 Constanza is really shy. She _____ in class. (not speak)
8 My mom _____ a lot about her children. (worry)
9 _____ you _____ me with this? (can / help)
10 Raul _____ very patient. (not be)

2 Rewrite the sentences and questions with the adverbs of frequency in the correct place.

1 We go for coffee after class. (sometimes)
_____
2 Do you talk to your best friend every day? (usually)
_____
3 My best friend is there for me, day or night. (always)
_____
4 How do you talk to your best friend? (often)
_____
5 My roommates are in our apartment. (hardly ever)
_____
6 Lucia works hard. (never)
_____

3 Put the words in the correct order to make sentences and questions.

1 your / often / friends / do / see / how / you ?
_____
2 usually / drink / doesn't / Luis / coffee
_____
3 evening / Sandra / every / studies
_____
4 me / friends / to / always / my / listen
_____
5 day / we / home / every / at / cook
_____
6 you / dentist / often / the / how / see / do ?
_____
7 week / bedroom / a / clean / times / I / my / three
_____
8 often / on / you / how / vacation / go / do ?
_____

◀ Go back to page 5

1C Present continuous

We use the present continuous to talk about things that are happening now.

My brother is taking a shower right now.
Are you reading a good book at the moment?

We also use the present continuous to talk about things that are temporary.

I'm staying at my parents' house this semester.
She isn't working in the office this month.

We form the present continuous with the verb *be* + the *-ing* form of the main verb.

▶ 1.12	I	he / she / it	you / we / they
+	I'm **reading** a book.	Daniel's **sleeping**.	We're all **wearing** glasses!
−	I'm **not working** in the office today.	My cousin **isn't staying** with me this week.	We **aren't using** this room now.
?	**Am** I **dreaming**?	**Is** she **studying** French this month?	**Are** you **watching** TV?
Y/N	Yes, I **am**. / No, I'm **not**.	Yes, she **is**. / No, she **isn't**.	Yes, we **are**. / No, we **aren't**.

We usually add *-ing* to the base form to make the *-ing* form.

Spelling rules for the *-ing* form

We usually add *-ing* to the base form. *play* ⇨ *playing*   *talk* ⇨ *talking*

When a verb ends in *e*, we omit the *e* before adding *-ing*.
take ⇨ *taking*   *live* ⇨ *living*

When a verb ends in consonant + vowel + consonant, we double the final consonant before adding *-ing*. *sit* ⇨ *sitting*   *plan* ⇨ *planning*

> **Look!** We often use the present continuous with time expressions, such as (*right*) *now, today, this week/month/year, at the moment*.
> *I'm studying economics now.*
> *Today, they're not working very much.*

Simple present and present continuous

We use the simple present to talk about things that are always true, and the present continuous to talk about things that are temporary.

Rebecca lives in Mexico City, but this month she's living in New York.

We use the simple present to talk about things that happen regularly and the present continuous to talk about things that are happening now.

I usually take the bus to work, but today I'm taking a taxi.

However, there are some verbs that describe a state rather than an action. We don't normally use these verbs in the present continuous.

Maria hates the new TV series. NOT ~~Maria is hating the new TV series~~.
My teacher doesn't think it's correct. NOT ~~My teacher isn't thinking it's correct~~.
I have a rental car at the moment. NOT ~~I'm having a rental car at the moment~~.

State verbs

Feelings	like, love, hate, want, prefer, need
Thoughts and opinions	know, believe, remember, forget, understand, think
States	be, exist, seem, look like, belong, own, have

1 Write sentences using the present continuous.

1 My sister / travel / in Asia / right now
_____

2 Ivan / not work / this week
_____

3 What / you / learn about / in your history class?
_____

4 They / plan / a trip to Mexico
_____

5 I / not shout
_____

6 you / use / that chair?
_____

7 she / wear / a scarf?
_____

8 I / not go running / this month
_____

2 Complete the sentences with the present continuous or the simple present form of the verbs in parentheses.

1 We can't have a picnic today. It _____ . (rain)
2 She often _____ her friends here. (meet)
3 Turn that music down! The children _____ . (sleep)
4 The trains are really busy because everyone _____ to work right now. (go)
5 It's amazing how much she _____ her mom. (look like)
6 Can you turn off the TV, please, if you _____ it? (not watch)
7 He _____ a suit to work, except when he has an important meeting. (not wear)
8 I can't talk while I _____ . I'll call you later. (drive)

3 Complete the text with the present continuous or the simple present form of the verbs in parentheses.

Ella Richards is the granddaughter of Keith Richards, who [1]_____ (play) guitar with the Rolling Stones. Ella is 18 and a model, and she [2]_____ (appear) in a series of ads for a fashion company at the moment. She [3]_____ (live) at home, with her mom, dad, and younger brother, but this week she [4]_____ (work) in London, and she [5]_____ (stay) at her grandmother's house. In our photo, she [6]_____ (wear) a black dress with flowers, and she [7]_____ (carry) a handbag. She says that when she's older, she [8]_____ (want) to be a spy!

◀ Go back to page 8

2A Simple past

We use the simple past to talk about completed actions in the past.

I bought a new camera yesterday.
Emma didn't come to work last week.
Did you see Lucia at the party?

We form negatives and questions with *didn't* and *did* + the base form of the verb.

▶ 2.1	Regular verbs	Irregular verbs
+	We **walked** to school yesterday.	We **took** a lot of photos.
–	I **didn't study** science in college.	He **didn't go** shopping last week.
?	**Did** he **use** his own camera?	**Did** you **meet** anyone interesting?
Y/N	Yes, he **did**.	No, I **didn't**.

We usually add *-ed* to regular verbs to make the positive form of the simple past.

Spelling rules for regular simple past positive forms
We usually add *-ed* to the verb. *play* ⇨ *played* *watch* ⇨ *watched*
When a verb ends in *e*, we add *-d*. *dance* ⇨ *danced* *live* ⇨ *lived*
When a verb ends in consonant + *y*, we change the *y* to *i* and then we add *-ed*. *study* ⇨ *studied*
When a verb ends in consonant + vowel + consonant, we double the final consonant and then add *-ed*. *stop* ⇨ *stopped* *plan* ⇨ *planned*

Many common verbs have irregular simple past positive forms.

go ⇨ *went* *have* ⇨ *had* *take* ⇨ *took*

Look! The verbs *be* and *can* are irregular in the simple past.
I was at the party.   *We could see the house.*
She wasn't here.   *He couldn't come to class.*
Were you happy?   *Could you speak French when you were younger?*
Yes, I was.   *No, I couldn't.*

Time expressions

We often use time expressions with the simple past to say when an action happened. Time expressions can go at the end or at the beginning of sentences.

Last year, the president traveled to Europe.
The president traveled to Europe last year.
NOT ~~The president traveled last year to Europe~~.

▶ 2.2	Time expressions
at + times	The train arrived **at 6 o'clock**.
in + seasons, months, years	They traveled **in the summer**. **In 2015**, we moved to Portugal.
last + *night/week/month/year*	**Last night**, I saw a good game on TV. We went there **last year**.
on + days, dates, *the weekend*	What did you do **on Monday**? Did you do anything special **on July 4th**? I went to the movies **on the weekend.**
seconds, minutes, hours, days, weeks, months, years + *ago*	**An hour ago**, Kevin was here. I saw him **three days ago.**
yesterday	I saw her **yesterday.**

1 Complete the sentences with the correct simple past form of the verbs.

1 They _____ to speak Spanish in Colombia. (learn)
2 _____ you _____ Hannah yesterday? (see)
3 We _____ this photo from the top of that building. (take)
4 I _____ to class last week. (not go)
5 _____ you _____ the movie? (enjoy)
6 How annoying! Elise _____ her e-mails last night. (not check)
7 _____ Paula _____ you on Monday? (call)
8 I _____ in a restaurant five years ago. (work)

2 A Write simple past questions.

1 what / you / do / yesterday?
_____
2 your sister / go / on vacation / with you / last year?
_____
3 when / you / finish / the project?
_____
4 you / have / a smartphone / ten years ago?
_____
5 when / Mario / take / the photo?
_____
6 where / be / you / on Monday / at 10:00 a.m.?
_____

B Match answers a–f with questions 1–6.

a I finished it a few days ago. _____
b Yes, I did. It was very expensive. _____
c I went to a friend's house and watched a movie. _____
d I was in my car, driving to work. _____
e No, she didn't. She stayed at home. _____
f He took it last month when he was in Poland. _____

3 Choose the correct options to complete the sentences.

1 We didn't take any photos *on / in / at* the summer.
2 I bought this phone a few years *ago / last / past*.
3 We moved to a new apartment *on / in / at* August.
4 Did you see Andrés in town *yesterday / last day / day ago*?
5 The concert started *in / on / at* 9:00 p.m.
6 Monica and Julieta went to the movies *in / at / on* Saturday.
7 Did your college course finish *in / on / at* July 5th?
8 They met in a café *ago / last / past* night.

◀ Go back to page 13

2C Question forms

When we ask for specific information, we use a question word, such as *who*, *where*, *when*, *how*, or *why*.

Where does Maria live?   *She lives in Germany.*
How did they get here?   *They came by car.*
Why are you wearing a coat?   *I'm wearing it because I'm cold.*

When we ask for a *Yes* or *No* answer, we don't use a question word.

Do you like coffee?   *Yes, I do.*
Did the train arrive late?   *No, it didn't.*
Is Ling Mai from China?   *Yes, she is.*

With most verbs, we use an auxiliary verb.

▶ 2.9 question word	auxiliary verb	subject	main verb
Where	**does**	your brother	**go** to college?
	Do	you	**remember** your elementary school?
How	**did**	your sister	**get** her first job?
	Did	Gustavo	**see** you yesterday?
Which book	**are**	you	**reading** right now?
	Is	Karla	**looking** forward to the trip?

With the verb *be*, we don't use an auxiliary verb and the subject comes after *be*.

▶ 2.10 question word	*be*	subject	
Where	**are**	you	from?
	Is	the meeting	in March?
Why	**was**	the computer	broken?
	Were	you	at the party?

> **Look!** We usually put prepositions at the end of questions, after the main verb.
> *Who did she get married to?* NOT ~~To who did she get married?~~
> *What are you worried about?* NOT ~~About what are you worried?~~

We use *how* in different ways when we ask questions.

How—to ask about the way of doing something
How do you travel to work?

How often—to ask about frequency
How often do you wash your hair?

How long—to ask about duration
How long is the movie?

How old—to ask about age
How old were you when you moved here?

How much/many—to ask about quantity
How much money do you have?

How + adjective—to ask about a specific quality
How deep is the swimming pool?

1 Put the words in the correct order to make questions.

1 often / gym / how / you / the / go / do / to
_____ ?

2 go / to / which / did / college / they
_____ ?

3 weekend / go / where / on / you / the / did
_____ ?

4 thinking / what / you / about / are
_____ ?

5 whose / today / it / is / birthday
_____ ?

6 to / work / how / get / she / does
_____ ?

7 who / you / at / are / looking
_____ ?

8 for / class / why / late / you / were
_____ ?

2 Write questions for the answers.

1 He was born in Belo Horizonte in Brazil.
Where _____ ?

2 They grew up with their grandparents.
Who _____ ?

3 She met her husband at a party.
Where _____ ?

4 They have five children.
How many _____ ?

5 He retired because of poor health.
Why _____ ?

6 At the moment, he's working on a new project.
What _____ ?

3 A Put the words from the box in the correct place to complete the interviewer's questions.

you	did	it	to	with	are

1 Where you from?
2 When you start singing?
3 What type of music do you listen?
4 Is difficult to write songs?
5 In the future, which musicians do you hope to work?
6 Do enjoy being famous?

B Match answers a–f with questions 1–6.

a I love all music—rock and pop, especially. ____
b I don't know. I just sing the songs. ____
c I was born in Puerto Rico, but I grew up in New York. ____
d I'm planning on working with Shakira soon. ____
e Yes, I do. I love it! ____
f I started singing classes when I was six years old. ____

◀ Go back to page 17

3A Comparatives, superlatives, (not) as ... as

Comparatives

We use comparative adjectives + *than* to compare things.

Helen is taller than Jason.
The train is more expensive than the bus.

We can also use *less* + adjective + *than* to compare things.

The train is less crowded than the bus. = The bus is more crowded than the train.
The subway is less expensive than the train. = The subway is cheaper than the train.

(not) as ... as

We use *as ... as* with adjectives to say two things are the same.

Sofia is as tall as Jasmine.   *The train is as fast as the bus.*

We use *not as ... as* with adjectives to say two things are different.

Sofia isn't as tall as Helen. = Sofia is less tall than Helen.
The bus isn't as expensive as the train. = The bus is less expensive than the train.

> **Look!** After comparatives or *(not) as ... as*, we can use an object pronoun or a subject pronoun + auxiliary verb.
> *Marcos is faster than me. / Marcos is faster than I am.*
> *Claudia is more relaxed than her. / Claudia is more relaxed than she is.*

Superlatives

We use superlative adjectives to say that something is more than all the others in a group.

Helen is the tallest in her class.
The train is the most expensive way to travel around this city.

We can also use *the least* + adjective to say something is less than all the others in a group.

It's the least dangerous way to travel. = It's the safest way to travel.

Spelling rules for comparative and superlative adjectives

When an adjective is one syllable, we add *-er / -est*.
fast ⇨ faster ⇨ fastest

When a one-syllable adjective ends in consonant + vowel + consonant, we double the final consonant and add *-er / -est*.   *hot ⇨ hotter ⇨ hottest*

When an adjective ends in consonant + *y*, we change the *y* to *i* and then add *-er / -est*.   *easy ⇨ easier ⇨ easiest*

When an adjective is two or more syllables, we use ***more/most*** + adjective.
comfortable ⇨ more comfortable ⇨ most comfortable

Some comparatives are irregular.   *good ⇨ better ⇨ best*
bad ⇨ worse ⇨ worst   far ⇨ further/farther ⇨ furthest/farthest

▶ 3.2

Comparatives	Fish is **healthier than** meat. I'm much **more/less patient than** you.
(not) as ... as	Melissa is **as friendly as** her sister. It isn**'t as warm as** it was yesterday.
Superlatives	This is **the fastest** car in the world. I bought **the most/least expensive** phone in the store.

1 Complete the sentences with the comparative or superlative form of the adjectives in parentheses.

1 The Torre Latino is the _____ place for a view of Mexico City. (good)
2 I can't believe you're _____ than me! (old)
3 My apartment is _____ from the park than yours (far)
4 I think Tokyo is the _____ city I know. (interesting)
5 Is Beijing _____ than Tokyo? (big)
6 Dubai is one of the _____ airports in the world. (busy)

2 Complete the second sentence with *(not) as ... as* so it means the same as the first sentence.

1 Your new apartment is bigger than your old apartment.
   Your old apartment is _____ your new apartment.
2 Moscow is more famous than São Paulo.
   São Paulo is _____ Moscow.
3 The subway and the bus are equally crowded.
   The subway is _____ the bus.
4 I think this part of town is livelier than downtown.
   Downtown is _____ this part of town.

3 Look at the information. Write three sentences using the adjectives in the boxes.

| Hotel Romeo $500 | Hotel Brooklyn $300 | Hotel Cruz $125 |

cheap   expensive

1 Hotel Cruz is _____ hotel.
2 Hotel Romeo is _____ hotel.
3 Hotel Brooklyn is _____ Hotel Romeo, but it isn't as _____ Hotel Cruz.

March 1, 10°   March 2, 15°   March 3, 25°

cold   hot

4 March 1 was _____ March 2.
5 March 3 was _____ day.
6 March 2 was _____ March 3, but it wasn't as _____ March 1.

Mumbai   Madrid   Buenos Aires

busy   quiet

7 Mumbai is _____ city.
8 Buenos Aires is _____ city.
9 Madrid isn't as _____ Mumbai, but it's _____ Buenos Aires.

◀ Go back to page 23

3C Past continuous

We use the past continuous to describe actions in progress at a particular time in the past.

I was sleeping at 7:00 this morning.
I was working at my desk when the telephone rang.

We form the past continuous with the simple past of the verb *be* + the *-ing* form of the main verb.

▶ 3.10	I / he / she / it	you / we / they
+	I **was watching** TV at 6:00 last night.	We **were walking** home when it started to rain.
–	It **wasn't raining** when I got to work.	The players **weren't playing** very well.
?	**Was** she **working** at this office when you met her?	**Were** you **living** here at the beginning of the year?
Y/N	Yes, she **was**. / No, she **wasn't**.	Yes, we **were**. / No, we **weren't**.

Past continuous and simple past

We use the simple past to describe completed actions in the past, for example a series of actions.

Yesterday, I woke up, I had breakfast, and then I took a shower.

| I woke up. | I had breakfast. | I took a shower. |

We use the past continuous with the simple past to describe an action that was in progress when a completed action happened.

The action in progress can continue.

I was having breakfast when I heard the new song on the radio. = I continued having breakfast.

I was having breakfast.

I heard the new song on the radio.

Or the action in progress may stop.

I was sleeping when the telephone rang. = I stopped sleeping.

I was sleeping.

The telephone rang.

We can also use two past continuous verbs together to show that two actions were happening at the same time.

I was cooking while Steve was doing his homework.

I was cooking.

Steve was doing his homework.

> **Look!** We often use **when** and **while** in sentences with the past continuous.
> *I broke my leg while I was playing soccer.*
> *I was playing soccer when I broke my leg.*
> *While I was playing soccer, I broke my leg.*

1 Complete the conversations with the past continuous form of the verbs in parentheses.

1. **A** _____ (you / watch) TV just now?
   B No, I wasn't. It was the radio.
2. **A** Why didn't you see Paula and Mark?
   B They _____ (walk) the dog.
3. **A** Why was the boss angry with Nigel?
   B He _____ (not work) fast enough.
4. **A** Why didn't you play tennis yesterday?
   B It _____ (rain) all day.
5. **A** Did you ask Thomas to come to the party?
   B Yes, I talked to him while we _____ (have) lunch.

2 Change one verb in each sentence to the past continuous.

1. We had dinner outside while we stayed in Rome.
   _____
2. When Lisa crossed the street, she dropped her phone and it broke.
   _____
3. We had dinner outside when it started to rain.
   _____
4. I didn't listen when the teacher told us about the exam next week.
   _____
5. While we sat in the taxi, we checked the address of the hotel.
   _____

3 Choose the correct form of the verbs to complete the text about a movie of Alastair Humphreys' new adventure.

Into The Empty Quarter

In September 2012, Alastair Humphreys [1]*trained / was training* for an expedition to the South Pole. Unfortunately, he [2]*found out / was finding out* that the trip couldn't take place because there wasn't enough money. So he [3]*had to / was having to* find a new adventure quickly. One day, he [4]*looked / was looking* through his adventure books when he [5]*found / was finding* the answer —a book named *Arabian Sands* about Wilfred Thesiger's trip across the Arabian desert in the 1940s. Alastair immediately [6]*contacted / was contacting* another explorer, Leon McCarron, and they started planning how to walk more than 1,600 kilometers across the desert. They [7]*began / were beginning* the trip in November 2012, and were home before the end of the year. But this time they [8]*filmed / were filming* all their adventures, too. *Into The Empty Quarter* is their story.

◀ Go back to page 27

117

4A *will*, *may*, and *might* for predictions

We use *will* and *won't* (=*will not*) + the base form to make predictions about the future. We usually use the contraction *'ll* after personal pronouns, such as *I, he, she*, etc. and after *there*.

It'll be sunny tomorrow.   *It definitely won't rain.*
There'll be lots of traffic tonight.   *She won't be here on time.*

We often use *probably* to say that the prediction is less sure. *Probably* comes after *will* and before *won't*.

I'll probably go to the gym tonight.
You probably won't see Karen tomorrow.

We use *may* and *might* + the base form to say that a prediction is possible. There is no difference in meaning between *may* and *might*.

He may be hungry when he gets home.
They might not serve any food on the flight.

We don't use *may* or *might* to make questions.

Will the exam be difficult? NOT *Might the exam be difficult?*

We can use *may* and *might* to reply to questions.

Will he get the job? He might. I'm not sure.
Will it rain tomorrow? It might, or it might not!

▶ 4.3	will	may	might
+	It'**ll rain** tomorrow.	It **may snow** tomorrow.	It **might be** windy.
–	She **won't pass** the exam.	Kelly **may not come**.	Jorge **might not arrive** on time.
?	**Will** she **be** the next president?		
Y/N	Yes, she **will**. / No, she **won't**.	Yes, she **may**. / No, she **may not**.	Yes, she **might**. / No, she **might not**.

Look! We often make predictions with *I think ...* or *I don't think ...* to show it is our opinion.
I think he'll win the race.
I don't think she'll lose her job. NOT *I think she won't lose her job*.

---

1   Write sentences using the correct form of *will, may*, and *might*.

1   It / probably / rain / tomorrow (will)
_____

2   You / need / your car (may not)
_____

3   I / don't think / we / see / you later (will)
_____

4   We / have time / to go for coffee? (will)
_____

5   She / come / to the meeting later (might)
_____

6   They / probably / go / on vacation next year (won't)
_____

7   I / think / there / be / lots of people / at the party (will)
_____

8   What do you think / happen? (will)
_____

2   Choose the correct words to complete the sentences.

1   They *will / might* go on vacation to Colombia, but they don't have much money, so they *'ll / might* probably just stay at home.

2   I don't think England *will / may* win the next World Cup. I'm sure it *will / may* be Germany.

3   I probably *won't / may not* go to the movies, but I *'ll / may* be able to meet you afterward. Can I text you later to let you know?

4   I'm sure *you 'll / might* pass your exam. *Will / Might* they tell you your grade right away?

5   It's certain that robots *will / may* become a part of all our lives. Who knows—a robot *will / may* even become president!

6   I know that *you 'll / might* really like Michael. You *'ll / might* meet him this weekend, although I'm not sure because his father's not well at the moment.

3   Complete the predictions with *will* or *won't* and the verbs in the box.

| buy   choose   come   become   exist   use |
| go shopping   increase   live   understand |

What will the world be like in 2050?

1   The world's population _____ to more than nine billion people.

2   Scientists _____ more about diseases and people _____ longer.

3   Parents _____ the sex of their baby.

4   We _____ oil and gas for electricity. Most of our energy _____ from solar power.

5   Some islands _____ anymore as sea levels rise. Some animals _____ extinct.

6   People _____ downtown. Instead, they _____ everything online.

◀ Go back to page 31

4C *be going to* and present continuous

We use *be going to* + the base form to talk about future plans.

What are you going to do tonight?
I'm going to watch a movie on TV.

▶ 4.7	I	he / she / it	you / we / they
+	I'm **going to look** for a new job.	The company**'s going to move** to a new office.	We**'re going to design** a new product.
−	I**'m not going to take** the bus tomorrow morning.	Hans **isn't going to buy** a new car.	My friends **aren't going to visit** me next year.
?	**Am** I **going to work** harder next year?	**Is** she **going to study** politics next year?	**Are** they **going to cook** dinner tonight?
Y/N	Yes, I **am**. / No, I**'m not**.	Yes, she **is**. / No, she **isn't**.	Yes, they **are**. / No, they **aren't**.

> **Look!** When the main verb is *go*, we usually omit *to go*.
> *Are you going (to go) swimming tonight?*
> *Maria is going (to go) abroad next year.*

When we talk about arrangements with a fixed place and time, we often use the present continuous.

What are you doing tonight?
I'm meeting Charlie and Susie downtown.

But it is also correct to use *be going to*.

What are you going to do tonight?
I'm going to meet Charlie and Susie downtown.

Future time expressions

We often use future time expressions with *be going to* and the present continuous. The time expressions usually come at the beginning or at the end of a sentence.

Sandra is going to help us next week.
Next week, Sandra is going to help us.

▶ 4.8	
next + week/month/year, etc.	We're going to buy a new house **next year**.
In ... two days'/five years' **time**	**In three weeks' time**, we're meeting with our colleagues from Colombia.
tonight	What are you doing **tonight**?
tomorrow	I'm not going to do anything exciting **tomorrow**.
the day after tomorrow	Peter is going to give a presentation at the conference **the day after tomorrow**.

1 Write sentences using *be going to*.

1 he / buy / some tickets for the soccer game
_____

2 the actor / make / a new TV series / next year
_____

3 they / go / to Spain / on vacation this year?
_____

4 she / not use / an architect
_____

5 where / you / sit?
_____

6 he / ask / his manager about the problem
_____

7 I / go / to the gym tonight
_____

8 you / drive or take the bus?
_____

2 Look at Kelly's day planner. Make sentences using the present continuous.

9:00 a.m.	new manager (Josie) starts
10:00 a.m.	introduce Josie to the team
~~11:00 a.m.~~	~~visit the factory~~
1:00 p.m.	have lunch with Andy
2:00 p.m.	pick up new sofa!
~~6:30 p.m.~~	~~go to yoga class~~ canceled

1 Kelly's new manager, Josie, _____ at 9:00.
2 At 10:00, Kelly _____ .
3 Is she _____ at 11:00? No, she isn't.
4 At 1:00, Kelly and Andy _____ together.
5 At 2:00, she _____ a new sofa.
6 She _____ her yoga class tonight. It was canceled.

3 Choose the correct options to complete the sentences.

1 Hi, Bob. What ____ on June 18th next year?
   a you are going to do   b are you doing
   c do you do

2 It's Mom's 70th birthday and we ____ a big party. You're invited!
   a 're having   b have   c 're going

3 The whole family ____ there, and lots of Mom's friends.
   a is being   b is doing   c is going to be

4 I'm sure everyone ____ a good time.
   a has   b is having   c is going to have

5 We want it to be a secret, so we ____ Mom.
   a are telling   b don't tell   c aren't going to tell

6 I ____ a big birthday cake for the party. Do you know a good pastry shop?
   a 'm going to order   b order   c 'm order

◀ Go back to page 34

5A *should/shouldn't*

We use *should* and *shouldn't* + the base form to ask for and give advice and recommendations.

Where should I go on vacation?
You should stay in this country.
You shouldn't go abroad. It's too expensive.

▶ 5.2	I / you / he / she / it / we / they
+	You **should see** a doctor.
–	Rachel **shouldn't drink** so much coffee.
?	**Should** I **buy** some new shoes?
Y/N	Yes, you **should**. / No, you **shouldn't**.

We often use *I think* and *I don't think* with *should* to show our opinion.

What do you think I should do?
I think you should stay in bed.
I don't think you should go out. NOT ~~I think you shouldn't go out.~~

Other ways of giving advice or recommendations

When we want to give strong advice (or warnings) we use the imperative.
Whatever you do, don't go outside. It's freezing!

For recommendations, we use *why don't you ...?* or *you could* + the base form.
Why don't you put a coat and hat on? It's cold outside.
You could stay inside, where it's nice and warm.

1 Complete the sentences with *should* or *shouldn't* and the verbs in parentheses.

1 He looks really tired. I think he _____ to bed. (go)
2 There's a great new restaurant in town. You _____ it. (try)
3 You _____ so fast. You'll get a stomachache. (not eat)
4 It's Andy's birthday. Do you think we _____ him a present? (buy)
5 She wants to get in shape. She _____ a gym. (join)
6 We _____ so much salt on our food. It's not good for our health. (not put)
7 There's a lot of traffic. I don't think you _____ so fast. (drive)
8 They _____ to him like that. It's rude. (not talk)

2 Complete the sentences with the correct form of *should* and the verbs in the box.

buy get get up lose spend study talk walk

1 A I'm always late for work.
  B You _____ earlier.
2 A I don't have much money right now.
  B I don't think you _____ those shoes, then.
3 A These pants don't fit me anymore.
  B Do you think you _____ some weight?
4 A I want to improve my English.
  B You _____ the summer in Canada.
5 A My brother wants to be an engineer.
  B He _____ math and physics in college.
6 A I'm stressed at work lately.
  B You _____ to your boss.
7 A You _____ home alone at night.
  B OK, I'll get a taxi.
8 A Do you think I _____ more exercise?
  B Yes, definitely.

3 Put the words in the correct order to make sentences.

1 what / I / don't / do / I / should / know
  _____

2 before / the / should / we / leave / house / 9:00
  _____

3 take / the / taxi / to / don't / a / airport
  _____

4 you / don't / homework / now / why / do / your?
  _____

5 job / for / Larry / another / look / could
  _____

◀ Go back to page 41

5C First conditional

We use the first conditional to talk about the result of a possible future action.

If you help me with my homework, I'll buy you coffee.

There are two parts to a first conditional sentence: an *if* clause to describe the possible future action, and the main clause to describe the result.

If it rains tomorrow, I'll take a taxi to the meeting.

    if clause   main clause

We can put either clause first with no change in meaning. However, if we put the main clause first, we don't use a comma between the two clauses.

If I get sick on vacation, I'll feel miserable.
I'll feel miserable if I get sick on vacation.

We form the *if* clause with *if* + simple present, and we form the main clause with *will* + the base form.

▶ 5.11	*if* clause	main clause
+	**If** I **pass** my driving test,	I**'ll buy** a car.
–	**If** they **don't invite** me to the wedding,	I **won't buy** them a present.
?	**If** you **take** the medicine,	**will** you **feel** better?
Y/N	Yes, I **will**. / No, I **won't**.	

We can also use *may* or *might* + the base form in the main clause to describe results that we are not sure about.

If I get the new job in Shanghai, I might move house.
She may come to the party if she finishes work early.

We use *can* + the base form or *will be able to* + the base form in the main clause to say that a result will be possible.

If I fix my bike, I can ride it to work.
He won't be able to bake a cake if he doesn't buy some eggs.

> **Look!** We can also use the imperative in the main clause to give people instructions for possible situations.
> *Please tell Carla about the new class if you see her tonight.*
> *If you use this computer, don't press this button!*

1 Choose the correct words to complete the sentences.

1 If she *passes / 'll pass* all her exams, her dad *is / will be* really proud.
2 If we *don't / won't* hurry up, we *miss / 'll miss* the bus.
3 I *am / 'll be* surprised if his plane *lands / will land* on time tonight.
4 If he *calls / will call*, *don't / won't* answer the phone.
5 I *tell / 'll tell* you a secret if you *promise / 'll promise* not to tell anyone.
6 She *is / 'll be* really disappointed if you *don't / won't* go to her party.
7 What *do / will* you say if he *asks / 'll ask* you to marry him?
8 If I *get / 'll get* lonely, *do / will* you give me a call?
9 He *'s / 'll be* really embarrassed if *he's / he'll be* late to his own wedding.
10 We *don't / may not* have time for lunch if the meeting *doesn't / won't* finish soon.
11 *Remind / Will remind* me if I *forget / 'll forget* to call the builder.
12 If you *don't / won't* leave now, I *call / 'll call* the police.

2 Write first conditional sentences.

1 I / write to you / if / I / have time
    _____

2 if / you / see him / you / give him this message, please?
    _____

3 she / not get her money back / if / she / lose the receipt
    _____

4 if / he / not get the job / he / be really miserable
    _____

5 if / you / not fix your car soon / the police / stop you
    _____

6 my mom / not forgive me / if / I / not remember her birthday
    _____

7 if / my phone/ ring / not answer it!
    _____

8 if / she / move to Italy / you / visit her?
    _____

9 if / you / go for a walk / it / help you to feel better
    _____

10 if / he / not get too nervous / he / do well on the exam
    _____

11 they / be late / if / they / not leave soon
    _____

12 if / I / stand here / you / take a photo of me?
    _____

6A Present perfect with *ever* and *never*

We use the present perfect to talk about experiences in our lives.

I've read Don Quixote.
He hasn't been to the U.S.
Have they done yoga?

We often use *ever* with questions and *never* instead of the negative to emphasize that we are talking about our lifetime.

Have you ever flown in a helicopter?
I've never eaten a hamburger!

We form the present perfect with the verb *have* and the past participle of the main verb.

▶ 6.3	I / you / we / they	he / she / it
+	I've **written** a novel.	Michelle **has been** to China.
-	They **haven't gone swimming** in the river.	Claude **hasn't seen** my new car.
?	**Have** you **tried** this new drink?	**Has** he **worked** as a chef?
Y/N	Yes, I **have**. / No, I **haven't**.	Yes, he **has**. / No, he **hasn't**.

In regular verbs, the past participle is the same as the simple past form.

I cooked pasta yesterday.
He played tennis with her last week.

I've never cooked dinner for her.
Have you ever played the saxophone?

In some irregular verbs, the past participle is different from the simple past form. For a full list of irregular verbs, see page 175.

I ate toast for breakfast this morning.
I saw Roberta at Ruth's party.

Have you ever eaten Chinese food?
I haven't seen that TV series.

Present perfect or simple past

We use the present perfect to talk about an experience in our lives and we use the simple past to talk about when a specific event happened.

I've met a movie star.
I met George Clooney in Mexico two years ago.

We often start a conversation with the present perfect. When we ask for more information, or give details, we use the simple past.

Have you ever been to Australia?
Yes, I have. I went there in 2014.
Who did you go with?
I went with my friend, Ella.

---

1 Complete the chart with the correct forms of the verbs.

	Base form	Simple past	Past participle
1	be		been
2	break	broke	
3		cried	cried
4		ate	eaten
5	drive	drove	
6	live		lived
7		sang	sung
8	speak	spoke	
9	stop		stopped
10	walk	walked	

2 Write sentences and questions in the present perfect.

1 you / ever / be / to New Zealand?
_____

2 I / never / eat / hamburgers
_____

3 she / walk / along the Great Wall of China
_____

4 my uncle / not give up / smoking
_____

5 you / ever / watch / the sun rise?
_____

6 we / never / play / rugby
_____

7 he / ever / ask / his boss for a pay raise?
_____

8 my sister / try / to learn English
_____

3 Choose the correct form (present perfect or simple past) to complete the conversation.

Rachel [1]*Have you ever learned / Did you ever learn* another language?

Sarah Yes, [2]*I have taught / I taught* myself Spanish about ten years ago.

Rachel So, [3]*have you ever been / did you ever go* to Spain?

Sarah No, but [4]*I've been / I went* to South America.

Rachel Really? When [5]*have you been / did you go* there?

Sarah Six years ago. [6]*I've been / I went* with John. It was our honeymoon.

Rachel That's great! [7]*Have you traveled / Did you travel* around a lot when you were there?

Sarah Yes, [8]*we've visited / we visited* Chile, Argentina, and Brazil. It was amazing!

◀ Go back to page 49

6C Second conditional

We use the second conditional to talk about impossible or very unlikely situations.

If I went climbing in the mountains, I'd take a first-aid kit. (but it's not likely that I'll go climbing in the mountains).

There are two parts to a second conditional sentence: an *if* clause to describe the situation and the main clause to describe the result.

If she had more money, she'd buy a new car.

    if clause   main clause

We can put either clause first with no change in meaning. However, if we put the main clause first, we don't use a comma between the two clauses.

If he spoke German, he would apply for the job.
He would apply for the job if he spoke German.

We form the *if* clause with *if* + simple past, and we form the main clause with *would* + the base form.

> **Look!** We often use *were* instead of *was* in the *if* clause with *I/he/she/it*.
> *If he were a little taller, the pants would fit him.*
> *I'd take a taxi if I were you.*

▶ 6.10	*if* clause	main clause
+	If I **knew** the answer,	I'**d tell** you.
−	If you **weren't** so impatient,	you **wouldn't have** this problem.
?	If it **were** cheaper,	**would** you **buy** it?
Y/N	Yes, I **would**. / No, I **wouldn't**.	

We use *could* + the base form or *would be able to* + the base form in the main clause to say that a result would be possible.

If Alex didn't have so much work, he could go to the party.
Sara would be able to help us if she were here.

Second conditional or first conditional

We can sometimes use either the first conditional or the second conditional, but it depends on if we think a situation is a real possibility, or if we think it's very unlikely/impossible.

If I get the job, I'll be really happy. = a real possibility
If I got the job, I'd be really happy. = very unlikely
I'll meet you later if I don't have to work late. = a real possibility
I'd meet you later if I didn't have to work late. = impossible

1. Match the two parts to make second conditional sentences.

   1 If you had a daughter,   _____
   2 I would speak perfect English   _____
   3 Your computer wouldn't do strange things   _____
   4 If you told people about your website,   _____
   5 What would you do today   _____
   6 If I wrote a book,   _____

   a it would be much more popular.
   b it would be about my childhood.
   c if you weren't at work?
   d if I came from the U.S.
   e what would you name her?
   f if it didn't have a virus.

2. Choose the correct form of the verbs to complete the conversation.

   A What [1]*did / would* you do if your company [2]*offered / would offer* you a job in Japan?
   B If that happened, I [3]*thought / 'd think* about it. If they [4]*paid / would pay* me more money, I [5]*'ll / 'd* probably go.
   A But [6]*wouldn't / didn't* you miss your family and friends if you went abroad?
   B Yes, but they [7]*can / could* visit me if I was in Japan. It [8]*were / would be* a great opportunity if I went.
   A I [9]*wouldn't / didn't go* ... not even if they [10]*doubled / would double* my salary!

3. Complete the sentences with the verbs in parentheses so they are true for you. Use the second conditional if the situation is less likely. Use the first conditional if the situation is possible.

   1 If it _____ (snow) this afternoon,
   _____ .

   2 If I _____ (pass) my English exam,
   _____ .

   3 If I _____ (see) my parents this evening,
   _____ .

   4 If my computer _____ (stop) working,
   _____ .

   5 If a reporter _____ (ask) me to appear on TV today,
   _____ .

   6 If I _____ (go) out with my friends after class,
   _____ .

◀ Go back to page 53

7A Present perfect with *yet* and *already*

We often use the present perfect with *yet* and *already*.

Have you been to the new café yet?
Yes, I've already been there.
No, I haven't been there yet.

We use *yet* in negative sentences and questions to talk about something that we expected to happen before now. *Yet* comes at the end of the sentence or question.

Have you written the report yet?
I haven't finished it yet.

We use *already* to talk about something that happened before now or earlier than we expected. *Already* comes before the main verb.

Do you want to go out for lunch?
No, thanks. I've already eaten.

We sometimes use *already* in questions instead of *yet*. *Already* comes between the auxiliary verb and the main verb or at the end of the question. *Already* is usually stressed to show surprise.

Have you already finished your science project?

We form the present perfect with the verb *have* and the past participle of the main verb. For a full list of irregular verbs, See page 175.

▶ 7.2	I / you / we / they	he / she / it
+	We**'ve already heard** the news.	The bus **has already left** the station.
-	They **haven't found** the keys **yet**.	He **hasn't paid** the bill **yet**.
?	**Have** you **been** to the mall **yet**?	**Has** she **spoken** to the police **yet**?
Y/N	Yes, I **have**. / No, I **haven't**. / **Not yet**.	Yes, she **has**. / No, she **hasn't**. / **Not yet**.

Look! In American English we can also use *yet* and *already* with the simple past:
We already gave him the papers.
The supermarket didn't open yet.
Did Helen already call you?

1 Complete the conversation with the words in the box.

> already   yet

A Watching TV again? What about your homework?
B I've ¹_____ done it.
A When did you do it?
B On the bus from school ... so now I'm watching the game.
A The game? Has it started ²_____?
B Yes! It just started, so you haven't missed anything ³_____.
A Great! Let me sit down. I want to watch this, too!

2 Choose the correct words to complete the sentences.

1 A I have to clean the kitchen tonight.
   B Don't worry. I've *yet / already* cleaned it this week.
2 A Has Flora passed her driving test *yet / already*?
   B Yes, and she only took five lessons!
3 A Can I speak to Julia, please?
   B She was here a minute ago, but I think she's *yet / already* left the office.
4 Teresa hasn't booked her flight *yet / already*. It will be very expensive!
5 A Should we watch *Titanic* tonight?
   B Do we have to? I've *yet / already* seen it about twenty times!
6 Have you used the new bike lane *yet / already*? It's much safer.
7 A I think we need to fill up the tank with gas.
   B It's OK. I've *yet / already* been to the gas station today.
8 He only joined the company a year ago, and they've *just / yet / already* promoted him twice!

3 Make sentences using *yet,* or *already*.

1 she / not pack / her suitcase (yet)
   _____

2 I / send you / a wedding invitation (already)
   _____

3 the game / start (already)
   _____

4 you / speak / to Charles? (yet)
   _____

5 I / can't buy / a new apartment (yet)
   _____

6 I / have / three cups of coffee today (already)
   _____

124

◀ Go back to page 59

7C Present perfect with *for* and *since*

We use the present perfect with *for* and *since* to talk about a situation that started in the past and is still true now.

How long have you lived in Brazil? NOT ~~How long are you living in Brazil?~~
I've lived here all my life. NOT ~~I'm living here all my life.~~

We use *since* to refer to a fixed point in time in the past when the situation started.

I've worked for this company since 2010.
I haven't spoken to Fred since last summer.
Have you known Mark since you were a child?

We use *for* to refer to the period of time the situation has been true.

Joseph has been a teacher for two months.
This computer hasn't worked for years!
Has the building been here for a long time?

We use *How long ...?* to ask about the length of time a situation has been true.

How long have you known your boyfriend?
We've known each other since last March.
How long has he been a doctor?
He's been a doctor for about two years.

We form the present perfect with the verb *have* and the past participle of the main verb. For a complete list of irregular verbs, see page 175.

▶ 7.12	I / you / we / they	he / she / it
+	I**'ve lived** in this part of the city **for** two years. They**'ve worked** together **since** 1990.	Sam**'s had** this car **for** over 20 years. It**'s been** much hotter **since** last weekend.
-	We **haven't spoken** to each other **for** a year. I **haven't gone** swimming in the ocean **since** I was a child.	Isabella **hasn't worn** her glasses **for** a long time. He **hasn't driven** a car **since** he had the accident.
?	**How long have** you **known** her?	**How long has** he **been** a teacher?

Present perfect or simple past

We use the simple past to talk about completed actions in the past. We can often give the same information in two different ways.

a period of time / an unfinished action	a point in the past / a completed action
I've lived in Uruguay for ten years.	I moved to Uruguay ten years ago.
Jo has known me since I was 16 years old.	Jo met me when I was 16 years old.
How long have you worked here?	When did you start working here?
I haven't eaten meat since 2010.	I gave up meat in 2010.

We use the simple past to talk about a time period that started and finished in the past.

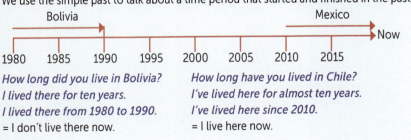

How long did you live in Bolivia?
I lived there for ten years.
I lived there from 1980 to 1990.
= I don't live there now.

How long have you lived in Chile?
I've lived here for almost ten years.
I've lived here since 2010.
= I live here now.

1 Put the times in the box in the correct column: *for* or *since*.

> 1997   9:30 a.m.   a couple of hours   a few seconds
> a long time   ages   April   five months
> he was a child   I finished college   last night
> most of my life   my accident   seventeen years
> several weeks   the middle of June   the weekend
> three centuries   Thursday

for	since

2 Write sentences using the present perfect form of the verbs in parentheses. Write one sentence with *for* and one with *since*.

1 I moved to Istanbul in the middle of July. It's the middle of December now. (live)
I've lived in Istanbul for five months.
I've lived in Istanbul since the middle of July.

2 I bought my own car when I was 19. I'm 23 now. (have)
_____
_____

3 The last time I was on an airplane was in August. That was six months ago. (not be)
_____
_____

4 I met my best friend when I was five. I'm 22 now. (know)
_____
_____

5 I gave up English in 2005. That was ages ago. (not study)
_____
_____

3 Choose the correct form of the verbs to complete the sentences.

1 He *didn't speak / hasn't spoken* to his mom since he *got back / 's gotten back* from his vacation.

2 I *bought / 've bought* this car in 2007, so I *'m having / 've had* it for more than ten years now.

3 I'm a sales manager and I *worked / 've worked* in this department for two years. Before that, I *worked / 've worked* in marketing from 2012 to 2015.

4 We *knew / 've known* each other for about ten years, in fact, since we *met / 've met* in college.

5 I *was / 've been* worried about Frank since he *lost / 's lost* his job.

6 He *lost / 's lost* his phone this morning, so I *'m not speaking / haven't spoken* to him for a few hours now.

7 I *lived / 've lived* in Chicago for two years, but then I *moved / 've moved* to Washington D.C., and I *lived / 've lived* here since then.

8 Their wedding *was / has been* in May, so they *are / 've been* married for nearly six months now.

◀ Go back to page 62

8A too, too many, too much, and (not) enough

We use *too, too many,* and *too much* to mean "more than necessary" or "more than is good."

This exam is too difficult. There are too many questions!

We use *too* before adjectives and adverbs.

That restaurant is too expensive.
She works too hard.

We use *too many* before countable nouns.

I drink too many cups of coffee.

We use *too much* before uncountable nouns.

I eat too much chocolate.

We can also use *too much* after a verb without an object.

He worries too much.

We use *enough* to mean "the right amount" or "sufficient." We can also use *not enough* to mean "less than necessary" or "less than is good."

Is your coffee sweet enough? I didn't have enough sugar for everyone.

Enough comes before countable and uncountable nouns.

He doesn't eat enough vegetables.
Have we got enough time?

Enough comes after an adjective or adverb.

The information isn't clear enough.
He didn't sing well enough to win the competition.

We can also use *enough* after a verb without an object.

I didn't sleep enough last night.

▶ 8.2	too / too many / too much	(not) enough
Countable nouns	You shouldn't watch **too many movies**.	We have **enough eggs** to bake two cakes.
Uncountable nouns	Jen drinks **too much coffee** in the morning.	Do you have **enough money** to buy those shoes?
Adjectives	The train is **too crowded** at rush hour.	The soup is**n't hot enough**.

1 Choose the correct words to complete the sentences.

1 She eats *too much / too many* candy.
2 They don't eat *enough vegetables / vegetables enough*.
3 Our apartment is *too much / too* small for a party.
4 He puts *too much / too many* sugar in his coffee.
5 Are you sure you're *well enough / enough well* to run a marathon?
6 You eat *too much / too many* junk food.
7 I don't have *enough money / money enough* to buy a new car.
8 These jeans are *too much / too* big for me now that I've lost weight.

2 Complete the sentences using *too, too many, too much,* and *enough.*

1 You eat _____ takeout meals. Don't you ever cook?
2 Don't cook the broccoli for _____ long.
3 My English isn't good _____ to have a conversation.
4 You drink _____ coffee. It isn't good for you.
5 I don't earn _____ money to buy a house.
6 I'm _____ tired to go out tonight.
7 My son spends _____ time playing computer games.
8 I have a stomachache. I ate _____ cupcakes.

3 Rewrite the sentences using the words in parentheses.

1 You should get more exercise. (enough)
You don't get enough exercise.
2 You eat more sugar than you should. (much)
_____
3 She's too young to drive. (old)
_____
4 It isn't quiet enough to work. (noisy)
_____
5 We need more gasoline. (enough)
_____
6 There are more cars on the road than there should be. (too)
_____

◀ Go back to page 67

8C *have to, not have to,* and *can't*

We use *have to* to talk about obligations and rules.

You always have to lock the door when you leave.
Amy has to wear formal clothes to work.

When we ask questions about obligations and rules, we usually use *have to*.

Do you have to start work early?
Why do we have to park the car here?

We use *don't have to* to say that something isn't necessary.

You don't have to speak English for this job, but it's useful.
Kasim doesn't have to work today. It's a holiday in Hong Kong.

We use *can't* to talk about things that are not allowed. We call this prohibition.

I can't eat any potato chips. I'm on a diet.
You can't start the exam until I say.

▶ 8.9	I / you / we / they	he / she / it
have to	I **have to work** late again tonight, unfortunately. Do you **have to take** the bus today? Yes, I **do**. / No, I **don't**.	Jackie **has to study** math in school. Does he **have to wait** a long time? Yes, he **does**. / No, he **doesn't**.
not have to	You **don't have to pay**–it's free!	He **doesn't have to wear** a uniform to school.
can't	I **can't be** late for the meeting.	Luke **can't eat** too much salt.

Look! Remember, *can't* and *don't have to* have different meanings.
You can't walk on the grass. = It's not allowed.
You don't have to walk on the grass—you can walk on the path. = it's not necessary. You can choose.

1 Make sentences using the positive (+), negative (–), or question form (?) of *have to*.

  1 What time / you / arrive / at the airport (?)

    _____

  2 My sister / study / English / in school (+)

    _____

  3 You / show / your passport / to enter the country (–)

    _____

  4 Lenny / cook / dinner / tonight (?)

    _____

  5 We / finish / the project / until next week (–)

    _____

  6 You / drive / on the left / in the U.K. (+)

    _____

2 Choose the correct words to complete the conversation.

  A What's wrong, David?
  B My brother [1]*can't / has to* go to the hospital tomorrow.
  A Oh no! Why does he [2]*can't / have to* go?
  B It's nothing serious. He [3]*has to / can't* have a blood test.
  A Does he [4]*have to / has to* spend the night there?
  B No, he [5]*hasn't / doesn't*. The worst thing is he [6]*doesn't have to / can't* eat anything for 24 hours.
  A I [7]*don't have to / can't* work tomorrow. I can give him a ride to the hospital, if you want.
  B Thanks, Ada. That's great. He [8]*has to / can't* be there at 10:00 a.m.
  A That's fine.
  B Great, he'll be happy he [9]*can't / doesn't have to* take the bus ... especially without any breakfast!

3 Look at the poster. Complete the rules for the swimming pool with the verbs in parentheses.

Downtown **Swimming Pool**

Adults: $3.00
Children: Free

  1 Adults _____ (pay) to use the pool.
  2 Children _____ (pay) to go swimming.
  3 You _____ (eat) by the pool.
  4 You _____ (take) a shower before you swim.
  5 You _____ (run) near the pool.

◀ Go back to page 71

9A *used to*

We use *used to* + the base form to talk about habits or situations that were true in the past, but aren't true now.

I used to ride my bike to school every day. = I don't ride my bike to school now.
I used to live in a small town. = I don't live there now.

We form the negative with *didn't* + *use to* + the base form.

I didn't use to drink so much coffee. (= I drink a lot now).
She didn't use to like spicy food. (= She likes it a lot now).

We form questions with *did* + *use to* + the base form.

Did you use to play on the school basketball team?
Why did you use to have two cars?

We can use the simple past instead of *used to*. The meaning is the same.

I used to have English classes at school = I had English classes at school.
She used to be shy when she was younger = She was shy when she was younger.

We don't use *used to* to talk about actions that only happened once.

I bought this shirt last year. NOT ~~I used to buy this shirt last year.~~
They started work at 9:00 this morning. NOT ~~They used to start work at 9:00 this morning.~~

▶ 9.1	I / you / he / she / it / we / they
+	I **used to like** reggae music when I was younger.
−	He **didn't use to be** as rich as he is now.
?	**Did** you **use to go** to the beach every day when you lived in Acapulco?
Y/N	Yes, I **did**. / No, I **didn't**.

Look! *Used to* only refers to the past. We use *usually* + simple present to talk about habits and situations that are true now.
Harry usually takes the bus to work.
He's not usually late for class.
How do you usually contact your family?

---

1 Read the text. Write sentences with *used to* or *didn't use to* and the verbs in parentheses.

He used to be rich!
George Kaltsidis lives in a small house in the north of England. He drives an old Ford Fiesta and wears a secondhand watch. However, believe it or not, George used to be a millionaire and lived a life of luxury. He wasn't happy, and last year he gave all his money away to charity. He's much happier now, he says. But what did his life use to be like?

1 He (live) in a small house. He (live) in an expensive apartment.
   He didn't use to live in a small house. He used to live in an expensive apartment.

2 He (drive) an old car. He (have) a new BMW.
   _____

3 He (be) very lonely because he (see) his family or friends very much.
   _____

4 He (wear) expensive clothes and he never (buy) secondhand things.
   _____

5 He (go) on luxury vacations, but he (enjoy) himself.
   _____

2 Complete the sentences with the positive, negative, or question form of *used to* and the verbs in the box.

have (x2)   play   work   argue   go   like   be

1 They _____ a house in Spain, but they sold it last year.
2 _____ you _____ a lot of sports when you were younger?
3 I _____ to the gym, but now I usually go three times a week.
4 _____ you _____ with your parents a lot?
5 Where _____ you _____ before you got this job?
6 She _____ long hair, but now she prefers it short.
7 I _____ fish, but I love it now.
8 There _____ a park here before they built those office buildings.

3 Complete the sentences with *used to* or the simple past form of the verbs in parentheses if *used to* is not possible.

1 Did you _____ a school uniform? (wear)
2 I _____ my arm when I was eight. I was ten. (not break)
3 I _____ badly behaved in school. (be)
4 My parents _____ a lot of money. (not earn)
5 I _____ a $50 bill on the sidewalk one day. (find)
6 My grandma _____ listening to the radio. (love)
7 I _____ a lot of computer games when I was a teenager. (play)
8 The first movie I _____ at a theater was *Titanic*. (see)

◀ Go back to page 77

9C The passive

Sentences can be either active or passive.

Active: *My brother wrote this book.*
Passive: *This book was written by my brother.*

We use the active sentence to focus on the person who does the action.

My brother wrote this book.

We use the passive sentence to focus on the action itself or on the thing the action affects.

This book was written by my brother.

We also use the passive when we don't know who does/did the action or it isn't important.

These coffeemakers are made in Italy.
My wallet was stolen yesterday.

We form the simple present passive with *am/is/are* + past participle of the main verb.
We form the simple past passive with *was/were* + past participle of the main verb.

Simple present passive: *Toyota cars are built in Japan.*
Simple past passive: *The buildings were destroyed five years ago.*

To say who does/did the action, we use *by*.

Lots of hotel towels are taken by tourists as souvenirs.
This building was designed in 1985, by a Chinese architect.

To form questions, we put the verb *be* before the subject.

Is your watch made of gold?
When was the book written?
Who was the music sung by?

▶ 9.12	Simple present passive	Simple past passive
+	The soccer games **are played** in the evening.	The movie **was directed** by Steven Spielberg.
−	The painting **isn't signed** by the artist.	Chess **wasn't invented** in Europe.
?	**Are** these cookies **made** with butter?	**Were** the workers **paid** last month?
Y/N	**Yes**, they **are. / No**, they **aren't.**	**Yes**, they **were. / No**, they **weren't.**

1 Write sentences in the simple present or past passive.

1 English / speak / here (simple present)
   English is spoken here.
2 This guitar / play / by Jimi Hendrix (simple past)
   _____
3 The soup / make / with fresh vegetables (simple present)
   _____
4 When / the photos / take? (simple past)
   _____
5 Who / the movie / direct / by? (simple past)
   _____
6 Credit cards / not accept / here (simple present)
   _____

2 Rewrite the sentences in the passive.

1 More than 162 million people use eBay.
   eBay _____ .
2 The Channel Tunnel connects Britain and France.
   Britain and France _____ .
3 Facebook bought WhatsApp for $22 billion.
   WhatsApp _____ .
4 Steven Spielberg didn't direct *Jurassic World*.
   Jurassic World _____ .
5 They make sushi with rice and raw fish.
   Sushi _____ .
6 Did Tolstoy write *War and Peace*?
   Was _____ .

3 Complete the text with the active or passive form of the verbs in parentheses.

HIDDEN TREASURE

Treasure Detectives is a British TV show and it [1]____ (watch) by more than 300,000 viewers. Each week, two different objects [2]____ (examine) very carefully by experts to find out if they are valuable treasures or copies of original works.

Robert Darvell [3]____ (contact) the show and [4]____ (ask) them to help him find out more about a painting he had. Robert's father [5]____ (buy) a box of objects, which included a small painting, for £30 at an auction in 2003. The painting [6]____ (keep) in a drawer for many years and eventually it [7]____ (give) to Robert.

After almost a year, Robert [8]____ (tell) the truth about the painting on live TV. The experts [9]____ (say) it was by the English artist, John Constable, and it was worth about £250,000! He was surprised, but very happy.

◀ Go back to page 80

10A Past perfect

We use the past perfect to describe an action that happened before another action in the past.

I arrived at the meeting late because I'd missed the train.
Justine hadn't studied for the exam, so she failed it.
Had you met Sergio before you started the job?

We form the past perfect with *had* + the past participle of the main verb.

▶ 10.5	Past perfect
+	He'**d forgotten** his wallet, so he couldn't buy anything.
–	We **hadn't tried** *ceviche* before we visited Peru.
?	**Had** you **trained** a lot before you ran the marathon?
Y/N	Yes, I **had**. / No, I **hadn't**.

Look! The contracted form of the past perfect is the same as the contracted form of *would*.
I'd seen him before. = I had seen him before.
I'd see him if I could. = I would see him if I could.

Narrative tenses

We usually use the past perfect with the simple past and the past continuous to show when actions happened.

When I got home, my husband cooked the dinner.

When I got home, my husband was cooking dinner.

When I got home, my husband had cooked dinner.

1 Match the two parts to make sentences.

1 Sofia had seen the movie before _____
2 Jeff felt very bad because _____
3 Susana hadn't had lunch, so _____
4 Paul had grown a beard, so _____
5 When I got to the station, _____
6 Anna had finished the report when _____

a I got to work this morning.
b she felt very hungry.
c and she said it wasn't very good.
d the bus had already left.
e I didn't recognize him.
f he'd forgotten his niece's birthday.

2 Complete the conversations with the past perfect form of the verbs in parentheses.

1 A Why did they walk to college today?
  B They _____ (have) a problem with the car.
2 A _____ you _____ (hear) about the problems at the airport before you left?
  B No, I hadn't. Luckily, they _____ (not make) any changes to my flight.
3 A Rita bought me a book for my birthday, but I _____ (read) it before.
  B It's my fault. She bought it because I _____ (recommend) it to her.
4 A Was Grandma pleased that the kids _____ (draw) a picture for her?
  B Yes, she was. They _____ (not do) one for her before.
5 A _____ Ricky _____ (look) everywhere before he canceled his credit card?
  B No, he _____ (not look) in his sports bag. He found it there this morning.

3 Complete the text with the simple past, past continuous, or past perfect form of the verbs in parentheses.

On April 21, 1980, Rosie Ruiz
1 _____ (cross) the finish line of the Boston Marathon with a time of 2:31:56–the fastest female time in Boston Marathon history. However, when she 2 _____ (receive) the winner's medal, some judges 3 _____ (become) suspicious because she 4 _____ (not sweat) very much. Then two students 5 _____ (say) that they 6 _____ (see) her join the race half a mile from the finish line. Later, photographer Susan Morrow said she 7 _____ (meet) Ruiz while she 8 _____ (ride) on the subway in her running clothes at the time of the New York marthon, six months earlier. The judges 9 _____ (discover) that Ruiz 10 _____ (do) the same thing to win the Boston Marathon.

◀ Go back to page 85

10C Reported speech

When someone speaks, we call what they say "direct speech." When we talk about what they said afterward, we call it "reported speech."

"I don't like the website." ⇨ *My boss said that he didn't like the website.*
"We reserved a room." ⇨ *They told me that they had reserved a room.*

We use the verbs *say* and *tell* to report speech. We use *tell* with a noun or a pronoun when we want to say who the person was speaking to. We can add *that* to reported speech sentences.

"I'm sorry." ⇨ *He said (that) he was sorry.*
⇨ *He told me (that) he was sorry.*

The tense of the verb usually changes when we report speech.

Direct speech		Reported speech
simple present	⇨	simple past
present continuous	⇨	past continuous
simple past	⇨	past perfect
present perfect	⇨	past perfect
past perfect	⇨	past perfect
am/is/are going to	⇨	was/were going to
will	⇨	would
can	⇨	could

Look! We also change pronouns and possessive adjectives in reported speech.
"I sold my car to Lenny." ⇨ *He said that he'd sold his car to Lenny.*
"We'll send you the letter." ⇨ *They said they'd send me the letter.*

▶ 10.12	Direct speech		Reported speech
simple present	"I drink too much coffee."	⇨	She told me she drank too much coffee.
present continuous	"We're studying for the exam."	⇨	They said they were studying for the exam.
simple past	"Karl didn't go to the store."	⇨	She said Karl hadn't gone to the store.
present perfect	"I haven't been to Paris."	⇨	He said he hadn't been to Paris.
past perfect	"We'd seen the movie before."	⇨	They said they'd seen the movie before.
going to	"Michelle is going to drive home."	⇨	He said Michelle was going to drive home.
will	"I'll open the letter."	⇨	He told me he'd open the letter.
can	"Ruby can't swim."	⇨	They told him Ruby couldn't swim.

1 Choose the correct words to complete the sentences.

1 My teacher *said / told* me that my English was improving.
2 The doctor *said / told* you had to stay in bed.
3 Victor *said / told* he had made a big mistake.
4 Someone *said / told* us that you had started a blog.
5 They *said / told* everyone they would win the game.
6 The newsreader *said / told* that scientists had discovered a new planet.

2 Rewrite these sentences in reported speech.

1 "I'll see you on Tuesday."
My mom told me _____.
2 "It's not going to rain this week."
The weather forecaster said _____.
3 "I've never eaten curry."
Julieta said _____.
4 "We saw your brother at the airport."
They told me _____.
5 "I hadn't heard the news."
Bobby said _____.
6 "I can't come to your wedding."
Ravi told me _____.
7 "I'm waiting for a phone call."
My boss said _____.
8 "I don't get much exercise."
Sandra said _____.

3 Write the direct speech for the reported sentences.

1 Sheila and Harold said that they wanted to tell me their news.

_____

2 They told me that they'd been on vacation to Egypt.

_____

3 They said they'd been excited because they'd never been there before.

_____

4 Sheila said that she'd never ride a camel again.

_____

5 Harold told me he was going to go back next year.

_____

◀ Go back to page 89

11A -ing and infinitive verb patterns

We often use two verbs together. The form of the second verb changes depending on the first verb.

I want to learn a new language.
I enjoy learning new languages.

After some verbs, we use the infinitive.

▶ 11.2	infinitive
decide	She decided to travel the world.
arrange	We've arranged to meet at the airport.
expect	I expect to have the results next week.
forget	Marcus forgot to buy any paper for the printer.
hope	He hopes to be here soon.
agree	They haven't agreed to lower the price.
can afford	He can't afford to go on vacation.
manage	The driver managed to stop the train.
learn	I'm learning to speak Italian.
offer	They offered to pay for the meal.
plan	We're planning to open a new office.
try	Patricia's trying to finish the project on time.
want	My sister wants to find a new job.
would like	I'd like to take a break now.
promise	Saul promised to help me with the work.

After other verbs, we use the -ing form.

▶ 11.3	-ing form
imagine	Can you imagine living until you're 150?
feel like	I feel like staying in bed all day.
enjoy	My son enjoys visiting his grandparents.
suggest	They've suggested installing some new software.
spend (time)	I spend a lot of time getting to work.
miss	She misses seeing her friends.
finish	Tony's finished building the wall.
hate	I hate being late.
keep	Jorge keeps making mistakes.
like	He doesn't like cooking dinner.
love	I love playing golf.
can't stand	Ramon can't stand sleeping in a tent.
mind	They don't mind getting up early.
look forward to	I'm looking forward to seeing you at the party.

> **Look!** After some verbs, we can use the infinitive or the -ing form, with no difference in meaning, e.g., *start* and *continue*.
> *It has started to rain.*   *It has started raining.*
> *He continued to study.*   *He continued studying.*

1   Choose the correct form of the verbs to complete the sentences.

1 Have you finished *to clean* / *cleaning* the kitchen?
2 Josh arranged *to meet* / *meeting* Natasha at the theater.
3 She promised *to do* / *doing* her homework.
4 I don't mind *to wait* / *waiting* for you.
5 They agreed *to fix* / *fixing* my dishwasher.
6 You should learn *to use* / *using* the computer.
7 We didn't expect *to see* / *seeing* them again.
8 He spent the whole morning *to sunbathe* / *sunbathing*.
9 Our teacher keeps *to give* / *giving* us lots of homework.
10 She offered *to help* / *helping me* with my English.
11 David suggested *to cancel* / *canceling* the meeting.
12 Don't forget *to bring* / *bringing* warm clothes.

2   Complete the conversation with the correct form of the verbs in parentheses.

Julia   Felipe and I have decided [1]_____ (move) back to Brazil.

Sophie   Really? I thought you liked [2]_____ (live) in France.

Julia   Yes, but we miss [3]_____ (see) our families and we'd like [4]_____ (have) our own house. We could never afford [5]_____ (buy) a place in Paris.

Sophie   When are you planning [6]_____ (leave)?

Julia   Well, we don't want [7]_____ (wait) too long, so we expect [8]_____ (go) some time in the next couple of months. I've already managed [9]_____ (find) a job, and Felipe is hoping [10]_____ (get) one soon.

Sophie   It won't be the same here without you. Do you promise [11]_____ (stay) in touch?

Julia   Yes, of course. And if you and Dan feel like [12]_____ (come) to Brazil on vacation, you'd be very welcome at our home in Rio.

Sophie   That sounds great. Don't forget [13]_____ (give) me your e-mail address before you go.

Julia   Don't worry, I won't. We're trying [14]_____ (plan) a party before we go so that we can say goodbye to everyone. Do you want [15]_____ (come)?

Sophie   I hate [16]_____ (say) goodbye to people, but yes, I'd love to come!

◀ Go back to page 95

11C Articles

We use articles (a, an, or the) before nouns. Sometimes we don't need to use an article.

▶ 11.13	articles
Indefinite article *a/an*	I have **a** pet dog and **a** pet cat.
Definite article *the*	**The** dog is much bigger than **the** cat.
No article	I love animals, especially dogs and cats.

We use the indefinite article *a/an*:

* to talk about a person or thing for the first time.
  I have two children–a boy and a girl.

* to talk about a person's job.
  My sister's an engineer.

* in expressions of frequency or measurement.
  I see him once a week.
  The fish costs $10 a kg.

We use the definite article *the*:

* if we have already mentioned the person or thing, or we know which one is referred to.
  The boy is named Alex, and the girl is named Lucy.

* if there is only one of the thing.
  The sun is setting.
  I'll check on the Internet.

* before some countries, especially if they have two words or are plural.
  I live in the U.S., but my brother lives in the Philippines.

* for specific places in a town.
  I went to the bank / the movie theater / the grocery store.

* for musical instruments.
  She plays the guitar.

* for superlatives.
  He's the fastest runner in the world.

We don't use an article:

* to talk about things in general (plural and uncountable nouns).
  Dogs are my favorite animals.
  Pollution is a big problem today.

* for some places we visit regularly.
  I'm not going to work today.
  He's working at home.
  She had to go to college.

* for meals, days of the week, months, and years.
  On Tuesday, I'm having lunch with Jack.
  August is my favourite month.

1 Complete the sentences with *a/an*, *the*, or – (no article).

1 We usually go to _____ movies once or twice _____ month.
2 I bought _____ new car yesterday, but this morning _____ engine won't start.
3 He's one of five brothers. _____ youngest brother is _____ doctor.
4 She flew from _____ Venezuela to _____ U.S.
5 Are you really scared of _____ spiders?
6 How long have you played _____ piano?
7 Neil Armstrong was _____ first man on _____ moon.
8 I hope you both find _____ happiness together.
9 What did you have for _____ breakfast this morning?
10 We have _____ dinner together three times _____ year.
11 She got _____ home from _____ work and went straight to _____ bed.
12 _____ Friday is _____ busiest day of _____ week for us.

2 Correct the mistakes or check (✔) the sentences if they are already correct.

1 Is she student? ☐
2 I'm staying in bed this morning. ☐
3 Why don't you ask her out for lunch? ☐
4 Excuse me, where is museum? ☐
5 It's beautiful day today. ☐
6 The life is hard sometimes. ☐
7 Our taxi driver was from Mexico. ☐
8 I went to bank this morning. ☐
9 My wife has never liked tomatoes. ☐
10 It's best present I've ever received. ☐

3 Complete the text with *a/an*, *the*, or – (no article).

Hexoskin is [1]_____ Canadian company founded in [2]_____ 2006. It wanted to create [3]_____ clothes that could record [4]_____ information about our bodies. That's why they developed [5]_____ smart shirt that contains lots of sensors. [6]_____ sensors collect data about the wearer's movements, heart rate, and breathing and send it to [7]_____ computer. Ariane Lavigne is [8]_____ Olympic athlete who uses it, and she says [9]_____ technology gives her [10]_____ advantage over other snowboarders.

◀ Go back to page 99

12A Defining relative clauses

We use relative clauses to say which person, thing, or place we are talking about.

He's the actor who was Sherlock Holmes on TV.
It's a machine that bakes bread.
That's the restaurant where I used to work.

We use the relative pronouns *who* or *that* to talk about people.

The man who sits next to me at work was sick today.
I saw the woman that works at the post office in the park.

We use the relative pronouns *that* to talk about things.

There are companies that plan weddings for people.
Louise enjoys movies that make her laugh.

In some cases it is possible to omit *that* entirely.

This is the sweater (that) he gave me for my birthday.

We use *where* to talk about places.

I want to visit the stadium where our team plays soccer.
Jorge works in the hospital where I was born.

▶ 12.2	defining relative clauses
To describe people	He's the teacher **who** taught me English. Did you see the children **that** were singing?
To describe things	That's the dog **that** bit me on the leg. I bought the flowers **(that)** she likes.
To describe places	I'll meet you in the square **where** we met last time.

Look! *Who, that,* and *where* refer to a person, thing, or place that's already been mentioned so we don't need to use another word again.
Snakes are the animals that ~~they~~ kill most people each year.
I'd prefer to see the doctor who ~~she~~ saw me last time.
Ronald went to the movie theater where we saw the Star Wars movie ~~there~~.

1 Complete the sentences with *who, that,* or *where*.

1 She opened the box _____ arrived this morning.
2 This is the nightclub _____ Nicola met her boyfriend.
3 There's a meeting at 2:00 p.m. for all employees _____ work in the sales department.
4 The office _____ she spends most of her time is in Kuala Lumpur.
5 The person _____ started this company is now a millionaire.
6 My father-in-law doesn't like movies _____ are too violent.

2 Add the correct words: *who, that,* or *where*. Then match the two parts to make sentences.

1 An umbrella is something ____*that*____ ___f___
2 A DJ is someone _____ ____
3 A hospital is a place _____ ____
4 A credit card is something _____ ____
5 An enemy is a person _____ ____
6 A passport is a document _____ ____
7 A department store is somewhere _____ ____
8 A selfie stick is something _____ ____
9 A single parent is someone _____ ____
10 A prison is a place _____ ____

a you go when you're sick.
b you use when you travel abroad.
c you use to take a photo of yourself.
d brings up a child without a partner.
e criminals are sent.
f ~~you use when it rains.~~
g plays music in a club or on the radio.
h you can buy lots of different things.
i someone hates.
j you use instead of cash to buy things.

3 Combine the pairs of sentences using *who, where, that,* or no relative pronoun. Remember not to use words that aren't necessary.

1 That's the restaurant. We're going there tonight.
   That's the restaurant where we're going tonight.
2 I know the man. He lives in that house.
   _____
3 Did you enjoy the movie? You watched it last night.
   _____
4 They're the neighbors. They have lots of parties.
   _____
5 We've reserved a room in the hotel. We stayed there last summer.
   _____
6 My sister-in-law works for a company. It develops apps.
   _____

◀ Go back to page 103

12C Uses of the *-ing* form and the infinitive

We use the *-ing* form after prepositions. In the negative, *not* goes before the *-ing* form.

Thanks for inviting me to your wedding.
I'm bored with not going out.
He's worried about failing his exam.

We also use the *-ing* form as the subject or object of a sentence. The *-ing* form functions as a noun.

Keeping in touch is so easy these days.
Reading is a great way to improve your English.
Not drinking soft drinks has helped me to lose weight.
John doesn't enjoy reading.
I love dancing.

We use the infinitive after adjectives. In the negative, *not* goes before the *to*.

I'm amazed to hear that they're going out with each other.
She was disappointed to lose the tennis match.
It's impossible not to laugh when you watch this movie.

We also use the infinitive to say why we do something (to express the purpose).

I went shopping to buy a new pair of shoes.
She left the office to meet a friend.
They're saving all of their money to get married.

> **Look!** We use *for + -ing* form to explain the function of things, but we use the infinitive to explain the purpose of actions.
> **Function:** *This button is for turning up the volume.*
> **Purpose:** *You press this button to turn up the volume.*

▶ 12.6	*-ing* form/infinitive
After prepositions	I'm interested **in buying** a new laptop.
As subject/object of a sentence	**Riding** a bike is a great way to stay in shape. I love **riding** my bike.
After adjectives	It's **easy to forget** he's only eighteen.
To express a purpose	We have to leave soon **to get there on time**.

1 Choose the correct words to complete the sentences.

1 Before *to say / saying* anything, please just listen to me.
2 She wants a better job *to earn / for earning* more money.
3 He's afraid of *to disappoint / disappointing* his father.
4 *To share / Sharing* photos is easy with Instagram.
5 I'm really sorry for *to miss / missing* your party.
6 I'm delighted *to tell / telling* you that we're getting married.
7 *To speak / Speaking* another language is really useful in business.
8 She's pleased *not to work / not working* for that company.
9 He asked me *to take care of / taking care of* his plants.
10 We thought about *not to go / not going* to the wedding.

2 Write sentences in the present tense using the *-ing* form or the infinitive.

1 Drink / too much coffee / not be / good for you
   Drinking too much coffee isn't good for you.
2 She really / enjoy / go to the movies
   _____
3 It / not be / expensive / eat / here
   _____
4 She / not be / afraid of / make mistakes
   _____
5 Cook / with friends / be / a nice way to relax
   _____
6 We / delighted / hear your news
   _____
7 He / not be / very good at / stay in touch
   _____
8 I / go / to the gym / stay in shape
   _____

3 Complete the text with the correct form of the verbs in the box.

> be   work   study   get   act

¹_____ happily married for over 50 years isn't easy, but that's what Paul Newman and Joanne Woodward were. In 1950, Paul was working for his family's business, but he was more interested in ²_____ , so at the age of 25, he went to Yale University ³_____ drama. He was lucky ⁴_____ a job as an actor in a play named *Picnic*, where he first met Joanne. After ⁵_____ together on the movie *The Long Hot Summer*, they got married. And the rest, as they say, is history.

◀ Go back to page 107   135

1A Personality adjectives

1 ▶ **1.1** Match sentences 1–8 with pictures a–h. Listen and check.

1 Rosa is very **shy**. She doesn't like talking to people she doesn't know. ____
2 Michael is very **funny**. He makes the children laugh. ____
3 Irene is very **patient**. She can wait for a long time and doesn't get angry. ____
4 Marco always buys me coffee when we go out. He's really **generous**. ____
5 Stefano is very **nice**. He's always happy to help me when I have a problem. ____
6 Jane watches TV all day, and she never cleans the house. I think she's **lazy**. ____
7 Arturo is very **polite**. He opens the door for us when we visit. ____
8 Sita always tells the truth about everything. She's very **honest**. ____

2 A ▶ **1.2** Match the adjectives in the box below with the definitions in the chart. Listen and check.

hard-working sociable dishonest serious
rude selfish mean impatient

	This type of person ...	adjective	opposite
1	only thinks about himself/herself.		
2	says and does things that hurt other people's feelings.		
3	works very hard.		
4	likes going out and meeting new people.		
5	doesn't like waiting for things.		
6	doesn't laugh very often.		
7	isn't very helpful to others.		
8	doesn't tell the truth.		

B Write the opposites of the adjectives in the right-hand column.

> **Look!** We say *What is he/she like?* when we ask about personality.
> *What is your teacher like?*   *She's shy, but she's very nice.*

3 Choose the correct adjectives to complete the sentences.

1 Children can be very *impatient / mean / dishonest*. They can say very bad things and make each other cry.
2 Paul prefers to be with people he knows. He's very *rude / patient / shy*.
3 I think Leo's *dishonest / rude / lazy*. He plays computer games all day, and he doesn't do any work.
4 Marco's very *selfish / impatient / lazy*. He drinks all the milk in the refrigerator and doesn't care about the rest of us.
5 Amanda hates waiting for the bus. She's so *impatient / mean / selfish*.
6 Anton is really *patient / generous / sociable* with his time and his money. He always buys me lunch when we get together.
7 Artur doesn't smile or laugh very much, and he thinks a lot about things before making decisions. He's very *hard-working / polite / serious*.
8 Sam's really *sociable / funny / nice*. He always makes us laugh when he tells us his stories.
9 Stella is a *lazy / dishonest / serious* person. She lies to people so they think she's clever.
10 Those children are very *polite / generous / honest*. If they break something, they always tell the teacher.

◀ Go back to page 4

1B Hobbies and socializing

1 ▶ 1.7 Match the two columns in each group to make phrases. Listen and check.

Online activities

1	download	_____	a	social media (e.g., Facebook)
2	go on	_____	b	about your opinions
3	blog	_____	c	music/movies/apps
4	play	_____	d	online
5	shop	_____	e	video games

Socializing

11	spend	_____	k	a club
12	get together	_____	l	out at night
13	meet	_____	m	time with the family
14	join	_____	n	new people
15	go	_____	o	with friends

Sports and games

6	stay	_____	f	soccer/chess
7	play	_____	g	Pilates
8	go	_____	h	in shape
9	do	_____	i	the gym/the swimming pool
10	go to	_____	j	running/swimming

Other hobbies

16	bake	_____	p	at home
17	learn	_____	q	a concert/the movies
18	relax	_____	r	an instrument/a language
19	go to	_____	s	coins/records/stamps
20	collect	_____	t	a cake/cupcakes/bread

2 Complete the sentences with the correct forms of the verbs in the box.

> meet   stay   relax   spend   go   join   shop   go on   get together   do

1 It's important to _____ time with your friends and family.
2 Why don't you _____ a tennis club?
3 Karen usually _____ online because she is very busy.
4 I took an English course to _____ new people.
5 I think swimming is the best way to _____ in shape.
6 Ned doesn't have many hobbies. He just _____ at home.

7 I hardly ever _____ social media. I prefer meeting people face-to-face.
8 Saturday night is a good time to _____ with my friends.
9 You need to be in very good shape to _____ gymnastics.
10 Martin _____ running every morning at 6:00.

◀ Go back to page 6

1C Useful verbs

1 ▶ 1.15 Complete the sentences with the correct forms of the verbs. Listen and check.

1 **wear / carry**
It's a beautiful day. Why are you _____ an umbrella and _____ a coat?

2 **take / give**
Could you _____ me to the party, please? Brian says he can _____ me a ride home.

3 **look / look like**
A: She _____ beautiful in that dress, doesn't she?
B: Yes, she _____ her mother.

4 **look forward to / expect**
I'm _____ seeing my cousins again. We _____ their flight to arrive at any minute.

5 **say / tell**
Don't _____ her about the party. Charlotte _____ that she loves surprises!

6 **miss / lose**
Here are our movie tickets. Don't _____ them! I don't want to _____ the beginning of the movie.

7 **hope / wait**
I'm _____ for you at the restaurant. I _____ you're not going to be late.

8 **win / earn**
He doesn't _____ very much money as a writer, although he _____ a lot of competitions.

9 **remember / remind**
I have to _____ to buy some eggs. If I forget, can you please _____ me?

10 **go back / come back**
My parents are _____ from Greece today. They had a fantastic time. They want to _____ next year!

2 **A** Choose the correct verb to complete questions 1–8.

1 Who do you *look like / look* in your family?
2 Are you *going back / coming back* to college in the fall?
3 What did you *take / give* for lunch today?
4 How do you usually *wear / carry* your things to class?
5 Do you always *remember / remind* to do your homework?
6 Do you ever *lose / miss* your cell phone?
7 Do you always *say / tell* your parents the truth?
8 Where do you *hope / wait* to be in 10 years?

B Match questions 1–8 with answers a–h.

_____ a Yes. We start in October.
_____ b Nothing! I forgot my lunch at home.
_____ c I use a small backpack.
_____ d Sometimes, but I usually put it in my pocket.
_____ e Of course! I'm very honest.
_____ f I want to own my own company.
_____ g No, I don't. Sometimes I forget.
_____ h My mother. We have the same eyes.

◀ Go back to page 9

3B Vacation activities

1 ▶ 3.5 Complete the chart with the words in the box to make phrases. Listen and check.

> a museum   on a guided tour   abroad   a seat on a train   a resort
> local attractions   sightseeing   camping   a hotel   a flight   a double room

go	visit	stay at	reserve/book

2 ▶ 3.6 Match the sentences. Listen and check.

1 We always **sunbathe** on the beach. _____
2 I usually **buy souvenirs** for my family. _____
3 You can **rent a car** for a week. _____
4 On vacation, we usually **eat out** every night. _____
5 Let's **have a barbecue** on the weekend. _____
6 I sometimes **pack my suitcase** a week before we go. _____

a It's expensive, but we like to try the local food.
b The weather looks good.
c That way I don't forget anything.
d The local market is the best place to find presents.
e I like relaxing and listening to the ocean.
f It's a good way to see the countryside.

◀ Go back to page 24

2A -ed/-ing adjectives

1 ▶ 2.5 Look at the pictures and complete the sentences with the -ed or -ing adjectives. Listen and check.

1 amazed / amazing

The magic show was _____!
I was _____. The magician did some incredible tricks.

2 relaxed / relaxing

I had a really _____ weekend.
I felt so _____ I took a nap on Saturday afternoon.

3 tired / tiring

What a long day! I'm very _____ now.
It's _____ being a mother.

4 interested / interesting

I'm _____ in Roman history.
Do you have any _____ books on the subject?

5 bored / boring

The class was very _____ this morning.
I was so _____, I fell asleep!

6 embarrassed / embarrassing

I was _____ when the computer stopped working. I couldn't give my presentation. It was very _____.

7 annoyed / annoying

I was _____ because Joe was playing loud music.
It's very _____ when people make a lot of noise.

8 disappointed / disappointing

I failed my driving test last week. I was really _____.
It's _____, but I can take the test again.

9 excited / exciting

I got my ticket for the music festival. I'm so _____!
It's always _____ to go to a live concert.

10 terrified / terrifying

I don't like this. I'm _____ of heights!
I didn't think cleaning windows would be so _____.

11 confused / confusing

These instructions are very _____.
I'm completely _____.
I don't know what this means.

12 surprised / surprising

Ana received a _____ e-mail this morning.
Ana was really _____ when she read the e-mail.

2 Choose the correct adjectives to complete the sentences.

1 The class was really *interested / interesting,* and all the students enjoyed it.
2 We were all *surprised / surprising* when we heard Katya's news.
3 The photos from the concert were really *disappointed / disappointing.*
4 Are you *excited / exciting* about moving abroad next year?
5 Horror movies are *terrified / terrifying.* I never watch them.
6 The exam questions were very *confused / confusing.* I didn't understand them at all.
7 I lost my phone, so I couldn't take any photos. It was very *annoyed / annoying.*
8 I was very *embarrassed / embarrassing* when I arrived late.

2C Life stages

1 ▶ 2.6 Match the phrases in the box with the pictures on the timeline. Listen and check.

> ~~be born~~ ~~die~~ get engaged graduate from college/high school get your driver's license go to elementary school get a divorce
> fall in love retire get married grow up have children finish school go to middle school start a career

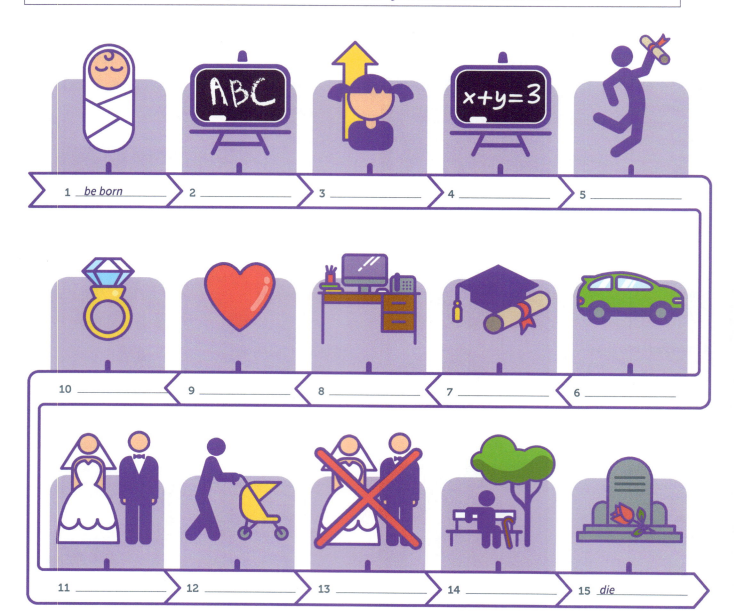

| 1 *be born* | 2 | 3 | 4 | 5 |

| 10 | 9 | 8 | 7 | 6 |

| 11 | 12 | 13 | 14 | 15 *die* |

2 Match the two columns to make sentences.

1 My grandmother was born ____
2 She grew up ____
3 She went to elementary school ____
4 She finished school when ____
5 She went to college ____
6 She started her career ____
7 There she met ____
8 They got married ____
9 They had two children— ____
10 My grandmother retired ____

a my grandfather, also a doctor.
b at the age of 65.
c she was 18, in 1961.
d my mother and my uncle.
e on April 14, 1961.
f in 1966, after getting engaged.
g when she was five.
h on a farm in Kentucky.
i as a doctor in a hospital.
j to study medicine.

3 Complete the text with the correct form of the life stages verbs.

1 My parents worked in lots of different countries, so I _____ with my grandparents in Miami.
2 Luca _____ to his girlfriend last week. The wedding is in May of next year.
3 I want to _____ in the summer. Then I can drive to college every day.
4 Sandra's parents _____ ten years ago, but they are still friends and see each other often.
5 Raul works in that hospital. He says almost 30 babies _____ there every day.

◀ Go back to page 16

3A Useful adjectives

1 ▶ **3.1** Match the adjectives in the box with the pictures 1–12. Listen and check.

ancient modern crowded famous busy lively messy polluted quiet ugly uncomfortable unusual

1 _____

2 _____

3 _____

4 _____

5 _____

6 _____

7 _____

8 _____

9 _____

10 _____

11 _____

12 _____

2 Choose the correct word to complete the sentences.

1 Our hotel room was really *uncomfortable / quiet*. We complained to the manager.

2 Petra is one of the most *lively / famous* archaeological sites in the Middle East.

3 You will love this restaurant; it's always very *lively / crowded*.

4 We went to the beach for our vacation but the water was really *polluted / messy*.

5 It's impossible to get on the buses at rush hour because they are so *lively / crowded*.

6 If you go to Egypt, don't miss the *ugly / ancient* temples in Luxor and Aswan.

7 We loved Vietnam. The streets were really *busy / messy* with all kinds of vehicles and people.

8 He went all around the world and all he bought me was an *ugly / ancient* key ring.

9 We went for a walk away from downtown and found some *quiet / messy* streets.

10 We saw some very *unusual / uncomfortable* animals when we went to Australia.

11 There is a new building downtown; it's really *lively / modern*.

12 The children's rooms are always *unusual / messy* when they're on summer vacation.

3 Complete the text with the correct adjectives.

My first trip to a foreign country was in 2015, when I visited Cambodia. My favorite place was Angkor Wat, which is one of the most ¹_____ archaeological sites in the world. There are hundreds of ²_____ temples from the 12th century in an area of over 1 km²! It's a very ³_____ place, but I'm very glad I went.

I went very early in the morning because it gets very ⁴_____ later in the day, and the buses get ⁵_____ . You can visit the site by yourself, or hire a guide who can show you around and explain everything. Remember not to wear ⁶_____ shoes, because you have to walk a lot!

◀ Go back to page 22

4A Jobs

1 ▶ 4.1 Match the words in the box with the pictures 1–12. Listen and check.

> lawyer accountant waiter/waitress receptionist surgeon firefighter
> scientist hairdresser journalist model salesperson farmer

1 _____

2 _____

3 _____

4 _____

5 _____

6 _____

7 _____

8 _____

9 _____

10 _____

11 _____

12 _____

2 ▶ 4.2 Match the words to make jobs. Listen and check.

1	fashion ____	a	guide
2	movie ____	b	designer
3	soccer ____	c	officer
4	police ____	d	coach
5	security ____	e	reporter
6	sales ____	f	guard
7	tour ____	g	person
8	news ____	h	director
9	travel ____	i	attendant
10	flight ____	j	agent

3 Complete the sentences with the correct jobs from exercises 1 and 2.

1 Whenever I have my hair cut, I always tell the _____ all my problems.

2 I didn't know where to go on vacation, but the _____ suggested some good places.

3 I was worried about the operation, but the _____ said everything would be fine.

4 I went to buy a new shirt and the _____ was very helpful.

5 The _____ might lose his job. The team has lost ten games now!

6 Why don't you speak to a _____ before you sign this contract?

7 My mother is a _____ . She works for a company that develops new medicines.

8 Our plane was full, but the _____ was very helpful.

9 The concert was really crowded, and a _____ said I couldn't go in.

10 I'm sure the company has financial problems. The _____ looks very worried!

4C Phrases about work

1 ▶ **4.11** Match the phrases with the pictures. Listen and check.

> agree on a salary   apply for a job   get a job offer
> get a pay raise   get a promotion   have an interview
> quit a job   see a job ad   start work   write a résumé

2 Complete the sentences with the correct form of the verbs from exercise 1.

1 I would like to _____ for the job of assistant manager.
2 I'm very bored at work. I'm going to _____ my job.
3 My husband _____ a pay raise last week, so we're going to buy an apartment.
4 It looks like a fabulous new job. When do you _____ work?
5 I _____ a job ad in the paper last week. It looks really interesting!
6 My sister _____ a promotion. Now she is the director. We're all very proud of her.
7 All the new jobs will be advertised next month. I need to _____ a résumé.
8 I _____ three job offers in one week! I'm not sure what to do!
9 She can't go to the meeting on Tuesday. She _____ an interview for a new job.
10 The interview went well and I want the job, but we can't _____ a salary.

3 ▶ **4.12** Match 1–8 with a–h to make expressions. Listen and check.

1 see	_____	a	interested in a career in …
2 send	_____	b	a degree in …
3 have	_____	c	a training course
4 take	_____	d	for an interview at any time
5 be	_____	e	for a salary between …
6 look	_____	f	as an intern
7 go	_____	g	a résumé, an application form
8 work	_____	h	an advertisement, an ad

4 Complete the letter with the words in the box.

> degree   interview   advertisement   salary   application   career

> Dear Sir/Madam:
>
> I saw your [1]_____ for the job of Software Engineer, and I'd like to apply. I am sending you my résumé and an [2]_____ form.
>
> I have a [3]_____ in Information Technology, and I am very interested in a [4]_____ in software development.
>
> I am looking for a [5]_____ of between $30,000 and $35,000 and I can go for an [6]_____ at any time during the next two weeks.
>
> I look forward to hearing from you.
>
> Best regards,
>
> Chloe Maxwell

1 _____

2 _____

3 _____

4 _____

5 _____

6 _____

7 _____

8 _____

9 _____

10 _____

◀ Go back to page 35

5A Health and medicine

1 ▶ 5.1 Complete the problems 1–16 with the words in the box. Listen and check.

> stomachache backache broke nosebleed burned cold cough cut
> earache flu headache hurts sore throat stressed temperature toothache

1 I _____ my hand.

2 I have a _____ .

3 I _____ my finger.

4 I _____ my leg.

5 I have a _____ .

6 I have a _____ .

7 I have a _____ .

8 I have a _____ .

9 I have a _____ .

10 I have an _____ .

11 I have a _____ .

12 I have a _____ .

13 I'm _____ .

14 My knee _____ .

15 I have the _____ .

16 I have a _____ .

2 Match problems 1–9 with possible solutions in the box. There may be more than one answer.

1 I don't feel well. I have a stomachache. _____
2 Those boxes were heavy. I have a backache now! _____
3 Ooh! I have a sore throat. _____
4 I'm worried about my nosebleeds. _____
5 I have a terrible headache. _____
6 I feel awful. I think I have the flu. _____
7 I'm stressed about work. _____
8 I burned my hand yesterday. It still hurts. _____
9 My foot hurts. I fell getting out of the car! _____

> see a doctor   call a friend
> take some pills   put some ice / cold water on it
> rest in bed   have some hot lemon and honey
> go lie down   talk to your boss
> have some chicken soup   put some cream on it
> go to bed early every night   eat healthy food

5B Collocations with *do*, *make*, *have*, and *take*

1 ▶ 5.5 Complete the diagrams with *do*, *make*, *have*, or *take*. Listen and check.

a break — a chance
1 _____ — a nap
your time — a deep breath

a list — a decision
2 _____ — an excuse
a mistake — an effort

a good time — a talk
3 _____ — some tea/coffee
an argument

something — Pilates
4 _____ — your homework
your best

2 Complete the sentences with the correct form of the verbs *do*, *make*, *have*, or *take*.

1 I _____ a bad argument with my parents last night.
2 Alvin always finishes his work late and _____ an excuse.
3 If you want to make good sushi, you have to _____ your time.
4 Don't _____ any mistakes or you'll have to start over.

5 To relax, she _____ Pilates every day after work.
6 We _____ a great time when we went to California.
7 Lisa _____ her best, but she failed the exam.
8 I don't have a reservation, but I'm going to _____ a chance and go.

◀ Go back to page 42

6A Phrasal verbs

1 ▶ 6.1 Match sentences 1–8 with the pictures a–h . Listen and check.

1 Can I **turn on** the air-conditioning? _____
2 I'm going to **find out** who did this. _____
3 Oh no! We've **run out of** milk! _____
4 Why did the car **break down** here? _____
5 Please **throw away** the empty bottles. _____
6 Can you **fill up** the car with gasoline, please? _____
7 You should **clean up** your bedroom. _____
8 I'm going to **look up** the word in a dictionary. _____

2 ▶ 6.2 Match the phrasal verbs in **bold** with their meanings a–h. Listen and check.

1 I don't want to **go on** with the course. It's boring.   a wait
2 If you want to get in shape you should **take up** running. b continue
3 I'm going to **take care of** my sister's children tonight.   c stop
4 You need to **fill out** this form to get a passport.   d start
5 Can you **give back** the money you owe me?   e return
6 You should **give up** smoking. It's bad for you.   f be with
7 If you **hold on** for five minutes, I'll come, too.   g complete
8 The snow will soon **turn into** water.   h become

3 Complete the sentences with the correct form of the phrasal verbs.

1 My car is awful. It _____ every month!
2 Yesterday, I _____ that I'm going to get a pay raise.
3 I'm going to _____ this pen. It's broken.
4 It rained at first, but then it _____ a beautiful day.
5 Two years ago, Colin _____ milk for health reasons.
6 The store _____ size 8 jeans yesterday.
7 Can you _____ my cat while I'm away on vacation?
8 I'm on my way! Please, _____ for another five minutes.

◀ Go back to page 48

5C Emotions and feelings

1 ▶ 5.10 Look at the pictures. Match sentences 1–12 with people a–l. Listen and check.

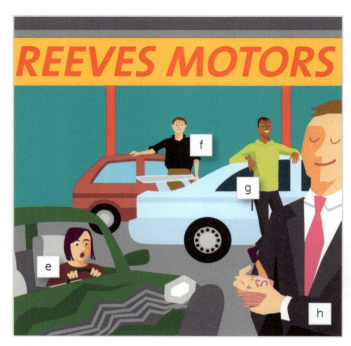

1 Roberto feels very **confident**. He thinks he'll get the job. ____
2 Mr. Wallace doesn't like his job. He looks **miserable**. ____
3 Karen isn't worried about the interview. She's very **calm** today. ____
4 Peter hates interviews. He gets very **nervous**. ____

5 Kevin's very **proud** of his expensive new car. ____
6 Joe's **envious** of Kevin's car. He can't afford a new one. ____
7 Mr. Reeves has made a lot of money. He's **delighted**. ____
8 Sally's very **upset** because she had a car accident. ____

9 Vikram loves his job. He's very **cheerful** today. ____
10 Lucia forgot Jess's birthday, and is one hour late. She feels **guilty**. ____
11 Jess is celebrating her birthday by herself. She feels very **lonely**. ____
12 Mr. Lee's **jealous**. He doesn't like his wife talking to Vincent. ____

2 Choose the correct words to complete the sentences.

1 I studied really hard for this exam. I'm *proud / confident / delighted* I will pass.
2 Claire's really *calm / guilty / upset* because her boss invited everyone to a party except her.
3 Patrick borrowed his neighbor's coffeemaker and broke it. He feels really *guilty / envious / miserable*.
4 I was *cheerful / delighted / confident* when I got a pay raise and a promotion at work.
5 I moved to the city last year. I see lots of people, but I still feel *envious / confident / lonely* sometimes.
6 My son won a writing competition. I'm very *proud / confident / delighted* of him.
7 My neighbor finishes work at 2:00 p.m. every day. I sometimes feel really *upset / envious / guilty* of her!
8 When she listens to classical music, she always feels very *cheerful / confident / calm*.
9 Jo doesn't like public speaking, but she's going to give a presentation this afternoon. She's really *lonely / nervous / upset*.
10 I feel *miserable / jealous / guilty*. My train was late, I lost my phone, and now it's starting to rain!
11 Malika's son is only 3 years old. He gets *guilty / lonely / jealous* when she plays with her friends' children.
12 My boss was very *cheerful / delighted / proud* today. She was singing a song when she came into the office.

◀ Go back to page 44

6C The natural world

1A Match the landscapes in the box with pictures 1–3.

> mountains   rainforest   coast

B ▶ **6.7** Match the words with the natural features a–r. Listen and check.

river	____
stream	____
rocks	____
branch	____
roots	____
wildlife	____

1 _____

cliff	____
ocean	____
waves	____
shore	____
lightning	____
thunderstorm	____

2 _____

cave	____
peak	____
valley	____
waterfall	____
lake	____
sunrise/sunset	____

3 _____

2 ~~Cross out~~ the word that is incorrect in each sentence.

1 I took a photo of the *sunset / sunrise / roots* because the sky was so pink.
2 We saw a snake sitting on a *branch / rock / stream*.
3 You can drink the water from *the ocean / a river / a stream*.
4 You can hear the *cave / thunder / waterfall* from a long way away.
5 He believes there are bears living in the *root / cave / valley*.
6 My feet got wet while I was walking along the *lake / shore / wildlife*.
7 She wants to climb up this *cliff / peak / wave*, but it's very difficult.
8 We didn't expect to see a *thunderstorm / ocean / wildlife* on our trip to the mountains.

3 Complete the sentences with words a–h.

1 One of the driest places in the world is Death ____.
2 In Acapulco, people dive into the ocean from high ____.
3 Cairo is on the banks of the Nile ____.
4 Niagara is an amazing ____ in the U.S. and Canada.
5 Every year, we drive along the Atlantic ____.
6 Surfers love going to Hawaii for its giant ____.
7 In 1963, a plane crashed when ____ hit it.
8 They say the Loch Ness Monster lives in a ____ in Scotland.

a	River
b	coast
c	lake
d	lightning
e	cliffs
f	Valley
g	waves
h	waterfall

◀ Go back to page 52

7A City features

1 ▶ 7.1 Match the words in the box with the pictures 1–14. Listen and check.

> apartment building   crosswalk   streetlight   street sign   sidewalk   bike lane
> fountain   tunnel   intersection   bridge   bench   trash can   statue   traffic lights

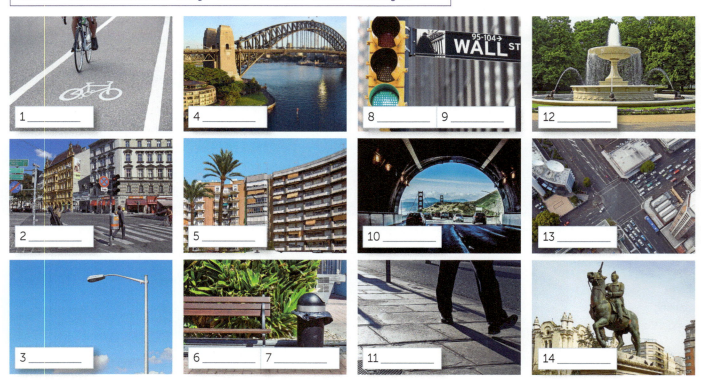

1 _____ 4 _____ 8 _____ 9 _____ 12 _____

2 _____ 5 _____ 10 _____ 13 _____

3 _____ 6 _____ 7 _____ 11 _____ 14 _____

2 Choose the correct options to complete the sentences.

1 The quickest way downtown is to go through the *bridge / tunnel*.
2 He stopped because the *streetlights / traffic light was* red.
3 Use the *crosswalk / trash can*—this street is dangerous.
4 This area is really dirty. I think it's because there aren't any *benches / trash cans*.
5 There's a big *statue / fountain* of a horse in the main square.
6 Follow the *street signs / sidewalk* to get to the national museum.
7 I don't like riding my bike here, there are no *apartment buildings / bike lanes*.
8 Go down this street and turn right at the *intersection / trash cans*.

◀ Go back to page 58

7B Transportation

1 ▶ 7.6 Match the words in the box with the definitions. Listen and check.

> parking lot   commuter   delayed   on time   parking space
> passenger   platform   public transportation   rush hour   traffic jam

1 The trains, subways, and buses people use to travel. _____
2 The area in a station where you get on and off a train. _____
3 A person traveling, but not driving. _____
4 Someone who travels to work each day. _____
5 An area or building where people leave their cars. _____
6 The time of day when most people are driving. _____
7 A place where you can leave a single car. _____
8 Slow or late. _____
9 A long line of cars that move very slowly. _____
10 Not early or late. _____

2 ▶ 7.7 Match the sentences. Listen and check.

1 The trains never **arrive on time**. _____
2 It **takes me** nearly two hours to get to work. _____
3 Can I **give you a ride** to the mall? _____
4 I work at a local school, so I usually **walk** _____
5 I prefer to **ride my bike** into town. _____
6 You need to **start out** earlier. _____
7 It's much quicker to **go by taxi**. _____
8 I have to **take a bus** and **the subway** to work. _____

a I'm going into town anyway.
b That's why I always have my breakfast on the way.
c You'll find one outside the station.
d I usually miss one of them!
e Last week I waited almost 50 minutes on the platform.
f I always talk to people on the way.
g You're always late for work!
h It's faster than walking and there are good bike lanes.

◀ Go back to page 60

8A Food and drink

1 ▶ **8.1** Match the words in the box with the pictures 1–20. Listen and check.

> tomato sauce   beef   shrimp   cereal   cucumber   salmon   lettuce   peppers   fruit juice   pineapple
> strawberry   lamb   tuna   cabbage   coconut   turkey   flour   peach   eggplant   apple pie

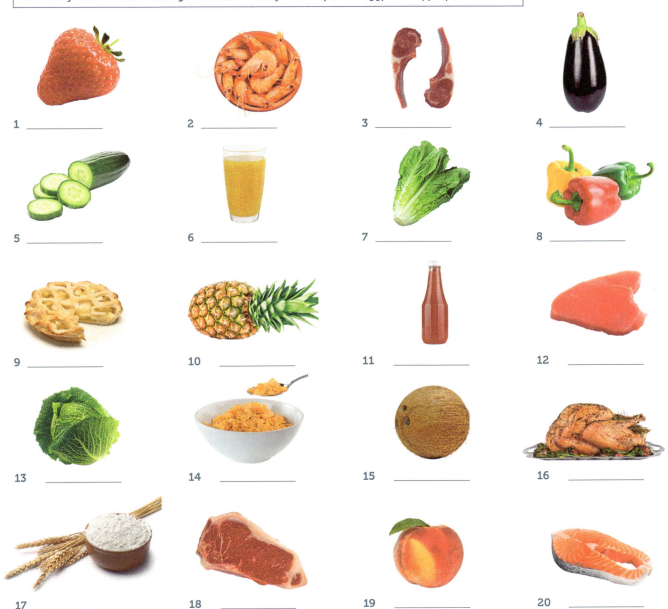

1 _____   2 _____   3 _____   4 _____

5 _____   6 _____   7 _____   8 _____

9 _____   10 _____   11 _____   12 _____

13 _____   14 _____   15 _____   16 _____

17 _____   18 _____   19 _____   20 _____

2 Complete the sentences with the words in the box.

> strawberries   tuna   cucumber   coconut   shrimp   fruit juice   beef   lettuce   apple pie   tomato sauce   flour   cereal

1 For breakfast, I usually have a bowl of _____ and a glass of _____ .

2 It's easy to bake bread. You just need _____ , water, and salt.

3 I'm allergic to seafood, I can't eat _____ .

4 The simplest pizza only has _____ and cheese on top.

5 It's difficult to open the shell of a _____ , but the milk inside is delicious.

6 My grandmother is going to bake an _____ for dessert tonight.

7 I'm going to make sushi tonight, so I need some rice and _____ .

8 She always has a salad with tomatoes, _____ , and _____ for lunch.

9 In the summer, I love eating _____ and cream!

10 I ate some amazing _____ steaks in Argentina.

◀ Go back to page 66

8C   Adjectives to describe food

1 ▶ 8.8 Complete the descriptions 1–8 with the words in the box. Listen and check.

> spicy unhealthy tasty raw fresh crunchy salty delicious sour
> disgusting healthy vegetarian bitter burned creamy sweet

1 You can't eat that _____ toast. It will taste _____ !

2 Sashimi is made with _____ fish. There's not much fat or salt, so it's very _____ .

3 I don't eat meat, so I ordered a _____ curry, but it was so _____ I had to drink a lot of water!

4 I know French fries are _____ , but mmm! They're very _____ !

5 I don't like black coffee—it's too _____ . I prefer a _____ hot chocolate.

6 In Morocco, they make tea with _____ mint and lots of sugar, so it's very _____ .

7 You can't eat these snacks quietly; they're too _____ . They're _____ , too, but perfect with a cold drink.

8 Oh no! I can't use this milk, It's a little _____ . My cake has to be _____ to win the competition.

2 Choose the correct words to complete the sentences.

1 A Do you remember those *tacos* we ate in Mexico that were full of chilli peppers?
  B I'll never forget that. They were so *burned / spicy / crunchy* that I started crying!

2 A How often do you go to the supermarket?
  B Hardly ever. I think the market is the best place to buy *fresh / raw / spicy* ingredients.

3 A Is something wrong with your cake?
  B Yes, I used too much sugar and now it's too *salty / tasty / sweet*.

4 A What's *lassi*?
  B Oh, you'll love it! It's a *disgusting / bitter / creamy* drink from India made with yogurt.

5 A I have some lettuce, cucumbers, and red peppers in the refrigerator.
  B Great! Then we can make a nice *crunchy / creamy / salty* salad for lunch.

6 A Do you like lemon juice?
  B No, I don't. It's too *spicy / sour / raw* for me.

9A Money verbs

1 ▶ **9.3** Complete the sentences with the words in the box. Listen and check.

> owe   borrow   can afford   charge   cost   earn   get paid
> be worth   own   pay back   save   spend   waste   lend

1 Excuse me, how much does this necklace _____?
2 In my opinion, soccer clubs _____ too much for tickets.
3 Waiters can _____ a lot of money from tips.
4 Can you _____ me $50 until I get paid next week?
5 He has a rare 1950s Rolex watch. It must _____ a fortune!
6 As well as their apartment in London, they _____ a house in Hollywood.
7 They _____ most of their money on clothes.
8 How much money do you _____ to the bank each month?
9 The car isn't ours yet. We still _____ the bank $5,000.
10 I've left all my money at home. Can I _____ $20, please?
11 Don't _____ your money on lottery tickets—you'll never win!
12 He's trying to _____ for an expensive trip next summer.
13 She's so rich that she _____ to buy anything she wants.
14 We normally _____ on the last day of the month.

2 Choose the correct words to complete the sentences.

1 Oh no, I've forgotten my wallet. Can you *borrow / lend / owe* me some money?
2 I can't go out tonight. I don't *earn / afford / get paid* until next week.
3 Excuse me, how much does this jacket *cost / worth / charge*?
4 I *spend / waste / save* almost half of my money on rent every month.
5 If you give me $200, I'll *borrow / owe / pay back* the money next week.
6 I bought the guitar for $500, but it's now *worth / cost / earn* almost double that.
7 My car is very old, but I can't *spend / afford / own* to buy a new one right now.
8 When I finish college, I will *owe / lend / charge* the bank more than $10,000.
9 I shouldn't go out this month. I need to *charge / earn / save* for a new computer.
10 Why did you *pay back / waste / earn* all your money on these comic books?

◀ Go back to page 77

9B Shopping

1 ▶ **9.5** Choose the correct verbs to complete the sentences. Listen and check.

1 Can I *pay by / pay with* credit card, or do I have to *pay on / pay with* cash?

2 I'd like to *exchange / return* this jacket—it's too big. Can I *exchange / return* it for a smaller one, please?

3 Can I *try on / fit* these shoes, please? I need to know how they *try on / fit* me.

4 You can *deliver / order* furniture online. Then the company will *deliver / order* it to your house.

2 ▶ **9.6** Match the words in the box with the definitions 1–12. Listen and check.

> dressing room   bargain   receipt   discount   sales   cash
> refund   cash register   window shopping   department store
> line   shopping center

1 A product that a store sells at a very good price. _____
2 A piece of paper that shows you have bought something. _____
3 A time when a store sells things at a lower price than usual. _____
4 The place in a store where you can try on clothes. _____
5 A place where people stand to wait for something. _____
6 The place where you pay for things in a store. _____
7 The money that is returned when a product isn't suitable. _____
8 An amount or percentage off the usual price. _____
9 Money in the form of bills and coins. _____
10 Looking at products in stores without buying anything. _____
11 A large store with areas selling different types of products. _____
12 A covered area with different stores. _____

3 Match the two parts to make sentences.

1 I'm going to try on these jeans ____
2 I'm sorry, I can't give you a refund ____
3 You can stand in this line for the cash register ____
4 This morning I went window shopping ____
5 I bought this handbag on sale for $15; ____
6 I bought it at the department store because ____
7 If I pay with cash, ____
8 I ordered these online last week, ____

a can you offer me a discount?
b in the dressing room.
c but you can only pay by credit card.
d it was a real bargain!
e if there's a problem, I can easily return it.
f but I'd like to exchange them for a different color.
g if you don't have the receipt.
h in the shopping mall.

◀ Go back to page 78

10A Sports and competitions

1 ▶ **10.2** Look at the soccer scores. Complete the text with the verbs in the box in the correct form. Listen and check.

> win   beat   score   lose   tie

On May 28, 2016, Real Madrid [1]_____ their rivals, Atlético, in the final of the UEFA Champions League. Ramos [2]_____ a goal first, but 65 minutes later, Carrasco managed to score again to [3]_____ the game 1–1. After extra time, Real Madrid was lucky to [4]_____ the game on penalties. Atlético was very disappointed to [5]_____ because in 2014, they had also lost to Real Madrid in the final.

> **Look!** We use *win* for a competition or award, and we use *beat* for another team or opponent.
> *Real Madrid won the Champions League.*
> *Real Madrid beat Atlético.*

Real Madrid   1 – 1   Atlético
Ramos (15)   Carrasco (79)
(5-3 on penalties)

2 ▶ **10.3** Match the words in the box with the pictures 1–10. Listen and check.

> athlete   crowd   player   medal   race   referee
> spectator   umpire   trophy   game

3 ▶ **10.4** Read sentences. 1—4. Match the verbs in **bold** with definitions a–d. Listen and check.

1 Over 200 countries **take part** in the Olympic Games every four years. ____
2 It's difficult to **cheat** in sports events, but some athletes still try. ____
3 Before you play any sports, you should always **warm up**. ____
4 I couldn't finish the marathon. I had to **give up** after 20 kilometers. ____

a break the rules to try to win a game or pass a test
b stop doing something because it's too difficult
c play in a game or competition
d do special exercises to prepare your body for sports

4 Choose the correct words to complete the sentences.

1 The *referee / umpire* showed three soccer players the red card.
2 I was injured because I didn't *give up / warm up* before the game.
3 My grandfather won a bronze *medal / race* in the Olympic Games.
4 The L.A. Lakers *beat / won* the Chicago Bulls by 123 to 118.
5 Serena Williams is a very successful *athlete / referee*.
6 Your team *cheated / scored*. This competition is for under 16-year-olds, but three of your players are 17 years old.
7 We *tied / lost* 0–0. It was a really boring game.
8 My sister was in the stadium, so when I watched the game on TV, I looked for her in the *crowd / spectator*.
9 The 100-meter *match / race* is my favorite part of the Olympics.
10 I'm terrible at tennis. I *beat / lost* my last match 0–6, 0–6, 0–6!

1 _____

2 _____

3 _____

4 _____

5 _____

6 _____

7 _____

8 _____

9 _____

10 _____

◀ Go back to page 84

10C Parts of the body

1 ▶ 10.9 Match parts of the body *a–x* with the words *1–24*. Listen and check.

1 foot ____ **2** knee ____ **3** toes ____ **4** ankle ____

5 finger ____ **6** wrist ____ **7** elbow ____ **8** hand ____
9 arm ____ **10** thumb ____

11 neck ____ **12** cheek ____ **13** chest ____ **14** lips ____
15 back ____ **16** chin ____ **17** forehead ____ **18** shoulder ____

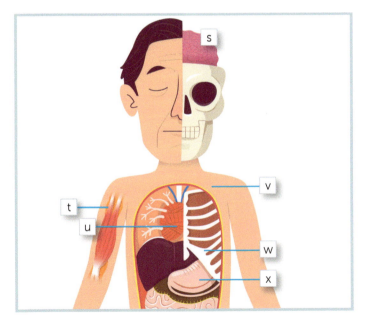

19 heart ____ **20** brain ____ **21** stomach ____
22 skin ____ **23** muscle ____ **24** bone ____

2 ~~Cross out~~ the word that is incorrect in each sentence.

1 I got injured playing football, and now I can't move my *cheeks / elbow / shoulder*.
2 She can't walk because she's hurt her *ankle / brain / toes*.
3 I can't write because something is wrong with my *fingers / lips / wrist*.
4 It was so cold, she was wearing a scarf around her *elbow / neck / shoulders*.

5 This shirt doesn't fit me because I have a big *chin / neck / chest*.
6 It's impossible for me to run a marathon because of my bad *ankle / fingers / knee*.
7 Put this cream on your *lips / muscles / bones* if they hurt.
8 You need to have a scan at the hospital to be able to see your *bones / heart / forehead* well.
9 In a warm-up, you have to stretch your *chin / arms / muscles*.

◀ Go back to page 88

11A Household items

1 ▶ 11.1 Match the words in the box with the pictures 1–20. Listen and check.

> oven sink blanket cushion dishwasher trash can comforter pillow refrigerator iron rug sheets stove
> faucet air-conditioning washing machine carpet chest of drawers central heating closet

1 _____

2 _____

3 _____

4 _____

5 _____

6 _____

7 _____

8 _____

9 _____

10 _____

11 _____

12 _____

13 _____

14 _____

15 _____

16 _____

17 _____

18 _____

19 _____

20 _____

2 Choose the correct word to complete the sentences.

1 Can you put these glasses in the *trash can / sink*, please? They're dirty.
2 We need new *pillows / cushions* for the sofa. What color would you like?
3 Let's move the *rug / carpet* to the middle of the room.
4 Could you turn on the *air-conditioning / central heating?* It's cold in here.
5 We have a new *dishwasher / washing machine*. My shirts are really clean these days!
6 Help me make the bed. Can you pass me the *sheet / blanket* to put on top?

◀ Go back to page 94

11B Housework

1 ▶ 11.6 Match the words in the box with the pictures 1–15. Listen and check.

> mop the floor   clear the table   set the table   water the plants   load the dishwasher   do the ironing   vacuum the carpet   wash the dishes
> sweep the floor   take out the trash   make the bed   dust the furniture   hang out the clothes   do the laundry   put away the toys

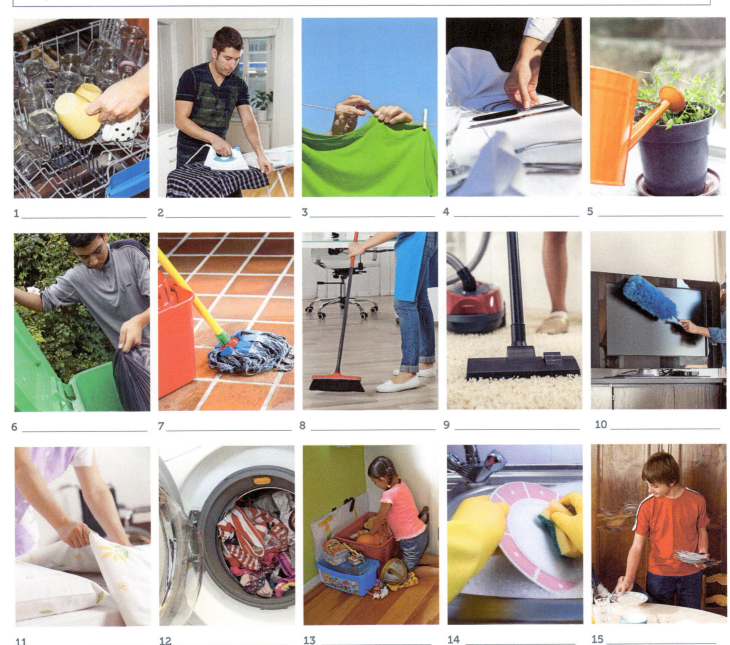

1 _____   2 _____   3 _____   4 _____   5 _____

6 _____   7 _____   8 _____   9 _____   10 _____

11 _____   12 _____   13 _____   14 _____   15 _____

2 Choose the correct word to complete the sentences.

1 The first thing I do every morning is *lay / make / change* my bed.
2 You have to *wash the dishes / do the laundry / hang out the clothes*. The dishwasher is broken.
3 I have lots of allergies, so if I don't *clear / do / dust* the furniture every day, I start to sneeze and cough.
4 These plants will die if you don't *wash / water / clear* them more often.

5 Can you *hang out / take out / water* the clothes, please? They're very wet.
6 My dog leaves hairs on the rug, so I have to *vacuum / mop / clear* it every day.
7 What a wonderful meal! Can you help me *mop / clear / set* the table?
8 My friends are coming over for dinner in twenty minutes, so I need to *clear / make / set* the table.

◀ Go back to page 96

155

11C Words to describe materials and clothes

1 ▶ 11.12 Complete the descriptions 1–10 with the words in the box. You will need to use some of the words more than once. Listen and check.

> denim cotton plastic leather silk fur wood glass wool metal

1 A _____ shirt. It's made of _____ .

2 A _____ coat. It's made of _____ .

3 Some _____ boots. They're made of _____ .

4 A _____ tie. It's made of _____ .

5 Some _____ shoes. They're made of _____ .

6 A _____ sweater. It's made of _____ .

7 A _____ necklace. It's made of _____ .

8 Some _____ jeans. They're made of _____ .

9 A _____ ring. It's made of _____ .

10 Some _____ beads. They're made of _____ .

2 ▶ 11.13 Match the adjectives with their opposites. Listen and check.

1 plain ____   a old-fashioned
2 formal ____   b loose
3 stylish ____   c striped
4 tight ____   d casual

3 Look at the pictures. Are the sentences true (T) or false (F)? Correct the false sentences.

1 Helen is wearing a formal jacket. ____
2 She's wearing a silk scarf. ____
3 She's wearing tight pants. ____

4 Joe is wearing casual clothes. ____
5 He's wearing a gray jacket. ____
6 He's wearing a plain tie. ____

7 He has a wood tennis racket. ____
8 He's wearing loose shorts. ____
9 He's wearing a plain T-shirt. ____

◀ Go back to page 98

12A Relationships

1 ▶ 12.1 Put the words in the box in the correct columns. Listen and check.

cousin only child roommate employer enemy stranger twin ex-husband stepsister bride colleague neighbor
in-laws boss girlfriend groom single parent relative employee business partner classmate brother-in-law

family	couple	work/study	home	other

2 Complete the sentences with the words from exercise 1.

1 Daisy and I work in the same office. She's my _____ .
2 I'm an _____ . I don't have any brothers or sisters.
3 Harry and Luke share an apartment. They're _____ .
4 Carolina got a divorce in 2013, but she still sees her _____ .
5 It was a lovely wedding. The _____ wore a long white dress, and the _____ wore a gray suit.

6 Our next-door _____ just sold his house.
7 He's very friendly. He doesn't have an _____ in the world.
8 Her husband died, so she's a _____ to Emma, her daughter.
9 This is my _____ . We're not identical, but we look alike.
10 People are really friendly here. A _____ helped me when I was lost.

◀ Go back to page 102

12C Relationship verbs

1 ▶ 12.5 Complete the sentences with the simple past form of the phrases in the box. Listen and check.

stay in touch go out (together) get back together ask (someone) out fall in love get along
have (something) in common become friends get married introduce get to know go on a date break up

Couple gets back together after 30 years

Hannah Mason from the U.S. and Gustavo Ramos from Argentina first met in 1985. They were both traveling around Canada after graduating from college. A friend ¹_____ Gustavo to Hannah, and they immediately ²_____ well. As they ³_____ each other better, they ⁴_____ good _____ . They discovered that they ⁵_____ a lot in _____ , including a love of travel.

Friendship turned to romance when Gustavo ⁶_____ Hannah _____ . They ⁷_____ to Gustavo's favorite restaurant in Montreal, and before long they ⁸_____ in _____ . They ⁹_____ together for the rest of the summer, but they ¹⁰_____ when Hannah returned to the U.S. and Gustavo went home to Argentina.

They didn't ¹¹_____ , and that could have been the end of the story. But, 30 years later, Gustavo moved to the U.S. and contacted Hannah. They realized they still cared for each other, so it wasn't long before they ¹²_____ . And their story ended happily when they ¹³_____ last year.

2 Choose the correct words to complete the sentences.

1 We don't *have / make / do* a lot in common; in fact, we're completely different!
2 I think I'm falling *on / in / for* love.
3 Are Charlie and Sarah really *leaving / going / getting* out together?
4 They're getting *marry / marriage / married* next year.
5 Do you get *along / in / out* well with your brother?
6 My boss introduced me *with / for / to* my future wife.
7 The first date that we went *to / in / on* together was to a rock concert.

8 They had a big argument and decided to break *up / off / out*.
9 We were classmates, but we only *became / got / came* friends after we graduated from high school.
10 I first *became / arrived / got to know* her when we worked together in Istanbul.
11 Has Sam ever asked you *out / up / off* for dinner?
12 James and I are thinking of *going / getting / joining* back together.
13 You'll have to *go / have / stay* in touch while you're away.

◀ Go back to page 106

1A Student A

1 Look at the activities and ask Student B questions with *How often ... ?* Write down his/her answers.

1 see the dentist   _____
2 go to the movies   _____
3 buy clothes   _____
4 check your phone   _____
5 exercise   _____
6 eat in a restaurant   _____

2 Answer Student B's questions using adverbs and expressions of frequency.

> always usually sometimes often hardly ever never
> once/twice/three times a day/week/month
> every day/week/month

3 Tell the class what you found out about your partner.

1C Student A

1 Look at pictures 1–4. Ask Student B questions to guess what is happening.

A *Is the woman in picture 1 going for a walk?*   B *No, she isn't.*

2 Answer Student B's questions about pictures 5–8.

2A Student A

1 Ask Student B *What did you do ... ?* with the time expressions. Add the correct prepositions, if necessary.

A *What did you do in the summer?*
B *I studied for my exams, but I got together with friends, too.*

> the summer yesterday 8:00 this morning last week 2015 two weeks ago

2 Answer Student B's questions.

2D Student A

1 Read sentences 1–5 to Student B and listen to his/her responses.

1 I fell down last week and broke my arm.
2 I got a new car for my birthday.
3 My brother found a wallet with $100 in it.
4 Yesterday was the best day ever!
5 I met someone famous yesterday.

2 Listen to Student B's sentences and respond to show you are interested.

B *I didn't get home from work until 10:00 p.m. last night.*
A *You poor thing! What happened?*

2C Student A

1 Ask Student B questions about your mystery person and complete the chart. Can you guess who she is?

When / born?		1935
Where / grow up?		Mississippi, U.S.
What / first job after finishing school?		Salesperson
How many times / get married?		Once–to Priscilla
Have / children?		Yes, a daughter named Lisa Marie
How / become famous?		Made lots of records, including "Jailhouse Rock" and "Can't Help Falling in Love"
When / die?		1977

2 Answer your partner's questions about Elvis Presley. Remember, don't use his name! Can Student B guess who he is?

3A Student A

1 Complete the sentences with the superlative form of the adjectives in parentheses and guess the answer. Student B will say if you are correct.

1 The _____ animals in the world are … (*dangerous*)

crocodiles   sharks   snakes

2 The _____ sports event was … (*popular*)

Brazil World Cup, 2014   Beijing Olympics, 2008   Superbowl XLVI, 2012

3 The _____ car in the world is … (*fast*)

Porsche 959   McLaren F1   Bugatti Veyron

4 The _____ place in the world is … (*noisy*)

Times Square, New York   Champs Élysées, Paris   Exchange Square, Hong Kong

2 Listen to Student B's sentences. Look at the information and say if he/she is correct. Give more information using comparatives, superlatives, and *(not) as … as*.

The Amazon isn't as long as the Nile, but it's longer than the Yangtze.

1 The Nile (6,853 km.); the Amazon (6,437 km.); the Yangtze (6,300 km.)
2 *Nafea Faa Ipoipo*, Paul Gauguin ($300 million); *The Card Players*, Paul Cézanne ($274 million); *The Grand Canal*, Claude Monet ($35 million)
3 Manila, the Philippines (41,014 people/km.^{2}); Cairo, Egypt (36,618 people/km.^{2}); Buenos Aires, Argentina (13,680 people/km.^{2})
4 The Beatles (265 million albums); Michael Jackson (175 million albums); Madonna (166 million albums)

4D Student A

1 You call a company to rent a car for one week. Call Student B and use the details below. Speak as quickly as possible!

Name: George Graddoll
Car: 5-door Subaru Impreza
Dates: Monday, March 1 (12:00)–Sunday, March 7 (18:00)
Credit card: Visa - CD25 5221 BZ55 Xy23

2 You work in a restaurant. Student B will call to reserve a table for tonight. Ask him/her questions and complete the form as accurately as possible.

Customer name: _____
Telephone number: _____
Number of people: _____
Time: _____
Special requirements: _____

3C Student A

1 Read the text about Harold Bride. Prepare questions for Student B. Use the answers to complete the story.

   1 What / Harold Bride's job?
   2 What / he / do / on April 14, at 11:40 p.m.?
   3 What / Captain Edward Smith / say?
   4 What / water / force into the ocean?
   5 What / he / send from the radio room?

2 Answer Student B's questions to help him/her complete the story.

THE STORY OF A SURVIVOR

Harold Bride was working on the *Titanic* when the ship sank over 100 years ago. He was a ¹ _____ who sent and received important information. He was on board when the ship began its voyage from Southampton on April 10, 1912.

On April 14, at 11:40 p.m., Bride ² _____ in his room when he heard a terrible noise. He woke up and went straight to the radio room to find out what was happening. Just after midnight, Captain Edward Smith came in and said that ³ _____ . He asked Bride to send an emergency signal to any other ships in the area. The nearest ship to respond was the *Carpathia*, but, unfortunately, it didn't arrive until after the *Titanic* sank.

While the *Titanic* was filling up with water, Bride continued to send messages. However, the equipment eventually stopped working, and Bride went to help release one of the last lifeboats. But the water forced the ⁴ _____ into the freezing ocean.

Bride held onto the damaged lifeboat and, after hours in the water, some sailors rescued him and took him onto the *Carpathia*. He was badly hurt, so he rested for a while, but later he went to the radio room and began to send ⁵ _____ .

4A Student A

1 Ask Student B questions with *will*. Check (✔) his/her answers in the chart.

Do you think ...	likely	possible	unlikely	impossible
you will move in the next five years?				
you will get a (new) job soon?				
you will become famous?				
you will live abroad in the future?				
you will learn to speak English fluently?				
you will do anything exciting this week?				

2 Answer Student B's questions using the phrases in the box. Give more information.

   B *Do you think you will go on vacation next summer?*
   A *Yes, I think I will. I'll probably visit my family in Miami.*

> Yes, I think I will.   Yes, I probably will.
> Yes, I may.   Yes, I might.
> I don't think I will.   I probably won't.
> I definitely won't.

4C Student A

1 Student B has applied for a job in your company. You call him/her to set up an interview. Look at your day planner and find a time to schedule the interview.

   B *I'm free on Monday afternoon. Can we have the interview then?*
   A *I'm sorry, I'm meeting with the marketing team. What about Monday morning?*

Monday	morning	
	afternoon	*meet with the Marketing team*
Tuesday	morning	
	afternoon	*visit the factory*
Wednesday	morning	
	afternoon	*meet with the managing director*
Thursday	morning	
	afternoon	
Friday	morning	*fly to Paris*
	afternoon	*have lunch with Peter*

5A Student A

1 Tell Student B about your problems and write down the advice that he/she gives you.

Your problems	Advice
I can't sleep at night.	
I burned my hand while I was cooking.	
I have a bad headache.	
I have a nosebleed.	
I want to lose weight.	

2 Student B will tell you about a problem. Give him/her some advice using the ideas from the box and your own ideas.

get some exercise	drink so much coffee	eat junk food
eat more fruit	go to bed	go to the hospital
go to work today	lie down	lose some weight
put a bandage on it	work so hard	put some cream on it
rest	see a doctor	talk to a friend
stay at home	take the day off work	

You should …   I think you should …   You shouldn't …
I don't think you should …

5C Student A

1 Read the beginnings of sentences 1–6 to Student B. He/She will complete the sentences.

1 If I don't feel well tomorrow morning …
2 If it snows this weekend …
3 If I'm invited to a costume party …
4 If I don't have any homework tonight …
5 If I have to cook dinner tonight …
6 If I'm stressed at work …

2 Listen to the beginnings of the sentences Student B reads to you. Choose the correct ending to complete the sentence and tell him/her.

… I might have a party to celebrate.
… I probably won't get a dog.
… I'll buy some new jeans.
… I'll take an aspirin.
… I might go to Cuba.
… I might get a promotion.

6A Student A

1 Complete the *Have you ever …?* questions with the past participles of the verbs in parentheses and ask Student B. He/She will always answer with *Yes, I have*. Ask him/her the simple past questions and decide if he/she is telling the truth.

2 Student B will ask you a *Have you ever …?* question. You should always answer with *Yes, I have*. He/She will ask you more questions. If it is true, tell the truth. If it is not true, invent the details.

	Have you ever …	Simple past
1	_____ on TV? (be)	What show were you on? What did you do? Did many people watch the show?
2	_____ something valuable by mistake? (throw away)	What was it? How much was it worth? Did you find it again?
3	_____ karaoke? (sing)	When did you sing karaoke? Which song did you sing? Did you sing it well?
4	_____ something and not given it back? (borrow)	What did you borrow? Who lent it to you? Were they angry about it?
5	_____ a dangerous animal? (take care of)	What kind of animal was it? Why did you have to take care of it? Did you have any problems?

6C Student A

1 Complete the sentences with the correct form of the verbs in parentheses. Decide if the sentence is true or false for you. Read your sentences to Student B.

1 If I _____ near the ocean, I _____ swimming every day. (live / go)
2 I _____ a friend $50 if he/she _____ to borrow it. (not lend / ask)
3 If someone _____ to steal my bike, I _____ them. (try / stop)
4 I _____ terrified if my friends _____ me to go mountain climbing. (be / ask)
5 If I _____ outside in a thunderstorm, I _____ under a tree. (be / hide)

2 Listen to Student B's sentences. Decide if they are true or false. He/She will tell you if you are correct.

B *If I had more money, I'd buy a new car.*
A *False.*
B *Yes, you're right. If I had more money, I'd go on vacation.*

7A Student A

1 Student B has recently moved to an apartment in another country. Find out if he/she has done these things.

A *Have you unpacked your things yet?*
B *Yes I have. The apartment looks great.*

1 unpack your things
2 set up the Wi-Fi
3 meet your neighbors
4 explore the local area
5 check out public transportation
6 open a bank account

2 You are going to Miami, Florida on vacation tomorrow. Look at your "to do" list and answer Student B's questions.

Things to do
find my passport	✓ (five minutes ago—on my desk)
pack the suitcase	✗
reserve a hotel room	✓ (Grand Beach Hotel, Miami)
buy some sunscreen	✓ (went to the store an hour ago)
ask friend to take care of pet	✗
decide what to do in Miami	✓ (city tour & shopping)

7C Student A

1 Complete the sentences with the present perfect form of the verbs in the box and *for* or *since*. Guess the correct options and tell Student B. He/She will tell you if you are correct.

have	collect	be	take

HOLLYWOOD FACTS

1 The Academy Awards ceremony has _____ place _____ 1929. The winner of the Best Actor award that year was *an American / a German / a Russian* actor, Emil Jannings.
2 The actor Johnny Depp _____ _____ *Barbie dolls / teddy bears / toy cars* _____ his daughter was little.
3 Hollywood actress Christina Ricci _____ _____ afraid of *plants / spiders / flying* _____ most of her life.
4 The actress Angelina Jolie _____ _____ *Chinese classes / a pilot's license / a pet snake* _____ more than ten years.

2 Listen to Student B's sentences and tell him/her if they are correct.

1 There has been a big Hollywood sign in Los Angeles since 1923, but the first sign said "Hollywoodland."
2 *Spider-Man* actor, Tobey Maguire, and Leonardo DiCaprio have known each other since they were children.
3 Actress Mila Kunis has played video games for many years.
4 Eva Marie Saint, who won an Oscar for *On the Waterfront* in 1954, has lived in Hollywood for over 60 years and still works as an actress.

8A Student A

1 You are going to cook a big meal for a group of friends. Student B will tell you what ingredients he/she has. Look at the list of ingredients and use the phrases in the box to help you reply.

Great, that's enough. That's too much. That's too many.
That's not enough. We (only) need ...

2 You are going to cook a big meal for a group of friends. Tell Student B what ingredients you have. He/She will tell you if you need more, less, or if it is enough.

I have 500 grams of shrimp.

INGREDIENTS
4 cans tomatoes
1.5 kg. beef
2 red peppers
3 onions
1 pineapple
500 g. strawberries
2 cartons vanilla ice cream
2 l. orange juice

8C Student A

1 You and Student B are starting work as cooks in a school cafeteria. Guess the missing words. Student B will tell you if you are correct.

SCHOOL KITCHEN GOLDEN RULES!

HYGIENE

1 You have to wear _____ at all times, but you don't have to wear gloves.

2 You can't wear _____ in the kitchen.

3 You have to wash your hands before starting to cook.

COOKING

4 You have to use _____ in all the dishes, and you can't use too much salt or sugar.

5 You have to wash all _____ , but you don't have to wash the meat.

6 You have to throw away _____ in the black trash cans.

MENU

7 You have to prepare one vegetarian dish every day.

8 You don't have to serve _____ on Fridays.

9 On Thursdays, you have to make a curry, but you can't make the sauce _____ .

10 On Wednesdays, you have to make a Chinese dish, but you can't make _____ .

8D Student A

1 Invite Student B to one of the events below. If he/she refuses, try another one.

Die Meistersinger von Nürnberg Fri 6:00 p.m.
Over four hours of German opera at the National Theater

Pencils through the ages Sat 11:00 a.m.
A talk about the history of pencils at the City Museum

Local chess competition Mon 1:00 p.m.
32 local players compete to win the tournament

Karaoke night Tue 7:00 p.m.
Sing your favorite songs all night

2 Student B is going to invite you to some events. Refuse as politely as possible every time.

9A Student A

1 Complete the quiz questions with *used to* and the verbs in parentheses.

Before they were famous

1 The singer, Madonna, _____ (work) in a donut shop. **True** or False?

2 The actor, Brad Pitt, _____ (dress up) as a chicken to advertise a fast-food restaurant. **True** or False?

3 The founder of Microsoft, Bill Gates, _____ (sell) hot dogs at his local baseball stadium. True or **False**? (He used to work as a computer programmer.)

4 The actor, Johnny Depp, _____ (feed) the penguins at a zoo in Kentucky. True or **False?** (He used to sell pens.)

5 The actor and comedian, Jim Carrey, _____ (live) with his family in a VW camper van. **True** or False?

6 The hip hop artist, Kanye West, _____ (work) as a salesperson in GAP. **True** or False?

7 The actor, Tom Cruise, _____ (work) as a chef in a Chinese restaurant. True or **False?** (He used to work in a hotel, carrying luggage for guests.)

8 Actress Julia Roberts and former U.S. president, Barack Obama, _____ (sell) ice cream. **True** or False?

2 Take turns reading your quiz questions to your partner. The correct answers are in **bold**.

9C Student A

1 Complete sentences 1–6 with the passive form of the verbs in parentheses.

1 Which famous article of clothing _____ by Dorothy in the movie *The Wizard of Oz*? (wear)
   a A pair of blue boots   b A green hat   c **A pair of red shoes**

2 When _____ the first *Superman* comic _____? (publish)
   a In 1901   b **In 1938**   c In 1959

3 In 2015, some drums that belonged to Ringo Starr from The Beatles were sold at auction. How much _____ they _____ for? (sell)
   a **$1.75M**   b $5.5M   c $800,000

4 Who _____ the picture *Guernica* _____ by? (paint)
   a Andy Warhol   b Salvador Dalí   c **Pablo Picasso**

5 Who _____ the movie *Star Wars: The Force Awakens* _____ by? (direct)
   a Steven Spielberg   b **J.J. Abrams**   c George Lucas

6 Who _____ the songs "Umbrella" and "Diamonds" _____ by? (sing)
   a Beyoncé   b **Rihanna**   c Lady Gaga

2 **A** Read your questions and the three possible answers to Student B. He/She has to answer. The correct answers are in **bold**.

B Try to answer Student B's questions.

10A Student A

1 A Guess the past perfect verbs to complete the sentences.

Kevin's roommates were really angry with him because ...
1 he _____ all the food in the refrigerator.
2 he _____ to the supermarket.
3 he _____ the dirty dinner dishes.
4 he _____ all the milk.
5 he _____ the kitchen.

B Read your sentences to Student B. He/She will tell you if you are correct.

2 Listen to Student B's sentences. Tell him/her if they are correct or not.

Last night, Miriam's friends planned a party for her. She was really surprised because ...
1 nobody had told her about it.
2 she hadn't seen some of her friends for years!
3 everyone had bought her a present.
4 she thought her friends had forgotten about her birthday.
5 all her friends had shouted "surprise!" when she came in.

10C Student A

1 You're a journalist. You interviewed Student B last week and took notes. Check the information with him/her and correct any mistakes.

A *Did you say that you were originally from South Africa?*
B *No, I told you that I was originally from Kenya.*

> *Student B*
> *is originally from ~~South Africa~~ Kenya.*
> *has lived in Argentina for ten years.*
> *is married and has two children.*
> *can't speak Spanish.*
> *is going to the U.S. next week.*
> *studied dance in the Netherlands.*

2 Student B is a journalist who interviewed you last week. Correct what he/she says using the information.

B *Did you tell me that you were Irish?*
A *No, I said that I was Scottish.*

> You're Scottish.
> You moved to Kyoto in 2010.
> You're learning to speak Japanese.
> You've been to China twice.
> You're going to take part in a marathon.
> You won't go to the Olympics next year.

10D Student A

1 You are a passenger at an airport. Follow the diagram and use the phrases in the box to have a conversation with the information desk assistant.

> Excuse me, I was hoping you could help me ...   I'd also like to ask about ...   Just one more thing.   Can I double check?
> Could you give me some information about ... , please?   Could I speak to someone about ... ?

Passenger (Student A)	Information desk assistant (Student B)
Ask if there's a delay on the 2:00 p.m. flight to Madrid. →	Apologize and explain that there is a 30-minute delay on this flight.
Ask which gate the flight is leaving from and how to get there. ←	Say that the flight leaves from gate A22. Offer to print out an airport map. Check to make sure the guest is satisfied. ←
Ask about a store that sells newspapers and magazines. →	Explain that there are lots of stores, but suggest one on the third floor that has lots of foreign language newspapers. ←
Thank the assistant. →	Respond politely.

2 You are a receptionist in a hotel. Respond to Student B in a helpful way. Make offers and suggestions and make sure he/she is satisfied.

Guest (Student B)	Receptionist (Student B)
Ask about the best way to get to the bus station. →	Greet the guest and explain that the quickest way is to take a taxi. Offer to call a taxi for the guest. ←
Thank the receptionist. Say that you need to be at the station at 4:00 p.m. ←	Check to make sure the guest is satisfied.
Ask the receptionist about a good place to have lunch. ←	Recommend a restaurant on Main Street. Give the guest a map and explain how to get there. ←
Thank the receptionist. →	

11C   Student A

1 A Complete the questions with the correct article: *a*, *an*, *the*, or – (no article).

1   Is _____ stress _____ big problem for you and your friends?

2   What's _____ best way to get _____ good job?

3   Have you ever been to _____ U.S. or _____ Canada?

4   What did you have for _____ dinner _____ last night?

5   Would you like to take _____ English classes on _____ Internet?

6   When was _____ last time you went to _____ movies?

B Ask Student B the questions and listen to his/her answers.

12A   Student A

1   Ask and answer questions with Student B to complete the crossword puzzle. Use the phrases in the box to make definitions with relative clauses.

B *What's 3 down?*

A *It's someone who is the leader of a country.*

> It's someone who/that ...   It's a place where ...
> It's something that ...

12C   Student A

1   Answer Student B's questions. Use the chart below. Tell him/her where you went and what you did.

B *What did you do yesterday?*

A *First, I went to the bank to take out some money.*

B *What did you do after that?*

Where	Why
the bank	take out some money
the mall	buy a new coat
the doctor	get some test results
the market	get some fish
a café	meet some friends
the airport	pick up a friend from Washington

2   Ask Student B questions about what he/she did yesterday. Write down his/her answers in the chart below.

A *What did you do yesterday?*

B *First, I went for a swim at the sports center.*

A *What did you do after that?*

Where	Why
the sports center	*go for a swim*
the office	
the garage	
the hospital	
the hairdresser's	
the movie theater	

12D   Student A

1   Thank, congratulate, or compliment Student B using phrases 1–5. Listen to his/her responses.

1   Wow, what a great presentation!

2   Your English is really good.

3   Thank you for dinner. It was delicious.

4   You found my wallet. Thanks a million!

5   Thanks so much for your help with the report.

2   Listen to Student B's ways of saying thanks or congratulations, or giving compliments.
Respond using the phrases in the box.

> Thanks, it's just a secondhand one, though.
> It was a pleasure. They're lots of fun.
> Thanks. Yours is really nice, too!
> Oh, it's just something I did when I was in college.
> It wasn't just me. We're a team.

1A Student B

1 Answer Student A's questions using the frequency adverbs and expressions.

> always usually sometimes often hardly ever never
> once/twice/three times a day/week/month
> every day/week/month

2 Tell the class what you found out about your partner.

3 Look at the activities and ask Student A questions with *How often ... ?* Write down his/her answers.

1 download music _____
2 send an e-mail _____
3 get angry _____
4 cook dinner _____
5 read a newspaper _____
6 dance _____

1C Student B

1 Answer Student A's questions about pictures 1–4.

   A *Is the woman in picture 5 going for a walk?*   B *No, she isn't.*

2 Look at pictures 5–8. Ask Student A questions to guess what is happening.

2A Student B

1 Answer Student A's questions.

2 Ask Student A *What did you do ... ?* with the time expressions. Add the correct prepositions, if necessary.

> December 31   an hour ago   the weekend   February   Friday night   last month

   B *What did you do last year on December 31?*
   A *I went to a street party with my friends and danced until midnight.*

2D Student B

1 Listen to Student A's sentences and respond to show you are interested.

   A *I didn't get home from work until 10:00 p.m. last night.*
   B *You poor thing! What happened?*

2 Read sentences 1–5 to Student A and listen to his/her responses.

1 I have a new job.
2 My car didn't start this morning.
3 My sister wants to get married on a beach next year.
4 I had a terrible day yesterday.
5 I won a trip to India in a contest.

2C Student B

1 Answer your partner's questions about Marilyn Monroe. Remember, don't use her name! Can Student A guess who she is?

When / born?		1926
Where / grow up?		California, U.S.
What / first job after finishing school?		Factory worker
How many times / get married?		Three times–to James Dougherty, Joe DiMaggio, and Arthur Miller
Have / children?		No
How / become famous?		She made lots of movies, including *Gentlemen Prefer Blondes* and *How to Marry a Millionaire*
When / die?		1962

2 Ask Student A questions about your mystery person and complete the chart. Can you guess who he is?

3A Student B

1 Listen to Student A's sentences. Look at the information and say if he/she is correct. Give more information using comparatives, superlatives, and *(not) as … as*.

Crocodiles aren't as dangerous as snakes, but they're more dangerous than sharks.

1 snakes (50,000 deaths/year); crocodiles (10,000 deaths/year); sharks (20 deaths/year)
2 Brazil World Cup, 2014 (700 million viewers); Beijing Olympics, 2008 (600 million viewers); Superbowl XLVI, 2012 (110 million viewers)
3 Bugatti Veyron (415 km./h); McLaren F1 (408 km./h); Porsche 959 (317 km./h)
4 Times Square, New York (80 decibels); Champs Élysées, Paris (79 decibels); Exchange Square, Hong Kong (78 decibels)

2 Complete the sentences with the superlative form of the adjectives in parentheses and guess the answer. Student A will say if you are correct.

1 The _____ river in the world is … (*long*)

Amazon River

Yangtze River

Nile River

3 The _____ city in the world is … (*crowded*)

Buenos Aires, Argentina

Manila, The Philippines

Cairo, Egypt

2 The _____ painting ever sold is … (*expensive*)

The Grand Canal, Claude Monet

Nafea Faa Ipoipo, Paul Gauguin

The Card Players, Paul Cézanne

4 The _____ musical artist is … (*successful*)

Madonna

Michael Jackson

The Beatles

4D Student B

1 You work for a rental car company. Student A will call to rent a car. Ask him/her questions and complete the form as accurately as possible.

Customer name: _____
Credit card: _____
Type of car: _____
Pick up date and time: _____
Number of days: _____

2 You call a restaurant to reserve a table for tonight. Call Student A and use the details below. Speak as quickly as possible!

Name: Lysandra Apostolakis
Phone number: 202-555-0110
Time: 7:00 (but may be late)
People: 8 adults, 4 children, 1 baby (need highchair for baby)

3C Student B

1   Read the text about Harold Bride. Answer Student A's questions to help him/her complete the story.

2   Make questions for Student A. Use the answers to complete the story.

  1   When / the *Titanic* / begin / its voyage?
  2   Why / he / go / to the radio room?
  3   What / name of the nearest ship?
  4   What / happen / while / Bride / send / the messages?
  5   What / Bride / hold onto / in the water?

THE STORY OF A SURVIVOR

Harold Bride was working on the *Titanic* when the ship sank over 100 years ago. He was a radio operator who sent and received important information. He was on board when the ship began its voyage from Southampton on
¹ _____ .

On April 14 at 11:40 p.m., Bride was sleeping in his room when he heard a terrible noise. He woke up and went straight to the radio room to ² _____ . Just after midnight, Captain Edward Smith came in and said that the ship was sinking. He asked Bride to send an emergency signal to any other ships in the area. The nearest ship to respond was ³ _____ , but, unfortunately, it didn't arrive until after the *Titanic* sank. While the ⁴ _____ , Bride continued to send messages. However, the equipment eventually stopped working and Bride went to help release one of the last lifeboats. But the water forced the lifeboat and the men into the freezing ocean.

Bride held onto the ⁵ _____ and, after hours in the water, some sailors rescued him and took him onto the *Carpathia*. He was badly hurt so he rested for a while, but later he went to the radio room and began to send personal messages from the survivors.

4A Student B

1   Answer Student A's questions using the phrases in the box. Give more information.

> Yes, I think I will.   Yes, I probably will.
> Yes, I may.   Yes, I might.
> I don't think I will.   I probably won't.
> I definitely won't.

  A   *Do you think you will move in the next five years?*
  B   *Yes, I might. My downtown apartment is very small, and I want to look for a bigger one.*

2   Ask Student A questions with *will*. Check (✔) his/her answers in the chart.

Do you think ...	likely	possible	unlikely	impossible
you will go on vacation next summer?				
you will travel abroad this year?				
you will make any new friends this month?				
you will earn a lot of money in your next job?				
you will live to be 100 years old?				
you will eat in a restaurant next week?				

4C Student B

1   You applied for a job at Student A's company. He/She calls you to set up an interview. Look at your day planner and find a time to have the interview.

  A   *I'm free on Monday morning. Can we have the interview then?*
  B   *I'm sorry, I'm visiting my aunt in the hospital. What about Monday afternoon?*

Monday	morning	*visit Aunt Emma in the hospital*
	afternoon	
Tuesday	morning	*see the dentist at 10:00*
	afternoon	
Wednesday	morning	
	afternoon	*go to Jenny's birthday lunch*
Thursday	morning	*take piano class*
	afternoon	
Friday	morning	
	afternoon	*play the piano at the jazz concert*

5A Student B

1 Student A will tell you about a problem. Give him/her some advice using the ideas from the box and your own ideas.

drink lots of water	drink so much coffee
eat so much chocolate	go on a diet
go to bed early	go to the pharmacy
go to the hospital	go to work today
hold it under cold water	hold your nose with a tissue
join a gym	move around too much
see a doctor	put some cream on it
take some pills	sit down for a few minutes
smoke	take some medicine

You should ...   I think you should ...
You shouldn't ...   I don't think you should ...

2 Tell Student A about your problems and write down the advice that he/she gives you.

Your problems	Advice
I feel tired all the time.	
I cut my hand on a piece of glass.	
I have a backache.	
I'm stressed.	
I have a stomachache.	

5C Student B

1 Listen to the beginnings of the sentences Student A reads to you. Choose the correct ending to complete the sentence and tell him/her.

... I won't make pasta.
... I might go as Superman.
... I'll probably watch a movie.
... I'll speak to my boss.
... I'll stay in bed.
... I might go skiing.

2 Read the beginnings of sentences 1–6 to Student A. He/She will complete the sentences.

1 If I go on vacation this summer ...
2 If I decide to get a pet ...
3 If my boss thinks I'm doing a good job ...
4 If I pass my exams ...
5 If I have a headache ...
6 If I go shopping on the weekend ...

6A Student B

1 Student A will ask you a *Have you ever ...?* question. You should always answer with *Yes, I have*. He/She will ask you more questions. If it is true, tell the truth. If it is not true, invent the details.

2 Complete the *Have you ever ...?* questions with the past participles of the verbs in parentheses and ask Student A. He/She will always answer with *Yes, I have*. Ask him/her the simple past questions and decide if he/she is telling the truth.

	Have you ever ...	Simple past
1	_____ an e-mail in English? (write)	When did you write it? Who did you send it to? Did you have any problems?
2	_____ all night to see the sunrise? (stay up)	Why didn't you sleep? How did you feel? What was it like?
3	_____ London? (visit)	When did you go there? Did you have a good time? What things did you see there?
4	_____ money your trip? (run out of)	Where did you go? Did you have any problems? How did you get more money?
5	_____ your house keys? (lose)	How did you get into your house? Do you know where you lost the keys? Did you find them again?

6C Student B

1 Listen to Student A's sentences. Decide if they are true or false. He/She will tell you if you are correct.

A *If I had more money, I'd buy a new car.*
B *False.*
A *Yes, you're right. If I had more money, I'd go on vacation.*

2 Complete the sentences with the correct form of the verbs in parentheses. Decide if the sentence is true or false for you. Read your sentences to Student A.

1 I _____ my friends if I _____ my driving test. (not tell / fail)
2 If I _____ a spider in the bathtub, I _____ and take it outside. (find / pick it up)
3 If I _____ a lot of money, I _____ it with my friends. (win / share)
4 I _____ an animal to eat if I _____ any other food. (kill / not have)
5 If I _____ , I _____ more free time. (not work / have)

7A Student B

1 You have recently moved to an apartment in another country. Look at your "to do" list and answer Student A's questions.

> **Things to do**
>
> meet your neighbors   ✓ (they're very nice)
> open a bank account   ✗
> explore the local area   ✓ (got back 15 minutes ago)
> unpack your things   ✓ (the apartment looks great!)
> set up the Wi-Fi   ✗
> check out pubic transportation ✓ (went this morning)

2 Student A is going to Buenos Aires on vacation tomorrow. Find out if he/she has done these things.

B *Have you bought some sunscreen yet?*
A *Yes. I went to the store an hour ago.*

1 buy some sunscreen
2 decide what to do in Buenos Aires
3 reserve a hotel room
4 find your passport
5 ask a friend to take care of your pet
6 pack your suitcase

7C Student B

1 Listen to Student A's sentences and tell him/her if they are correct.

1 The Academy Awards ceremony has taken place since 1929. The winner of the Best Actor award that year was a German actor, Emil Jannings.

2 The actor Johnny Depp has collected Barbie dolls since his daughter was little.

3 Hollywood actress Christina Ricci has been afraid of plants for most of her life.

4 The actress Angelina Jolie has had a pilot's license for more than ten years.

2 Complete the sentences with the present perfect form of the verbs in the box and *for* or *since*. Guess the correct options and tell Student A. He/She will tell you if you are correct.

> know   play   be   live

HOLLYWOOD FACTS

1 There _____ _____ a big Hollywood sign in Los Angeles _____ *1923 / 1953 / 1973*, but the first sign said "Hollywoodland."

2 *Spider-Man* actor, Tobey Maguire, and *Leonardo DiCaprio / Kanye West / Joaquin Phoenix* _____ _____ each other _____ they were children.

3 Actress Mila Kunis _____ _____ *golf / video games / chess* _____ many years.

4 Eva Marie Saint, who won an Oscar for *On the Waterfront* in 1954, _____ _____ in Hollywood _____ over 60 years and still works as *a designer / an actress / a musician.*

8A Student B

1 You are going to cook a big meal for a group of friends. Tell Student A what ingredients you have. He/She will tell you if you need more, less, or if it is enough.

I have six cans of tomatoes.

2 You are going to cook a big meal for a group of friends. Student A will tell you what ingredients he/she has. Look at the list of ingredients and use the phrases in the box to help you reply.

> Great, that's enough.   That's too much.
> That's too many.   That's not enough.
> We (only) need ...

INGREDIENTS
1 whole salmon
500 g. shrimp
1 lettuce
1 cucumber
250 g. butter
1 l. milk
200 g. flour
1 coconut

8C Student B

1 You and Student A are starting work as cooks in a school cafeteria. Guess the missing words. Student A will tell you if you are correct.

SCHOOL KITCHEN GOLDEN RULES!

HYGIENE

1 You have to wear <u>a hat</u> at all times, but you don't have to wear _____ .

2 You can't wear <u>jewelry</u> in the kitchen.

3 You have to wash _____ before starting to cook.

COOKING

4 You have to use <u>fresh ingredients</u> in all the dishes, and you can't use _____ .

5 You have to wash all <u>raw fruit and vegetables</u>, but you don't have to wash the _____ .

6 You have to throw away <u>all burned food</u> in the black trash cans.

MENU

7 You have to prepare _____ every day.

8 You don't have to serve <u>salad</u> on Fridays.

9 On Thursdays, you have to make a _____ , but you can't make the sauce <u>too spicy</u>.

10 On Wednesdays, you have to make _____ , but you can't make <u>sweet-and-sour sauce</u>.

8D Student B

1 Student A is going to invite you to some events. Refuse as politely as possible every time.

2 Invite Student A to one of these events. If he/she refuses, try another one.

Black-and-white night   Thur 6:00 p.m.
Enjoy three movies from the 1930s at Roxy Movie Theater

Crazy burger buffet   Fri 7:00 p.m.
Eat as many hamburgers as you want for $12

Ballroom dancing lessons   Sat 11:00 a.m.
Learn how to dance the waltz and cha-cha-cha

Benches of the world   Sat 5:00 p.m.
An exhibition of Michael Lamb's photographs of benches

9A Student B

1 Complete the quiz questions with *used to* and the verbs in parentheses.

Before they were famous

1 Famous singer, Beyoncé, _____ (sweep up) hair in her mom's beauty salon. **True** or False?

2 The actress, Jennifer Aniston, _____ (clean) salmon in a fish factory. True or **False**? (She used to clean toilets.)

3 The Australian actor, Hugh Jackman, _____ (teach) gym class at a school in England. **True** or False?

4 The actor, Tom Hanks, _____ (sell) popcorn and peanuts at his local movie theater. **True** or False?

5 The singer, Lady Gaga, _____ (work) in a library. True or **False**? (She used to work in a Greek restaurant.)

6 The actor, Sylvester Stallone, _____ (clean) the lions' cages at Central Park Zoo in New York. **True** or False?

7 The Rolling Stones singer, Mick Jagger, _____ (be) a firefighter in London. True or **False**? (He used to work in a hospital.)

8 The Russian billionaire, Roman Abramovich, _____ (sell) plastic ducks in a market. **True** or False?

---

2 Take turns reading your quiz questions to your partner. The correct answers are in **bold**.

9C Student B

1 Complete sentences 1–6 with the passive form of the verbs in parentheses.

1 What famous articles of clothing _____ by Harrison Ford in the *Indiana Jones* movies? (wear)
   a A hat and raincoat   b **A hat and leather jacket**   c A baseball jacket and cap

2 When _____ the first Sherlock Holmes story _____? (publish)
   a In 1810   b **In 1887**   c In 1935

3 In 2011, one of Marilyn Monroe's dresses was sold at auction. How much _____ it _____ for? (buy)
   a $1.3M   b $3.2M   c **$4.6M**

4 Who _____ the sunflower pictures _____ by? (paint)
   a **Vincent Van Gogh**   b Henri Matisse   c Salvador Dalí

5 What type of car _____ by the mad scientist Doc Brown in the *Back to the Future* movies? (drive)
   a A Lamborghini   b A Ferrari   c **A DeLorean**

6 Who _____ the movies *Titanic* and *Avatar* _____ by? (direct)
   a **James Cameron**   b Steven Spielberg   c Ridley Scott

2 **A** Try to answer Student A's questions.

   B Read your questions and the three possible answers to Student A. He/She has to answer. The correct answers are in **bold**.

10A Student B

1 Listen to Student A's sentences. Tell him/her if they are correct or not.

Kevin's roommates were really angry with him because ...
1 he had eaten all the food in the refrigerator.
2 he hadn't been to the supermarket.
3 he hadn't washed the dirty dinner dishes.
4 he had drunk all the milk.
5 he hadn't cleaned up the kitchen.

2 A Guess the past perfect verbs to complete the sentences.
Last night, Miriam's friends planned a party for her. She was really surprised because ...
1 nobody _____ her about it.
2 she _____ some of her friends for years!
3 everyone _____ her a present.
4 she thought her friends _____ about her birthday.
5 all her friends _____ "surprise!" when she came in.

B Read your sentences to Student A. He/She will tell you if you are correct.

10C Student B

1 Student A is a journalist who interviewed you last week. Correct what he/she says using the information.

A *Did you say that you were originally from South Africa?*
B *No, I told you that I was originally from Kenya.*

> You're originally from Kenya.
> You've lived in Argentina for eight years.
> You're married and have one child.
> You can speak Spanish fluently.
> You're going to the U.S. next week.
> You studied dance in Belgium.

2 You are a journalist. You interviewed Student A last week and took notes. Check the information with him/her and correct any mistakes.

B *Did you tell me that you were Irish?*
A *No, I said that I was Scottish.*

> *Student A*
> *is ~~Irish~~ Scottish.*
> *moved to Tokyo in 2010.*
> *is learning to speak Japanese.*
> *hasn't been to China before.*
> *is going to take part in a 10-km. race.*
> *will go to the Olympics next year if it's possible.*

10D Student B

1 You work on an information desk in an airport. Respond to Student A in a helpful way. Make offers and suggestions and make sure he/she is satisfied.

Passenger (Student A)	Information desk assistant (Student B)
Ask if there's a delay on the 2:00 p.m. flight to Madrid.	Apologize and explain that there's a 30-minute delay on this flight.
Ask which gate the flight is leaving from and how to get there.	Say that the flight leaves from gate A22. Offer to print out an airport map. Check to make sure the guest is satisfied.
Ask about a store that sells newspapers and magazines.	Explain that there are lots of stores, but suggest one on the third floor that has lots of foreign language newspapers.
Thank the assistant.	Respond politely.

2 You are a guest staying at a hotel. Follow the diagram and use the phrases in the box to have a conversation with the receptionist.

> Excuse me, I was hoping you could help me ...   I'd also like to ask about ...   Just one more thing.   Can I double check?
> Could you give me some information about ... , please?   Could I speak to someone about ... ?

Guest (Student B)	Receptionist (Student A)
Ask about the best way to get to the train station.	Greet the guest and explain that the quickest way is to take a taxi. Offer to call a taxi for the guest.
Thank the receptionist. Say that you need to be at the station at 4:00 p.m.	Check to make sure the guest is satisfied.
Ask the receptionist about a good place to have lunch.	Recommend a restaurant on Main Street. Give the guest a map and explain how to get there.
Thank the receptionist.	Respond politely.

11C Student B

1 A Complete the questions with the correct article: *a*, *an*, *the*, or – (no article).

1 Do you have _____ pet? What's _____ pet's name?
2 How many times _____ year do you see _____ dentist?
3 Do you like _____ reading? Are you reading _____ book right now?
4 What time do you usually go to _____ bed at _____ night?
5 What's _____ worst food you've ever had in _____ restaurant?
6 Do you know anyone who is _____ architect or _____ designer?

B Ask Student A the questions and listen to his/her answers.

12A Student B

1 Ask and answer questions with Student A to complete the crossword puzzle. Use the phrases in the box to make definitions with relative clauses.

A *What's 3 across?*
B *It's a place where you can play soccer or go for a walk.*

> It's someone who ...   It's a place where ...
> It's something that ...

12C Student B

1 Ask Student A questions about what he/she did yesterday. Write down his/her answers in the chart below.

B *What did you do yesterday?*
A *First, I went to the bank to take out some money.*
B *What did you do after that?*

Where	Why
the bank	*to take out some money*
the mall	
the doctor	
the market	
a café	
the airport	

2 Answer Student A's questions. Use the chart below. Tell him/her where you went and what you did.

A *What did you do yesterday?*
B *First, I went to the sports center to go for swim.*
A *What did you do after that?*

Where	Why
the sports center	go for a swim
the office	finish a report
the garage	fix my car
the hospital	visit my uncle
the hairdresser's	have my hair cut
the movie theater	see the new *Batman* movie

12D Student B

1 Listen to Student A's ways of saying thanks or congratulations, or giving compliments. Respond using the phrases in the box.

> No problem. I enjoyed working on it!
> It was no trouble at all. It was in my car.
> Do you think so? I didn't have much time to practice.
> Thanks, but I still need to improve.
> Well, thank you for coming to visit us!

2 Thank, congratulate, or compliment Student A using phrases 1–5. Listen to his/her responses.

1 Did you paint this picture? It's fantastic.
2 I'm very grateful for your help at this difficult time.
3 I love your watch! It's cool.
4 Thanks for taking care of the children.
5 Congratulations on your new car.

6D All students

1 You're going on a trip to a rainforest for one week. You can only take six of the items with you. Decide which are the most useful.

tent　　　　mosquito net　　　　flashlight　　　　first-aid kit　　　　water-purifying kit　　　　sunscreen

knife　　　　food　　　　compass and maps　　　　insect repellent　　　　cooking equipment　　　　rope

2 In groups of four, discuss which six items you will take. Try to take turns politely.

11A Both students

1 In pairs, complete the sentences with the infinitive or the *–ing* form of the verbs in parentheses.

Tell me about …

1 something important you need _____ this week. (do)
2 a place you're planning _____ soon. (visit)
3 something you spend a lot of time _____ . (do)
4 a person you'd like _____ more often. (see)
5 something you can't afford _____ , but would love to have. (buy)
6 a household chore you can't stand _____ . (do)
7 a movie you're looking forward to _____ at the movie theater. (see)
8 a mistake you keep _____ in English. (make)
9 a food you would miss _____ if you lived in another country. (eat)
10 someone you expect _____ later today. (see)

2 In pairs, take turns asking and answering the questions.

A *Tell me about something important you need to do this week.*
B *I need to buy a birthday card for my mom. What about you?*
A *I need to take my car to the garage.*

3A Quiz results

For each answer A, score 0 points. For each answer B, score 1 point.

0–1 points = tourist. You're happiest sunbathing on a beach.

2–3 points = traveler. You like to do something more unusual on vacation.

4–5 points = adventurer. The best vacation for you is six months in the jungle!

5C Quiz results

For each answer A, score 0 points. For each answer B, score 1 point. For each answer C, score 2 points. For each answer D, score 3 points.

0–3 = Oh dear, you're really miserable right now. Are you upset about something? If you talk to your friends or family, you'll feel better.

4–7 = You're not very happy right now. If you do something you enjoy, maybe you'll feel more cheerful.

8–11 = Great news, you're happy! If you're friendly and smile at everyone today, you'll make them feel happier, too!

12–15 = You're extremely happy! Are you delighted about something? What's the secret to feeling so happy?

6C Quiz results

How many answers did you get right?

0–1 = You probably wouldn't survive if you went on a weekend camping trip. It's safer for you to stay at home.

2–3 = If you were in a difficult situation, you'd probably survive, but don't take any risks. Always find out about the dangers of a place before you go.

4 = Wow! You'd know what to do if you were in the wild. If you could choose an exciting place for an adventure, where would you go?

6D Quiz results

How many times did you answer yes?

0–2 = You don't like taking risks. Be careful, if you always play it safe, you might miss out on opportunities in your life.

3–4 = You're happy to take a risk, but not too many. That's probably the best way to be.

5–6 = You're a real risk-taker! It can be exciting, but watch out, it can be dangerous, too!

Infinitive	Simple past	Past participle	Infinitive	Simple past	Past participle
be	was, were	been	make	made	made
become	became	become	meet	met	met
begin	began	begun	pay	paid	paid
bite	bit	bitten	put	put	put
break	broke	broken	read (/rid/)	read (/red/)	read (/red/)
bring	brought	brought	ride	rode	ridden
build	built	built	ring	rang	rung
buy	bought	bought	rise	rose	risen
choose	chose	chosen	run	ran	run
come	came	come	say	said	said
cost	cost	cost	see	saw	seen
do	did	done	sell	sold	sold
dream	dreamed/dreamt	dreamed/dreamt	send	sent	sent
forbid	forbade	forbidden	sleep	slept	slept
forget	forgot	forgotten	speak	spoke	spoken
forgive	forgave	forgiven	spend	spent	spent
get	got	gotten	stand	stood	stood
give	gave	given	steal	stole	stolen
go	went	gone	stick	stuck	stuck
grow	grew	grown	swim	swam	swum
have	had	had	take	took	taken
hear	heard	heard	teach	taught	taught
hide	hid	hidden	tell	told	told
hold	held	held	think	thought	thought
keep	kept	kept	throw	threw	thrown
know	knew	known	understand	understood	understood
learn	learned	learned	wake	woke	woken
leave	left	left	wear	wore	worn
let	let	let	win	won	won
lose	lost	lost	write	wrote	written

58 St Aldates
Oxford
OX1 1ST
United Kingdom

ISBN: 978-84-668-2755-3
Twenty-first reprint: 2024

© Richmond / Santillana Global S.L. 2017

Publishing Director: Deborah Tricker
Publisher: Simone Foster
Media Publisher: Sue Ashcroft
Content Developer: David Cole-Powney
Editors: Debra Emmett, Helen Ward, Ruth Cox, Emma Clarke, Fiona Hunt, Eleanor Clements
Proofreader: Peter Anderson
Design Manager: Lorna Heaslip
Cover Design: This Ain't Rock'n'Roll, London
Design & Layout: Lorna Heaslip, Oliver Hutton, Gabriela Alvarez
Photo Researcher: Magdalena Mayo
Learning Curve video: Mannic Media
Audio production: Tom, Dick and Debbie
App development: The Distance
Americanization: Diane Hermanson, Jennifer Wise

We would also like to thank the following people for their valuable contribution to writing and developing the material:
Alastair Lane, Bob McLarty, Claire Thacker, Louis Rogers, Rachael Roberts, Pamela Vittorio (Video Script Writer), Belen Fernandez (App Project Manager), Rob Sved (App Content Creator)

Illustrators:
Simon Clare; Dermot Flynn c/o Dutch Uncle; Guillaume Gennet, Julien Kern and Liav Zabari c/o Lemonade; Joanna Kerr c/o New Division; Piers Sandford c/o Meiklejohn; The Boy FitzHammond and Beverley Young, c/o NB Illustration

Photos:
J. Jaime; J. Lucas; 123RF/ lightpoet; ALAMY/IanDagnall Laptop Computing, John Birdsall, Chuck Place, Granger Historical Picture Archve, All Canada Photos, Cofiant Images, ONOKY - Photononstop, Action Plus Sports Images, Arcaid Images, Jasminko Ibrakovic, Image Source Salsa, Radius Images, Pat Behnke, Ann Cutting, 360b, Heritage Image Partnership Ltd, Roger Bamber, Cultura Creative (RF), Blend Images, RosaIreneBetancourt 10, Nick Gregory, BSIP SA, Trinity Mirror / Mirrorpix, Wavebreak Media ltd, Torrontonian, Joy Sunny, SWNS, TP, IanDagnall Computing, PhotoEdit, Ammentorp Photography, Peter Barritt, Cliff Hide Stock, greenwales, caia image, eye35.pix, Carlos Guerra, Janine Wiedel Photolibrary, Peter Titmuss, Richard Heyes, Motoring Picture Library, Helen Hotson, Cephas Picture Library, ACORN 1, tommaso altamura, Steve Davey Photography, Image Source, Bill Cheyrou, Agencja Fotograficzna Caro, Kreative Photography, Imagedoc, Lou-Foto, Julie g Woodhouse, allesalltag, Stefano Carvoretto, MAX EAREY, wareham.nl (sport), Duncan Snow, Wilawan Khasawong, Brian Overcast, Design Pics Inc, Westend61 GmbH, Anton Stariskov, Elina Manninen, Aflo Co., Ltd., Alan Smith, Classic Image, Photos 12, D. Hurst, MBI, AF archive, PjrTravel, FineArt, moodboard, DonSmith, Jeramey Lende, epa european pressphoto agency b.v.; BNPS (BOURNEMOUTH NEWS & PICTURE SERVICE)/ Rijksmuseum/ BNPS; CATERS NEWS AGENCY/ Caters News

Agency; GETTY IMAGES SALES SPAIN/Lumi Images/Dario Secen, Graham Monro/gm photographics, Jetta Productions, Thomas_EyeDesign, Photos.com Plus, David M. Benett, Astrid Stawiarz, Mark Metcalfe, CARL DE SOUZA, Alistair Berg, Toby Burrows, Sam Edwards, Dave Hogan, Barcroft, Maskot, Bloomberg, Bettmann, Don Arnold, Kari Lehr, PETER MACDIARMID, RENE SLAMA, Boston Globe, CHRISTOPHE ARCHAMBAULT, Caiaimage/Paul Bradbury, Image source, Paul Chesley, Thinkstock; HIGHRES PRESS STOCK/AbleStock.com; ISTOCKPHOTO/SeanShot, Pali Rao, oztasbc, jojoo64, SondraP, MollyNZ, Geber86, xijian, vgajic, sturti, olaser, miralex, mergez, alexsl, HASLOO, SolStock, DONOT6, Getty Images Sales Spain, Devasahayam Chandra Dhas, monkeybusinessimages, Osmany Torres Martín, alessandroguerriero, AleksandarGeorgiev, Tommaso Altamura, Nicolas McComber, warrengoldswain, travellinglight, stevecoleimages, Robyn Mackenzie, German-skydiver, digitalskillet, Wavebreakmedia, Petar Chernaev, Jaroslav Frank, wundervisuals, Squaredpixels, LuckyBusiness, Julia Nichols, Drazen Lovric, Dean Mitchell, elenaleonova, PeopleImages, Elenathewise, Dieter Meyrl, Daniel Ernst, Cathy Yeulet, ozgurdonmaz, mediaphotos, Yuri_Arcurs, Visiofutura, Jason Poole, David Sucsy, Bulent Ince, nataistock, bluehill75, calvindexter, MartialRed, Juanmonino, FangXiaNuo, Joel Carillet, FSTOPLIGHT, DeluXe-PiX, DeanDrobot, g-stockstudio, zhudifeng, pixdeluxe, milanfoto, dolgachov, cindygoff, SteveTram, OcusFocus, robertcicchetti, Maxiphoto, Kaan Ates, Huchen Lu, Anna Bryukhanova, Halfpoint, CactuSoup, yipengge, mihailomilovanovic, urbancow, rcaucino, pepifoto, lucky336, kyoshino, denphumi; MAYANG MURNI ADNIN; NASA/ NASA; REX SHUTTERSTOCK/Jonathan Player, ABC Inc/ Everett, Peter Brooker, Kippa Limited, Pixelformula, Newspix; SHUTTERSTOCK; SHUTTERSTOCK NETHERLANDS,B.V.; Project Jacquard/Levi's Strauss; Library of Congress/wikipedia; Carpigiani Gelato University; Niccolo Casas /EMBR labs; Optomen Television Ltd.; courtesy of Alex Deans; Pauline Van Dongen; Alastair Humphreys; freepic.com; Ringly Inc.; Jon Barlow; Dave Homcy; ARCHIVO SANTILLANA; Images used under licence from ©Shutterstock.com

Cover Photo: Jon Barlow

We would like to thank the following reviewers for their valuable feedback which has made Personal Best possible. We extend our thanks to the many teachers and students not mentioned here.

Brad Bawtinheimer, Manuel Hidalgo, Paulo Dantas, Diana Bermúdez, Laura Gutiérrez, Hardy Griffin, Angi Conti, Christopher Morabito, Hande Kokce, Jorge Lobato, Leonardo Mercato, Mercilinda Ortiz, Wendy López

The Publisher has made every effort to trace the owner of copyrighted material; however, the Publisher will correct any involuntary omission at the earliest opportunity.

Printed in Brazil by Forma Certa
Lote. 800411